Wright state

The Woman War Correspondent, the U.S. Military, and the Press

The Woman War Correspondent, the U.S. Military, and the Press

1846–1947

Carolyn M. Edy

LEXINGTON BOOKS
Lanham • Boulder • New York • London

Published by Lexington Books
An imprint of The Rowman & Littlefield Publishing Group, Inc.
4501 Forbes Boulevard, Suite 200, Lanham, Maryland 20706
www.rowman.com

Unit A, Whitacre Mews, 26-34 Stannary Street, London SE11 4AB

British Library Cataloguing in Publication Information Available

Library of Congress Cataloging-in-Publication Data

Names: Edy, Carolyn M., author.
Title: The woman war correspondent, the U.S military, and the press, 1846-1947 / Carolyn M. Edy.
Description: Lanham, MD : Lexington Books, [2017] | Includes bibliographical references and index.
Identifiers: LCCN 2016044773 (print) | LCCN 2016047202 (ebook) | ISBN 9781498539272 (cloth :
    alk. paper) | ISBN 9781498539289 (Electronic)
Subjects: LCSH: War correspondents--United States--History. | Women war correspondents--United
    States--History. | War correspondents--United States--Biography. | Women war correspondents--
    United States--Biography. | World War, 1939-1945--Women. | World War, 1939-1945--Journal-
    ists. | World War, 1914-1918--Women. | World War, 1914-1918--Journalists. | Women and war.
Classification: LCC D799.U6 E39 2017 (print) | LCC D799.U6 (ebook) | DDC 070.4/
    4994053092520973--dc23
LC record available at https://lccn.loc.gov/2016044773

∞™ The paper used in this publication meets the minimum requirements of American
National Standard for Information Sciences Permanence of Paper for Printed Library
Materials, ANSI/NISO Z39.48-1992.

Printed in the United States of America

For Lucy

Contents

List of Figures

Preface and Acknowledgments

One thing I have come to value in researching this book is that what you can't find is often as important as what you find. The holes in a story may tell a story all their own, or they may just guide you to the real story. At the same time, just like that essential item that is only lost until you give up on ever finding it—when it will suddenly appear—just because you don't find something does not mean it can't be found. The search for answers (if not materials) is what drives any historical study, along with the knowledge that these answers are never within any one person's reach, nor the product of any one person's search.

The idea for this book began nearly a decade ago in an archive after I was looking for something I never found but instead discovered something else, entirely unrelated. I came across a brief note that a woman named Inez Robb had written to chastise columnist Robert Ruark for using one of her anecdotes as his own. I had never heard of Robb, and neither had anyone else I asked. And yet a search in ProQuest historical databases seemed to reveal that Robb had gained military accreditation in 1942 as the first woman war correspondent. Additional searches led me to claims of so many other "first" women war correspondents. I began to read books about war correspondents, and the more I learned, the more questions I had. This book answers some of those questions, as well as others that emerged along the way, but I would also encourage readers to find and read the three "first" books on women war correspondents, by three women who blazed this trail for me: Nancy Caldwell Sorel, Lilya Wagner, and Julia Edwards.[1]

I am thankful to the many people who gave me advice, helped me find materials, or offered me encouragement and support, but I am equally thankful to others whose contributions lay in helping me set boundaries, eliminate false leads, and rule things out. One who fits in the former category, even while making me appreciate those in the latter category all the more, is Jan Boles, archivist of the Robert E. Smylie Archives at The College of Idaho. The fact that an unprocessed collection of Inez Robb's papers existed, along with the fact that I could just as easily have overlooked them entirely without Boles' help, was a great gift. But it also was the kind of windfall that is troubling—just how many troves of unprocessed materials are out there, and can you ever stop looking? Another archivist to whom I would like to extend special thanks is Francesca Pitaro, who helped me navigate the Associated Press Corporate Archives even when my requests were broader than necessary and included materials that I have had to set aside for future projects.

I would also like to thank the archives and individuals who shared photographs and materials with me for use in this book, including Alison Perry, Patricia Perry, and Brian Scruby; Benjamin Phillips IV and the Phillips Family Archive; Charles Deering McCormick Library of Special Collections, Northwestern University Library; Denver Public Library; Douglas County Historical Society; Kenneth Spencer Research Library, University of Kansas Libraries; Library of Virginia; Sophia Smith Collection, Smith College; Robert E. Smylie Archives, The College of Idaho; San Diego Air & Space Museum; Arthur and Elizabeth Schlesinger Library on the History of Women in America, Harvard University; the National Archives at College Park; and the Associated Press Corporate Archives.

I am grateful to everyone who helped me at each stage of this project, including my friends and colleagues at Appalachian State University, as well as the many faculty members and classmates at the University of North Carolina–Chapel Hill who helped me in classes, reading groups, and throughout my dissertation.

I am also thankful to have had many thoughtful and generous readers along the way, including Maurine Beasley, W. Fitzhugh Brundage, Jacquelyn Dowd Hall, Frank Fee Jr., Jean Folkerts, Charlie Frieberg, Barbara Friedman, Kathleen Kearns, Nancy Oates, Michael Sweeney, and Betty Winfield. I would also like to thank Sarah Arneson for her help formatting images.

My research benefitted from the generous support of the Triad Foundation, the College of Fine and Applied Arts at Appalachian State University, a Schlesinger Library grant, a Mary Gardner Research Award, a Minnie S. and Eli A. Rubinstein Research Award, and the Joseph L. Morrison Award for Excellence in Journalism History.

In the most literal sense, this book would not exist without Lexington Books and the support, encouragement, and editorial assistance that I have received from Brian Hill and Eric Kuntzman.

Since I first started this project, my daughter Lucy has nearly doubled in age (in time to help me with last-minute research and proofreading), all the while offering me encouragement, inspiration, and purpose. Since that time, too, our family has almost tripled, in size as well as in our daily potential for laughter, camaraderie, and adventure. I am so thankful for Charlie, Alyssa, Elaina, and Lucy, and for all of our family members, far and wide. With any luck, now that this book is complete, I will have more time to spend with each of you.

NOTE

1. Nancy Caldwell Sorel, *The Women Who Wrote the War* (New York: Arcade Pub., 1999); Julia Edwards, *Women of the World: The Great Foreign Correspondents* (Boston: Houghton Mifflin, 1988); and Lilya Wagner, *Women War Correspondents of World War II* (New York: Greenwood Press, 1989).

Abbreviations

AEF	Allied Expeditionary Forces
AGWAR	Adjutant General, War Department
CBI	China-Burma-India
CCS	Combined Chiefs of Staff
ETO	European Theater of Operations
GHQ	General Headquarters
JCS	U.S. Joint Chiefs of Staff
OSS	Office of Strategic Services
PRD	Public Relations Division
PRO	Public Relations Officer
SEAC	Southeast Asia Command
SHAEF	Supreme Headquarters, Allied Expeditionary Forces
SWPA	Southwest Pacific Area
WAAC	Women's Army Auxiliary Corps
WAC	Women's Army Corps
WASP	Women Airforce Service Pilots
WAVES	Women Accepted for Voluntary Emergency Service
WD	War Department
WRENS	Women's Royal Naval Service

Chapter One

Introduction

The *Chicago Tribune*'s chief Berlin correspondent from 1925 to 1941 smoked a pipe, spoke more than five languages, had a seemingly uncanny ability to drink German officials under the table, and used covert tactics to scoop reporters worldwide on the impending death of Weimar Germany's first president, on Hitler's plans for world war, and, finally, on confirmation of Hitler's death. [1]

The *New York Times* correspondent who won the 1937 Pulitzer for foreign correspondence was among the first to predict for American readers the rise and wrath of a young, vastly underestimated Mussolini and had once procured a six-hour interview with Stalin at a time when he refused to speak with all other foreign reporters. [2]

Neither of these individuals—both of whom were women—had originally aspired to be a "newspaperman," yet a strong education, affinity for languages, and knowledge of world affairs, as well as extensive travel experience, earned them recognition and respect among world leaders—and readers. The highest compliment a female reporter could receive from her male colleagues, for much of the twentieth century, was to be called a "newspaperman." Sigrid Schultz, the first woman bureau chief for the *Chicago Tribune*, was honored in 1969 by the Overseas Press Club with a plaque acknowledging her life's work: "To a tough competitor, staunch friend, honest reporter. She worked like a newspaperman." Of her sex, her work, and her field, Schultz later said, "I insist that the only thing that counts is efficiency, which is a fact that the leading newspapermen believe." [3]

Both Schultz and Anne O'Hare McCormick, the Pulitzer Prize–winning *New York Times* correspondent, were rare individuals as, arguably, were most of the women who wrote about war in the early twentieth century and lived up to their personal ambitions instead of societal expectations. Yet

1

Schultz and McCormick were rare even among the small percentage of women whom the United States accredited as World War II correspondents. Scholars, journalists, and members of the general public are far more likely to have heard about or read about the women war correspondents who were valued as "newspapermen," such as McCormick and Schultz, than the majority of the nearly two hundred women war correspondents, who were called upon by editors and the United States military to cover the war from a feminine point of view.

Whichever angle they took, though, female war correspondents are easily lost in the larger picture of World War II correspondents, as well as among the vast array of books published by and about World War II correspondents. While stories by women correspondents and anecdotes about their lives and their work exist within larger works about women in wartime and women in journalism, few works have addressed the history of early women war correspondents as a group. Furthermore, the few works that have done so are, primarily, compelling stories about the lives of extraordinary women. Missing from these works is a broader picture of the accreditation of women war correspondents and their coverage of war, along with persuasive claims about the meaning of their work in terms of the war, the world, their profession, or their audience. Also missing from these works, notably, is a focus on the woman's angle of the war. Works about war correspondents in general and female war correspondents in particular largely dismiss or overlook this angle—the coverage itself, its gendered meanings, and even the many writers who covered it. Instead, most works focus on the ways in which women compared to their male colleagues. But few people viewed or treated these women as equals of their male colleagues. Even today, when women are as likely as men to be United States correspondents in war zones, female correspondents have reported being wary of drawing attention to the fact that they are women—for fear of assault on the job or concern that editors might take them off of the job for their own safety.[4] A study that considers the category of "woman war correspondent," during a time when the media, the government, and the public were constructing new roles for women and the press during wartime, is overdue.

The purpose of this book is to provide a history of the women whom the U.S. government accredited as war correspondents, while exploring the construction, by the press, the public, and the military, of the category of "woman war correspondent" and the concept of a woman's angle of war up through the end of World War II. Relying on cultural historical methods, this book explores government documents, as well as the writings of American men and women within the media, the United States military, and the public. While this book considers the lives and work of all women who were accredited by the U.S. government as war correspondents during this time period, its primary focus is upon the majority who worked for print media. Most women who worked as war correspondents before the end of World War II were writing for newspapers, magazines, or wire services; the technology available at that time, along with radio standards that favored live news coverage, greatly limited war reporting for broadcast. This book considers the ways the concept of a "woman war correspondent" might have influenced or been influenced by war, military regulations, societal norms, politics, and the media. By providing a history of the woman war correspondent and the woman's angle of war and by answering other unexplored questions about the military's acceptance and accreditation of women as war correspondents through World War II, this book informs our understanding of the history of women in journalism, government control of journalists, and gender identities in times of war, while providing further insight into the experiences of women reporting in conflict zones.

Like many projects, this one began with a deceptively simple question that existing texts could not answer, and led me to more questions than I could answer in one book. I set out to understand the United States military's reasons for accrediting women as war correspondents and confining them to the woman's angle during World War II. The question seemed straightforward, especially because so many secondary sources summarized this phenomenon in one paragraph—as though it was a documented fact throughout World War II that applied to all women who worked as war correspondents. Similarly, these same works described a handful or two of trailblazing women who worked as war correspondents before the 1930s, so I also assumed it was reasonable, as well as necessary, to attempt to understand the press' and the military's treatment of women who worked as war correspondents before World War II. I soon realized that, perhaps because I had overestimated the military and underestimated women, I had not appreciated the challenge or the opportunities my research questions presented. The number and variety of women, in the nineteenth and early twentieth centuries, who worked as war correspondents—and were recognized as such by the military and the press—far exceeded my expectations and broadened the scope of my research considerably.

BACKGROUND

Women and Journalism

Early historians who considered women in journalism began with contributory histories—finding the notable, exceptional woman who could be considered significant even when viewed through the value systems of male-dominated newsrooms. While uncovering the stories of exceptional women in journalism was important to our understanding of journalism history, it did less to inform the experiences of the majority of women journalists. Marion

Marzolf's *Up from the Footnote: A History of Women Journalists* is one example of an early work that sought to add women's stories to the record by providing biographical accounts of exceptional women.[5] Marzolf's work, and other early studies of women journalists, expanded our understanding of women in journalism, but as Maurine Beasley and other journalism historians pointed out, this literature needed deepening as much as it needed widening.[6] Also similar to early women's historians, early historians of women in journalism relied upon the value systems and measures of significance established by male-dominated newsrooms to determine their subjects of study. They often limited their focus to "hard news" reporting—stories about the world traditionally dominated by men, such as stories about crime, politics, and business. The late Catherine Covert noted that the field of journalism history, like any discipline, could be blind to its own paradigms and assumptions. Women journalists have long been measured, by historians and fellow journalists alike, according to a male standard of their work, the standard Covert defined as involving three principles: autonomy, winning, and change—in other words, by their ability to cover hard news topics and "scoop" the competition with breaking, front-page news stories.[7] Covert noted the need for journalism historians to see past the traditional values that defined success in male-dominated newsrooms to consider those values often dismissed as defining "soft news"—stories about the world traditionally dominated by women, such as human-interest stories or stories about social lives, style, and housekeeping. Women who aspired to be successful "newspapermen" typically tried to avoid soft news or the women's pages, but so, it seems, did many of the historians and biographers who first wrote about the heroines of journalism. The idea of a woman's page, or even women's news, has held conflicting meaning for many women: the woman's section presented new opportunities to women who were grateful for work of their own, while also representing confinement to women who saw greater opportunities outside of women's news.

Delving deeper into the work of women journalists requires historians to consider the broader scope of their work, but it also requires historians to consider the totality of women's experience, to consider the interrelationships and influences of male and female colleagues, employers, readers, and government officials. Studies that have considered the broader picture have shown the ways in which, as Jean Marie Lutes explained in her book *Front Page Girls,* early women reporters "functioned as both agents and pawns."[8] Editors often hired them for their ability to entertain readers and to provide a female perspective—as a stunt reporter or "sob sister"—as much as for their writing and reporting abilities. As Lutes explained, "By becoming the news, female reporters created fictions of themselves that far outlasted—in scope, depth, and impact—the fleeting news value of the stories they covered."[9]

This ability to provide what editors touted as the female perspective or the woman's angle helped to expand roles available to women by feminizing those roles—so that society viewed the role of reporter as one that could be fulfilled by women as well as men, even if society was not ready to change its view of women themselves. In fact, by the 1940s, this approach or strategy was nothing new. Throughout the history of women's struggle for societal rights, recognition, and privilege, women have by turns emphasized that they are similar to men and different from men. For example, during the suffrage movement, women argued at once that they were equal to men, thus deserved equal treatment, and that they were different from men, thus deserved a voice. Early women writers gained access to newspapers by covering domestic subjects eschewed by men. They often, as historian Patricia Bradley noted, used women's news as their "Trojan horse into forbidden encampment," their entry point to covering subjects such as politics, war, or sports. [10] Like women's news, the woman's angle increased professional opportunities for women journalists, but it also held them back. Women who strove to be taken seriously as journalists equal to men often resented having to cover "women's news" or the woman's angle. Scholars have largely overlooked coverage of the woman's angle, as well as the work and lives of women who did not resent its limitations, perhaps because those who covered it seemed to reflect and perpetuate stereotypes women sought to overcome. Much remains to be done to more fully explore women's progress in the history of journalism—both as the professionals and individuals affected by gender discourse and as the professionals and individuals affecting mass-mediated messages about gender.

Women, War, and Journalism

In the last three decades, gender analyses of war have not only helped dispel the "age-old story of war as men's business,"[11] they have continued to complicate and illuminate our knowledge and beliefs about war, citizenship, and politics.[12] Scholars have shown citizenship and gender to be inextricably bound together, especially during times of war, when governments and individuals depend upon the construction and emphasis of gendered meanings to rationalize violence and oppression and to promote nationalism.[13] Nations at war often emphasize and promote gender differences among their own citizens to boost national morale, while alternately diminishing and exploiting gender differences among their enemies to dehumanize and demonize them.[14] The actions of government agencies, employers, and individuals during and directly after World War II revealed that most Americans valued the preservation of gendered identities more than prospects of convenience, efficiency, or material gain. Government propaganda and media representations of men, women, and citizenship during World War II conveyed war as necessary for the protection and preservation of women, children, and family life—normalcy—while promoting the binary ideals of male aggression and action versus female peace and passivity.[15] These messages prescribed specific and gendered codes of conduct as essential to the outcome of the war. Loose-talking or loose-behaving women could cause the United States to lose the war, as could women who wasted leftovers, used too much sugar, or refused to work for the war effort, according to so many propaganda posters.[16] The United States government called on women, as the nation's caregivers, to help with rationing food and resources, controlling information, supporting and repairing male morale (and morality), selling war bonds, growing victory gardens, sustaining the ideal of home and hearth, watching for anyone who might be hindering the war effort, and filling new and vacant jobs in men's absence.[17] Of these activities, filling new and vacant jobs represented the most dramatic "paradox" of change and continuity for women during World War II.[18] Though the United States had determined that "mixed gender units performed better than all-male units" and that "demands of military efficiency called for assigning women to combat," the United States military never permitted American women to fight.[19] Instead, the United States employed women in noncombatant roles, such as clerical work, that could free men to fight, which some men resented because they felt it left them as "cannon fodder."[20] In addition to prohibiting women from "the inner circle"[21] of war, the United States military also prevented women from sharing the same status or benefits with men. Women who served in the Women's Army Auxiliary Corps, later the Women's Army Corps, suffered from public resentment and suspicion as well as the resentment of their male colleagues.[22] When, in 1943, the Army was preparing to recognize the WAACs officially as women in service to the Army (eliminating their "auxiliary" status), rumor campaigns about promiscuity and a high rate of pregnancy among the WAACs fueled public scrutiny and suspicion.[23] The Air Force considered its 1,000 WASPs, or Women Airforce Service Pilots, to be indispensable for the nation's noncombat missions, such as test runs and deliveries.[24] Yet the Air Force also considered these women to be civilians and had little use for their skills and experience after the war ended, when so many experienced male veteran pilots needed the work.[25] Thirty-eight women died while working as WASPs, and the rest who found themselves unemployed after the war received neither military benefits nor veteran status until 1977, when Congress finally recognized the WASPs and their service to the nation.[26]

Most historical works about women journalists that consider war correspondents provide anecdotes, biographical entries, and general summaries of women's experiences and their work. Numerous biographies, autobiographies, and anthologies focus on the experiences and writings of women war correspondents, but just a few works have addressed the history of early women war correspondents as a whole: former war correspondent Julia Edwards published *Women of the World: The Great Foreign Correspondents* in 1988; Lilya Wagner, now a fundraising professional and education researcher, published her master's thesis, *The Women War Correspondents of World War II,* in 1989; journalist Nancy Caldwell Sorel dedicated nine years to researching and writing *The Women Who Wrote the War,* which she published in 1996. In presenting the story of women who worked as World War II correspondents, each of these books draws from and expands upon the previous one, so that the third, *The Women Who Wrote the War,* provides the fullest picture of United States women war correspondents and their experiences during World War II.[27] A journalist herself, Sorel drew from her interviews of countless World War II correspondents and their family members and former colleagues, as well as from extensive archival and manuscript research, published war correspondence, biographies, and autobiographies.[28] Her book, like the two shorter works by Wagner and Edwards, conveys vivid personal stories of accredited women war correspondents, describing their relationships, hopes, and fears to round out the picture of these women to include much about their personal lives. Written for general audiences, the literature about women World War II correspondents is full of dramatic adventures and rare personalities, and often includes excerpts of exceptional war coverage. Yet for all of their value, the works that contribute to our knowledge of the history of women war correspondents still leave much ground uncovered. For instance, while books that mention women war correspondents may mention the woman's angle, their focus tends to rest upon the women who most often wrote like "newspapermen," covering the hard news topics, such as battles, military strategy, diplomacy, and political conflict—upon whether these women proved themselves capable of doing a man's job and doing it well. Contextual information regarding women and war-time journalism is scattered throughout each text, but much more must be gleaned from works that focus on women's history or that consider war correspondence in general—those same works whose omission of women inspired the few books that focus on women war correspondents. These works about early women war correspondents have made invaluable contributions to journalism history, as well as to our nation's history, and yet they leave many questions unanswered about the military's and the press' acceptance of women as war correspondents and the woman's angle of war.

THEORY AND APPROACH

Women and gender relationships are often absent from histories of war, citizenship, work, mass communication, and individual wartime experiences. Yet considering gender identities and the relationships of men and women

continues to reveal new ways of understanding the past. Women themselves—as well as gender identities, roles, and relationships—are directly
and indirectly essential to the topics of war, citizenship, work, and mass
communication, as well as to any study of an individual's life. Studies that
consider gender have broadened our understanding of history, not only for
the answers they have provided but for the questions and concerns they
continue to provoke. As Joan Wallach Scott concluded in 2008:

> Two decades of research has made it abundantly clear that . . . "gender con-
> structs politics." . . . But oddly, or perhaps predictably, there are fewer ques-
> tions posed about the ways in which "politics constructs gender," about the
> changing meanings of "women" (and "men"), and about the ways they are
> articulated by and through other concepts that seemingly have nothing to do
> with sex (such as war, race, citizen, reason, spirituality, nature, or the univer-
> sal).[29]

The premise for Scott's conclusion, as well as the premise for most studies that consider gender, is a belief that fixed gender categories do not exist.
Gender as a category is fluid, deriving significance and meaning from context. Traits or tasks that individuals or groups define and value as masculine
in one time or place, they might well define and value as feminine in another
time or place. Each individual constructs gender through his or her perceptions and experiences, which in turn depend upon and influence structures of
power, as well as the needs and desires of individuals in power within any
given society. As Judith Butler has argued: "There is no gender identity
behind the expressions of gender; . . . identity is performatively constituted
by the very 'expressions' that are said to be its results."[30] Thus, a look at
individual women or women as a group should consider gender, defined by
Scott as "an entire system of relationships that may include sex, but is not
directly determined by sex nor directly determining of sexuality."[31] How
individuals and groups construct, express, and perceive gender can have
grave implications for the lives of individual men and women, as well as for
communities and nations. Scott has called for historians to explore these
"subjective meanings of women and men as categories of identity," rather
than grouping individuals in binary categories as men or women, assuming
they share an identity or common goals, beliefs, and experiences.[32] If an
individual's sex is socially and culturally constructed, then a look at female
journalists alone could be as inadequate as a consideration of male journalists
alone. Likewise, setting two separate works side by side, such as a history of
male journalists and a history of female journalists, does not provide the
same understanding as a consideration of men and women together. A look at
gender can, as Scott has called for more historians to do, explore the subjective meanings of these women's identities in terms of their shifting roles and
ambitions.[33] And yet, any exploration of women's identities must go beyond

sex and gender. Historians and others too often use the term "women" to mean white women, while using the term "blacks" to mean black men, as Elizabeth Spelman and others have noted.[34] In any study, just as historians should consider the gender constructions and interactions of both sexes simultaneously and interactively, they must also consider, when applicable, the intersecting and similarly fluid categories of race and class.[35] Any consideration of a group's shared attributes and experiences risks overlooking the uniqueness of individuals, or the ways in which they may or may not identify with multiple groups. Iris Marion Young has drawn from Jean-Paul Sartre's ideas of serial collectivity to argue that scholars must consider gender in terms of "serial collectives" rather than binary groups.[36] Considering individuals in terms of a series of collectives defined by shared conditions, Young argued, allows scholars to compare these conditions and individuals without implying that all members of any group share common attributes, identities, or objectives. While I kept these concepts of intersectionality in mind as I researched and wrote this book, the fact remained that the same barriers that stood in the way of all women journalists were often insurmountable for women of color or of limited economic means or social connections. As this book will show, the vast majority of early women war correspondents, up through World War II, were well educated, well connected, and white. Nonetheless, I did explore a diverse range of sources while considering what (and who) was missing from each part of the story or set of documents, as well as the extent to which, as so many historians have shown, the opportunities long heralded for women during wartime only existed for certain women, in certain ways, while often creating additional barriers for other women.

Scholars continue to debate the extent to which World War II brought about societal change for women or just accelerated changes already under way. Scott argued that scholars of women's history should pay less attention to "watersheds and the impacts of events on women" and instead should be asking subtle and arguably more complex questions "about processes of politics, about interconnections between economic policy and the meanings of social experiences, about cultural representations of sexual difference and their presence in political discourse." These questions, Scott argued, "permit historians to maintain a perspective that at once makes women visible as historical actors, as subjects of the narrative," while offering new readings of subjects in which women traditionally were overlooked.[37] Whereas it is useful to understand the subjective meanings of women's progress in any history, the history of women in the profession of journalism seems to hold particular significance because women journalists were so well poised to influence gender discourse. Not only were women journalists seeking professional status in a male world, where they might earn wages for their work and work alongside men as equals, they also gained a voice through journalism and a chance to perform the role of "woman as journalist" for the world.[38]

How they used this voice and this performance, in turn, could have broad implications for men and women, as well as society as a whole. As women reported what they saw and did as war correspondents, they contributed to the discourse of citizenship and gender, two concepts that are inextricably bound together to form a "set of social practices,"[39] especially during times of war.

This book, as a historical study of the press' and the military's acceptance and accreditation of U.S. women war correspondents, should deepen our understanding of gender, war, and journalism. It also should contribute to a greater understanding of women war correspondents that can, in turn, help future scholars consider the impact that these correspondents' milestones, setbacks, and writings might have had on the profession of journalism as a whole or on women's perceptions of themselves, or even how these women might have influenced how men perceived themselves, their work, and the women around them. Understanding the ways that the U.S. military controlled or influenced journalism and journalists through World War II therefore also should contribute to our understanding of history. Historians themselves rely upon, and generally trust, the writings of journalists as primary sources, the "raw material" that allows them to secure "a durable, accurate, and reliable recounting of the past."[40] Scholars have shown that wartime reporting is often unreliable. Noting that few civilians understood the truly gruesome nature of war, historian Paul Fussell explained that even war correspondents "who perceived these horrors kept quiet about them on behalf of the War Effort."[41] Embedded reporters had an obligation to the troops to which they were attached, and they had their own feelings of patriotism to honor as well. Thus an understanding of the government's control and influence of women war correspondents during World War II should also contribute to a more reliable understanding of history.

This book provides a cultural and social history of the United States military's acceptance of women as official war correspondents up through World War II. Rather than focus on individual stories of exceptionalism or heroism, it seeks a broader understanding of the interactions among the press, the military, and the majority of women who worked as war correspondents. It considers the woman's angle and its influence on the process by which women gained accreditation and access to theaters of war by considering the viewpoints and recollections of the writers, their audiences, and their colleagues, as well as those who had control over their work—such as their superiors within the military and the press. While the primary focus of my research was on the years in which the United States actively fought in World War II, from December 7, 1941, to September 2, 1945, I also considered the time period from 1846 to 1940 in order to document the emergence of the woman's angle of war and women's early attempts to attain accreditation before World War II. In addition to government documents, my research considered private papers of government officials and journalists, records of newspaper and magazine publishers and broadcast corporations, as well as newspaper articles, memoirs, and other published works by and about war correspondents. The purpose of this study was not only to contribute to the history of women who worked as early war correspondents, but also to consider the emergence of the woman's angle of war and the category of "woman war correspondent," and the influence these two concepts had on women's work as journalists and war correspondents. [42]

NOTES

1. Julia Edwards, *Women of the World: The Great Foreign Correspondents* (Boston: Houghton Mifflin, 1988), 62–70 (Edwards noted that Sigrid Schultz paid bartenders to serve her nonalcoholic drinks "that looked like the real thing," 63); and Lilya Wagner, *Women War Correspondents of World War II* (New York: Greenwood Press, 1989), 99, 102.

2. Awards of Pulitzer Prizes, Columbia University in the City of New York, Anne McCormick, General Correspondence, January to May 1937, Anne O'Hare McCormick papers, Manuscripts and Archives Division, The New York Public Library; Edwards, *Women of the World*, 75, 77–79; and Ishbel Ross, *Ladies of the Press: The Story of Women in Journalism by an Insider* (New York: Harper, 1936), 367.

3. Edwards, *Women of the World*, 71.

4. Judith Matloff, "Unspoken: Foreign Correspondents and Sexual Abuse," *Columbia Journalism Review* (May/June 2007), 22–23; see also ed. Hannah Storm and Helena Williams, *No Woman's Land: On the Frontlines with Female Reporters* (London: International News Safety Institute, 2012).

5. Marion Marzolf, *Up from the Footnote: A History of Women Journalists* (New York: Hastings House, 1977).

6. Maurine Beasley, "Recent Directions for the Study of Women's History in American Journalism," *Journalism Studies* 2, no. 2 (2001): 207–20.

7. Catherine L. Covert, "Journalism History and Women's Experience: A Problem in Conceptual Change," *Journalism History* 8, no. 1 (Spring 1981): 2–6.

8. Jean Marie Lutes, *Front Page Girls: Women Journalists in American Culture and Fiction, 1880-1930* (Ithaca, NY: Cornell University Press, 2006), 6.

9. Ibid., 11.

10. Patricia Bradley, *Women and the Press: The Struggle for Equality* (Evanston: Northwestern University Press, 2005), 113.

11. Miriam Cooke, "Wo-Man, Retelling the War Myth," in *Gendering War Talk*, ed. Miriam Cooke and Angela Woollacott (Princeton: Princeton University Press, 1993), 178.

12. See, for example, Gisela Bock, "Equality and Difference in National Socialist Racism," in *Feminism and History*, ed. Joan Wallach Scott (New York: Oxford University Press, 1996); Kathleen Canning, "Gender and the Politics of Class Formation: Rethinking German Labor History," *American Historical Review* 97, no. 3 (June, 1992): 736–68; Jean Bethke Elshtain, *Women and War* (New York: Basic Books, 1987); Emily S. Rosenberg, "Gender," *Journal of American History* 77, no. 1 (1990): 116–24; and Mrinalini Sinha, "Gender and Nation," in *Feminist History Reader*, ed. Sue Morgan (New York: Routledge, 2006).

13. Kathleen Canning and Sonya O. Rose, "Gender, Citizenship, and Subjectivity: Some Historical and Theoretical Considerations," *Gender and History* 13, no. 3 (November 2001): 427–43.

14. Cooke, "Wo-Man, Retelling the War Myth," 178; Marianne Hirsch and Leo Spitzer, "Gendered Translations: Claude Lanzmann's Shoah," in ed. Cooke and Woollacott, *Gendering War Talk*, 4; Maureen Honey, *Creating Rosie the Riveter: Class, Gender, and Propaganda during World War II* (Amherst: University of Massachusetts Press, 1984); and Leila J. Rupp,

Mobilizing Women for War: German and American Propaganda, 1939–1945 (Princeton: Princeton University Press, 1978).

15. Amy Bentley, *Eating for Victory: Food Rationing and the Politics of Domesticity* (Urbana: University of Illinois Press, 1998); D'Ann Campbell, *Women at War with America: Private Lives in a Patriotic Era* (Cambridge: Harvard University Press, 1984); William H. Chafe, *The Paradox of Change* (New York: Oxford University Press, 1991); Susan Gubar, "'This Is My Rifle, This Is My Gun,' World War II and the Blitz on Women," in eds. Margaret Randolph Higonnet, Jane Jenson, Sonya Michel, and Margaret Collins Weitz, *Behind the Lines: Gender and the Two World Wars* (New Haven: Yale University Press, 1987), 227–59; Susan M. Hartmann, *The Home Front and Beyond* (Boston: Twayne Publishers, 1982); Honey, *Creating Rosie the Riveter*; and Rupp, *Mobilizing Women for War*.

16. Sonya Michel, "American Women and the Discourse of the American Family during World War II," in Higonnet et al., *Behind the Lines*, 154–67; Rupp, *Mobilizing Women for War*; and Bilge Yesil, "'Who Said This Is a Man's War?': Propaganda, Advertising Discourse and the Representation of War Worker Women during the Second World War," *Media History* 10, no. 2 (2004): 103–18.

17. Karen Anderson, *Wartime Women: Sex Roles, Family Relations, and the Status of Women during World War II* (Westport, CT: Greenwood Press, 1981); Bentley, *Eating for Victory*; D'Ann Campbell, *Women at War with America*; Chafe, *The Paradox of Change*; Hartmann, *The Home Front and Beyond*; Marilyn E. Hegarty, *Victory Girls, Khaki-Wackies, and Patriotutes: The Regulation of Female Sexuality during World War II* (New York: New York University Press, 2008).

18. Chafe, *The Paradox of Change*, 233.

19. D'Ann Campbell, "Women in Combat: The World War II Experience in the United States, Great Britain, Germany, and the Soviet Union," *The Journal of Military History* 57, no. 2 (April 1993): 301.

20. Hartmann, *The Home Front and Beyond*, 39. For more about the "release-a-man" campaign and its public response, see Campbell, *Women at War with America*, 40.

21. Elshtain, *Women and War*, 183.

22. Ann Allen, "The News Media and the Women's Army Auxiliary Corps: Protagonists for a Cause," *Military Affairs* 50 (April 1986): 77–83; Campbell, *Women at War with America*, 35–37; and Leisa Meyer, *Creating G.I. Jane: Sexuality and Power in the Women's Army Corps during World War II* (New York: Columbia University Press, 1996), 33–50.

23. Allen, "The News Media and the Women's Army Auxiliary Corps"; Campbell, *Women at War with America*, 35–37; and Meyer, *Creating G.I. Jane*, 33–50.

24. Hartmann, *The Home Front and Beyond*, 46–47.

25. Ibid.

26. Ibid.

27. Edwards, *Women of the World*; Nancy Caldwell Sorel, *The Women Who Wrote the War* (New York: Arcade Pub., 1999); and Wagner, *Women War Correspondents of World War II*.

28. Phone interview with Nancy Caldwell Sorel, October 9, 2009.

29. Joan W. Scott, "Unanswered Questions," *American Historical Review* (December 2008): 1423–24.

30. Judith Butler, *Gender Trouble: Feminism and the Subversion of Identity* (New York: Routledge, 1990), 34.

31. Joan Wallach Scott, *Gender and the Politics of History* (New York: Columbia University Press, 1999), 32.

32. Ibid., 6.

33. Ibid.

34. Elizabeth Spelman, *Inessential Woman: Problems of Exclusion in Feminist Thought* (Boston: Beacon Press, 1988).

35. Kimberlé Crenshaw, "Demarginalizing the Intersection of Race and Sex: A Black Feminist Critique of Antidiscrimination Doctrine, Feminist Theory and Antiracist Politics," *University of Chicago Legal Forum* (1989): 139–67.

36. Iris Marion Young, *Intersecting Voices: Dilemmas of Gender, Political Philosophy, and Policy* (Princeton: Princeton University Press, 1997), 33–36.

37. Joan W. Scott, "Women and War: A Focus for Rewriting History," *Women's Studies Quarterly* 12, no. 2 (Summer 1984): 3.

38. As Butler has stated, "identity is performatively constituted by the very 'expressions' that are said to be its results," in *Gender Trouble*, 34.

39. Canning and Rose, "Gender, Citizenship, and Subjectivity," 441.

40. Barbie Zelizer, "Why Memory's Work on Journalism Does Not Reflect Journalism's Work on Memory," *Memory Studies* 1 (2008): 79.

41. Paul Fussell, *Wartime: Understanding and Behavior in the Second World War* (New York: Oxford, 1989), 285–86; and Zelizer, "Why Memory's Work on Journalism," 79.

42. David Paul Nord, "The Practice of Historical Research," in *Mass Communication Research and Theory*, eds. Guido H. Stempel III, David H. Weaver, and G. Cleveland Wilhoit (Boston: Allyn and Bacon, 2003), 70.

Chapter Two

"A Womanly View of War," 1846–1910

> The *London Post* has sent a woman to Africa as its war correspondent. We shall now learn what the women there wear.[1]
>
> —*Saturday Evening Post*, 1881

The term "war correspondent" describes an individual who travels to the site of a war to report news about that war for a medium that will reach a public audience. Individuals around the world have communicated aspects of battle with one another since the beginning of time.[2] Yet the role and image of the professional war correspondent, as we understand the term today, were born and raised in the nineteenth century. Among the first of this "luckless tribe" of journalists may well have been the reporter who claimed such a title for himself, William Howard Russell of *The Times of London*.[3] While Russell was by no means the first to report on war, scholars have largely agreed that his critical, independent reports about the British army from the battlefield of the Crimean War represented the start of something new.[4] Russell's war correspondence in 1854 was "the beginning of an organized effort to report a war to the civilian population at home using services of a civilian reporter," historian Phillip Knightley noted, which was "an immense leap in the history of journalism."[5] The 1850s may have been the dawn of an organized effort, yet these early efforts at war correspondence were highly unorganized, governed more by trial and error than by any professional standard.

Of all the American women whom journalists and historians have described as war correspondents, Jane Cazneau may have been among the earliest to have reported on war from behind battle lines, when she wrote about the Mexican-American War for the *New York Sun* in 1846, writing under the pseudonym "Cora Montgomery."[6] Another, Margaret Fuller, is better known today and has frequently been described as the first woman war correspondent, a label attributed to her writings about the Roman revolution for the *New-York Tribune* in 1849.[7] Fuller and Cazneau were exceptional women for their time, and publishers and the public took seriously their reports and views of war and politics. Yet even as so-called firsts, neither of these women was alone. Scholars, journalists, biographers, and others, writing throughout the past 150 years, have given the title "first woman war correspondent," with no qualifier, to more than two dozen women whose war reporting began some twenty to one hundred years later.[8] In the late nineteenth and early twentieth centuries, American newspaper and magazine articles described more than seventy women as "war correspondents" (see Appendix 1). While many of these women might not fit such a billing on closer scrutiny, it does appear that at least one woman reported on every major battle that engaged American military as well as several foreign conflicts in which the United States had no role.

If the mid-nineteenth century was the infancy of war correspondence, then the time between the Civil War and World War I was its "golden age," as well as, as Knightley has described it, "an inglorious fifty-year free-for-all," with little-to-no military regulation or censorship.[9] It was also a time when war correspondents were heroic symbols and even well-paid celebrities.[10] Frederic Hudson, writing a survey of journalism in 1872, noted society's reverence for war correspondents, calling them the true historians of war and opening a chapter about them with the following exclamations: "The war correspondent! How much would be lost without him! How many noble deeds and gallant actions have disappeared with the smoke of battle for want of a reporter!"[11] This "free-for-all" of war reporting meant the title of war correspondent was also up for grabs. The U.S. military did not have a formal process for accrediting war correspondents before World War I, other than to write letters of introduction or to grant rights of travel and accommodation. During the Civil War, war correspondence often consisted of entirely biased, exaggerated reports, written by reporters who may not have been anywhere near the action, who sought to prove their loyalty, build the morale of their own side, and outdo competing reporters rather than provide an accurate account of the war.[12] Just as reporters could write about war, firsthand, without earning a "war correspondent" label, news accounts often used the term "war correspondent" to describe writers whose subjects related to war, whether or not they witnessed violence or military operations. Lillie Devereux Blake and Laura Redden were women writers whom newspapers billed as war correspondents during the Civil War, despite the fact that both women remained in Washington, D.C., and based much of their work on interviews or opinions rather than on firsthand accounts of battle.[13] The press also labeled Emily Briggs (who often wrote under the pseudonym "Olivia"), Susan Dickinson, and Lottie Bengough McCaffrey as Civil War correspondents, yet I have been unable to find any war reporting with their bylines and no woman appears in any military list of Civil War correspondents.[14] As a means, perhaps, of sensationalizing their stories, newspapers often labeled writers as war correspondents when writing about them—and yet, more often than not, newspapers published the actual news of war with no byline. Thus, it is difficult if not impossible to consider the full contribution of women war correspondents in the nineteenth and early twentieth centuries. For this time period, and this portion of my study, I focused upon the bylined work of women whom American newspapers and magazines billed as war correspondents, as well as the articles written about these women and their work.

Coinciding with a war reporting free-for-all was a rising interest among newspaper publishers in presenting the woman's angle to reach more women readers, who in turn could draw more department-store advertising revenue.[15] In 1872, Hudson devoted a chapter of his survey of journalism to women, explaining their rise in the profession as follows: "They can frequently do what men can not accomplish. These female journalists, pure and bright, are the growth of the last fifteen years in America. They are now to be seen every where—in every large city where influential papers are printed."[16] In the late nineteenth century, journalism was among the few careers readily available to women that could offer the intellectual and economic satisfaction available to men. In September of 1894, Margaret Welch, a *New York Times* reporter who spoke at the annual meeting of the American Social Science Association, declared some aspects of newspaper work "almost ideal for women," because journalism was one of the only professions that allowed women to "command a fair salary while learning the business."[17] Women who wanted to break into the field could submit their work to editors to be published piecemeal, while persuading editors to offer them future assignments as special correspondents, or "specials." As Edwin Shuman explained in his 1894 guide for aspiring journalists, one of the best ways for women to enter newspaper work at that time was to become a special correspondent.[18]

> The special furnishes a broad but thorny road to newspaperdom that is open to all, because anybody, rich or poor, at home or in a strange land, can at least try it. It is therefore, generally speaking, the best free-for-all highway that we have. And there seem to be about as many women as men who reach distinction by it.[19]

Shuman noted that women who had reached such distinction included Fannie Brigham Ward, a correspondent who wrote lengthy articles, syndicated nationally, about war in South America, Central America, and Cuba in the 1890s.[20] At a time when women could not vote, own property, or travel alone without drawing suspicion, most of the women that newspapers and magazines described as war correspondents in the nineteenth and early twentieth centuries did not work in such a capacity until they were more than thirty years old and either divorced, widowed, or estranged from their husbands, and more than half were childless. Women often traveled with medical units, assisting nurses while they worked as correspondents, though many women also traveled with letters of permission from military officials.[21] While a woman writer's presence at any battle made news, often syndicated nationally, one report seemed to have little bearing on another so that newspapers often described each of more than a dozen women who reported on battles in the 1890s as the first and only woman war correspondent.

News reported by women war correspondents in the mid- to late-nineteenth century is rare and hard to find. Most war reporting in the nineteenth century either lacked any byline, with news often appearing in compiled reports, or appeared under the generic byline "special correspondent." Yet, news stories and briefs remarking on the existence of a woman war correspondent are easier to find. Even women who enjoyed notoriety for having "scooped" or otherwise outdone a man in war correspondence saw the novelty of their experience as a woman overshadow the content and significance of any news they reported. For example, newspapers reported that Teresa Dean, "a bright young widow" (who was twice divorced and, by all accounts I have found, never widowed),[22] was covering the Sioux Indian War in 1891 for the *Chicago Herald* and had published "advance news of the operations of the army, which Gen. Miles acknowledged to be correct, though he said he could not understand where she got the information."[23] The article went on to explain: "This was an experiment in journalism, sending out a woman as war correspondent, but it was a successful one, even though she was 'only a woman.'"[24]

In fact, Dean arrived at the Pine Ridge agency in South Dakota in January 1891, shortly after the battle of Wounded Knee, and she noted with alarm and some amusement that her presence seemed to be the only threat encountered by the other war correspondents, whose imagined roles far exceeded their actual assignments. "They were wonderfully equipped—to the very teeth—with revolvers, knives, and belts and ammunition," Dean noted in an unpublished memoir. "They looked a formidable army in themselves. I felt awfully inferior-looking in my heavy gray ulster." (See figure 2.1.) The men objected to her presence as unnecessary—they were covering the war just fine without her—and told her it was too dangerous for a woman. Dean noted the security of the camp at Pine Ridge and told them she was in no danger. She also assured them that she was no competition: Her writing was "not that of rushing any news to the office" but would instead be her own impressions of the situation. Dean observed that the man most insulted by her presence was the man with the "cowboy-hat-brim a little wider than the others, his revolvers, knives, and belts more conspicuous, and his manner the wild Western Hero!"[25] Whereas, Dean noted, the correspondent who escorted her

Figure 2.1.   In January 1891, the *Chicago Herald* sent Teresa Dean to cover the Sioux Indian War at Pine Ridge, where she said men exaggerated their roles as war correspondents in the "Wild West." The larger photograph shows a group of war correspondents taking time out from covering the Sioux to pose with William "Buffalo Bill" Cody.
   Source: Dean photographs reproduced with permission of Charles Deering McCormick Library of Special Collections, Northwestern University Library; group photograph reproduced with permission of Denver Public Library.

to her first meeting with General Nelson Miles was secure enough in his masculinity "not to resent the coming upon the danger zone one tame looking bit of femininity to lessen the glory awaiting scouts, heroes, dare-devils, and correspondents." This self-assured reporter was in the minority, however, and the other men decided that a group photograph of war correspondents at Pine Ridge also was "no place for a woman," Dean later recalled, and so they excluded her from the photograph and the chance to "go down in illustrated history."[26] But it appears that Dean did get the last word, winning notoriety for her widely published claims that the men embellished, exaggerated, and, in some cases, made up their stories, and that they were busier dressing the part and taking photographs of themselves than gathering news.[27] Dean continued to write extensively, often critically, about the U.S. military and battles in Cuba, China, and the Philippines and took pride in her position as a war correspondent, while noting that she preferred the title of "special correspondent" and thought it more fitting—"for modesty's sake, there being such brilliant real war correspondents out in the field."[28]

Another reporter who questioned the accuracy and significance of being labeled a war correspondent was Susette LaFlesche, a woman well versed in conflicting identities. The daughter of an Omaha Indian chief, LaFlesche often wrote under the name of "Bright Eyes"—which was the English translation of her given name, "Inshtatheamba"—even after she married Thomas Henry Tibbles, an editor of the *Omaha World-Herald*. In December 1890, one month before Teresa Dean arrived at the Pine Ridge Agency, the *Omaha World-Herald* and *Chicago Express* hired Tibbles and Bright Eyes as war correspondents to cover the Sioux Indian conflict. The couple had decades of reporting experience between them, and yet they both found the prematurity of the term "war correspondent" unsettling. They knew about the rising tensions between the Sioux and the white settlers, but they did not believe the tension would lead to war. When they arrived at Pine Ridge for their assignment, as Tibbles recalled in his autobiography, they found an "amazing state of affairs."

> Though there had been no outbreak of any kind, the place was jammed with "war correspondents" who were expected to produce thrilling "war news."
>
> Hanging around the hotel day after day, they constantly dispatched new inflammatory stories made out of whole cloth. Burning arrows were being fired into the agency building; the Indians were perpetrating horrors in every direction—according to those writers. Yet in that peaceful agency the Sioux crowded the trader's store, the children went to school. The congregation worshipped as usual, and rations were distributed methodically.
>
> Bright Eyes and I chose to stay in an Indian household, where we could hear facts instead of fiction. Here the Sioux men all called on us and kept us informed of every event in the tribe and the whole Sioux nation. They con-

firmed our theory that, except for that sudden craze for ghost-dancing in ghost shirts, all was peaceful.[29]

When a battle did break out in the last week of December, Tibbles and Bright Eyes witnessed the aftermath and wired their reports to their editors. Syndicated news stories about the attack rarely featured bylines beyond "Special Correspondent," but many credited a portion of the news to "Bright Eyes," with no further explanation as to her identity or her role, as seen in the following news brief, copied here in its entirety.

> At headquarters of the Department of the Platte Sunday night a dispatch was received from General Brooke, which stated that Major Whitesides, in command of a battalion of the Seventh Cavalry, had captured Big Foot and his entire band near the head of Porcupine creek. About 150 bucks surrendered. General Brooke also telegraphed that the hostiles in the Bad Lands had surrendered, and would reach Pine Ridge on Tuesday. Bright Eyes sent word Saturday night that half the hostiles had left the Bad Lands and were within a few hours' march of the agency. It is now apparent that the Indian trouble in the Northwest is rapidly approaching a termination.[30]

Like Bright Eyes, more than a dozen women who served as war correspondents in the nineteenth and early twentieth centuries did so while accompanying husbands, fathers, or brothers who were members of the military or were war correspondents themselves (see Appendix 1). Josephine Miles Woodward was thirty-five, with a husband and two sons, ages ten and thirteen, when she traveled in 1896 to Cuba for the *Cincinnati Commercial Gazette* to cover the Spanish-American War.[31] One trade journal, the *Fourth Estate*, in a news brief headlined "A Clever Correspondent," credited Woodward's upbringing in Indian Territory, as the daughter of a military colonel, with preparing Woodward for her assignment in Cuba.

> Mrs. Josephine Miles Woodward, of the staff of the *Cincinnati Commercial Gazette*, is in Cuba for her paper. Mrs. Woodward is a clever writer, and her pen has descriptive powers that are unusual. She may not be able to see much of the life of the insurgents in camp and on the march, but the *Commercial Gazette*'s readers will, however, be given an opportunity to read letters descriptive of life in Havana that will be full of spirit and color. Mrs. Woodward is very familiar with army life, having lived for years with her father in the army posts on the frontier.[32]

News by Woodward ran locally with her byline, but readers outside of Cincinnati would have been more likely to read brief accounts about Woodward herself, without knowing what war reporting, if any, she contributed to their daily news. Most of the accounts describing Woodward's work as a war correspondent were short, yet favorable. The *Chicago Daily Tribune* printed

Figure 2.2.   Susette "Bright Eyes" LaFlesche Tibbles covered the Sioux-Indian
conflict for the *Omaha World-Herald* and *Chicago Express*.
   Source: Reproduced with permission of Douglas County Historical Society.

ONLY WOMAN WAR CORRESPONDENT.

The Versatile Mrs. Colby.

Mrs. Clara Bewick Colby, who has as many titles to fame as Richard Harding Davis has medals, has added to the list. She is the only woman war correspondent at the front. She has gone to Cuba with a regular correspondent's pass, accompanying her husband, Brigadier General Colby.

Mrs. Colby is editor of the Woman's Tribune, lecturer on suffrage, civics, dress reform" and literature, ex-professor of Latin, founder of a public library and officer in many women's clubs.

Figure 2.3.   Clara Bewick Colby. Although more than a dozen women covered the Spanish American War in 1898, individual newspapers touted each one as the "first and only" woman war correspondent. (Above, the newspaper has spelled her name wrong.)
   Source: New York Evening Journal, August 10, 1898. Chronicling America, Library of Congress.

a brief under the headline "To Send Society Editor to Cuba. Cincinnati Newspaper Makes a New Departure in the War Line," and noted "Mrs. Woodward has ability, tact, and energy."[33] A few news accounts that ran nationally with Woodward's byline included a brief in which she reported on an interview with General Valeriano Weyler and another brief in which she reported the public execution of ten prisoners in Havana.[34]

"Yellow journalism," or the often sensationalistic, self-promotional, and questionable tactics used by newspaper editors in the late nineteenth century to compete for advertisers and readers, did not cause the United States to go to war with Spain, as historian W. Joseph Campbell made clear in his 2001 study.[35] Yet this desire for attention-grabbing headlines likely did influence the military and the press to allow hundreds of writers to cover the war.[36] By 1898, at least twelve women had gained permission—along with, in at least several cases, military accreditation—to travel to Cuba to cover war news for their publications (see Appendix 1). The United States War Department issued Anna Benjamin "War Correspondent's Pass No. 226," which was signed by the Secretary of War and which certified that on May 12, 1898, she had been "duly accredited to the War Department as a correspondent," and that military commanders should "permit him to pass freely, so far as in their judgment it is proper and expedient to do so, and to extend to him such aid and protection, not incompatible with the interests of the service, as he may require."[37] Newspaper articles and other accounts describe the following fifteen women as war correspondents covering the Spanish-American War, once again noting mistakenly that each of these women was the first or only one to do so: Anna Benjamin, Cecil Charles (Lily Curry), Clara Bewick Colby, Teresa Dean, Mary Francis, Margherita Arlina Hamm, Annabel Lee, Kate Masterson, Sadie Kneller Miller, Nora O'Malley, Elsie Reasoner, Fannie Brigham Ward, Kit Blake Watkins, Katherine White, and Josephine Woodward.[38]

Bylined articles of these women seem to have been rare, with newspapers instead making the women themselves the focus of stories within the women's section of a newspaper, often as brief items with no byline, and often accompanied by an illustrated portrait.[39] Most of the writings about these early women war correspondents were written in a light tone that reflected the surrounding content of the women's pages. The items described the women and their work in favorable, if not promotional, terms. These women war correspondents were most often described as being attractive, bright, and plucky—as being cheerful despite rough conditions and capable of holding their own without special treatment.[40] Articles often noted that these women were small, slight, or otherwise diminutive in shape or stature, even while being exceptionally active or energetic.[41] They were not what a reader might expect, these articles explained before offering an account of the correspondents' feminine attributes and habits as proof.

Figure 2.4.   Elsie Reasoner covered the Spanish-American War in Cuba.
Source: The St. Paul (Minnesota) Globe, June 19, 1904. Chronicling America, Library of Congress.

A woman's stated purpose for war correspondence, according to articles that mentioned it at all, was to provide a female perspective of war. Yet the official reason for a woman's travel often differed from the actual reason. For example, Elsie Reasoner found it easiest to travel to Cuba as a volunteer with the nurses, so while some articles explained that her intention was to cover the war (and quoted Reasoner as saying she wanted to learn whether war really was hell), other articles reported that her journalistic role was secondary to her volunteerism.[42] Few articles described the work women were doing, beyond labeling them as war correspondents. One exception was a half-page feature about Reasoner's marriage to fellow war correspondent Lester Ralph. The article began with a description of Reasoner at work, covering the Spanish-American War in Cuba:

> She is a slip of a girl, only five feet tall—just like a china doll—and she seemed entirely out of place on the battlefield. But as the shells shrieked and the Mauser bullets sang, she walked cheerfully around, watching the wounded men fall, and then after she had helped them, asking them questions about it.[43]

Men who relished the title of war correspondent and looked for opportunities to earn it resented women whose work might redefine their own. As Teresa Dean, in her unpublished memoirs, explained in an anecdote about war correspondent Kathleen "Kit" Blake Watkins, a reporter who was in Cuba in 1898 covering war for the *Toronto Mail*, many newspapermen and military officials saw only one purpose for female war correspondents: "Only for the sensation of a woman being at the front or trailing along—and it was a time too serious for sensations!"[44] True to prediction, Watkins did create a stir when she covered the Spanish-American War for the *Toronto Mail*, though, by some accounts, she also dug up several stories missed by her male colleagues. But while her stories ran locally or without bylines, the story about her presence was syndicated to newspapers in Canada, the United States, and England.

> "I got a lady war correspondent," he said triumphantly, "And I guess that takes the pot." We looked incredulous. "It's true, sure," he said. "She came on the train this morning from Washington with a full hand of papers from the War Department, and I tell you she's going through with the outfit."
> A lady war correspondent! The idea was too comic. We could not believe it.[45]

The war correspondent who authored this article, making Watkins the subject of his own breaking news story, lauded her reporting skills before mocking himself and his colleagues for their initial reaction.

A lady war correspondent! We looked at one another in doubt and indignation. After all, we said, there were limits to the sphere of woman's usefulness. What kind of a newspaper proprietor was it, anyhow, who would send a tenderly nurtured lady around amid the hardships and rigors, the bullets, and the yellow fever germs of a Cuban war?

"For her own sake," said the experienced war correspondent solemnly, "this thing ought to be stopped right now." "For her own sake,"—the unnecessary use of the phrase rather betrayed us, for at the back of our minds, as we lay back on the cushioned lounges, sipping ice water, there was a feeling which we did not care to recognize, that we had a right to be a little indignant for our own sakes.[46]

While women recalled male war correspondents as often uncooperative and resentful of their presence, only rarely did any article convey a negative assessment of women's work as war correspondents. A *London Exchange* article, which ran in American newspapers in 1899, chastised and mocked Lady Mary Howard, a war correspondent covering the South African War for the *London Telegraph*, for "skedaddling at the first hint of real live warfare to a comfortably secure place in the rear, where she was safe from shot and shell and all other realisms that might have perturbed her peace of mind."[47] After forgiving Howard her self-preservation instinct, the article resumed its lecturing tone, arguing that war correspondents must have personal knowledge of war and that "if Lady Mary wasn't willing to acquire this knowledge, whatever the risk, she should have stayed at home."[48] Before ending with a disparaging pronouncement of all female war correspondents, the article concluded that Howard may well have been useful after all: "While failing to get any 'copy' herself she nevertheless furnished delightful 'copy' to her male co-worker. Perhaps this is, after all, the real province of the woman war correspondent."[49]

Most of the writings by women billed as war correspondents during the late nineteenth century would not have competed for front page billing with the writing done by men at this time. Women who did cover war, and whose stories had bylines, often wrote about conditions for soldiers, such as sanitation, medical care, rations, clothing, and supplies, as well as conditions for civilians.[50] Other women whose writing was billed as war correspondence would have been more aptly identified as foreign correspondents or travel writers. These women wrote first-person accounts of landscapes, culture, and events, or they wrote extended political analyses.[51]

Women who worked as war correspondents continued to furnish delight throughout the early 1900s—not only for their critics, colleagues, and readers but for military troops as well. Newspapers and magazines described soldiers' surprise at seeing female war correspondents and even military units that were unprepared for such visitors—but not unwelcoming.[52] An article about Eleanor Franklin, who covered the Russo-Japanese War for the *Atlanta*

Constitution in 1905, ran in multiple daily papers along with her portrait and a description calling her "the only duly accredited newspaper woman in the Far East, that part of the world unsuccessfully besieged by correspondents for so long."[53] The premise of the article was an anecdote describing how Franklin's employer had inadvertently simplified her task of gaining access to Japanese government officials—by shocking them with the news that they would be visited by a *woman* war correspondent.

> When it was learned that she had been sent to the Far East for the harmless purpose of studying the Japanese methods of relief, charitable, and prison work occasioned by the war, as well as those features of the national life that are at all times interesting to the world at large, they [Japanese government officials] were so relieved that her greatest requests seemed reasonable, and she is now, through the personal direction and assistance of Baron Nakashima, confidential Secretary to the Prime Minister, preparing a series of articles that will be of the greatest possible interest.[54]

Yet news that a woman was reporting on war in Morocco generated much alarm at the *Army and Navy Journal*, as well as a call for action—despite the fact that by 1910 more than two dozen American women had reported from war zones over the course of six decades. "We are prepared already to shed tears for the unfortunate Army officers of the future," the journal stated after announcing the existence of a female war correspondent and explaining that "what one woman does to attract attention is imitated by others of her sex."[55] The article reminded readers that military officials were at work on a code to control newspaper correspondents and stated that such a code must prevent the otherwise inevitable consequences of having war described "in the emotional chronicles of a female war correspondent," which were likely to include "'pitiful' tales of discontented privates, who suddenly discover that field rations are not like what mother used to cook, and other 'inhumanities of war.'"[56] Such sentimentalism would weaken "the strong masculine hold on our destiny"—what's more, "peace societies would spring up in every little town," and it would become exceedingly difficult for the public to understand the need to sustain an adequate military.[57] The *New York Times* responded with apparent joy to these hysterical claims in an editorial titled "Women Will Jump at the Chance." After first mocking the fears expressed by the *Army and Navy Journal*, calling it "that usually courageous journal," the *New York Times* column responded by stating that if women wanted to be war correspondents, "Well, let 'em! Why not?"[58]

NOTES

1. "Femininities," *Saturday Evening Post*, April 30, 1881.

2. Joseph Mathews, *Reporting the Wars* (Minneapolis: University of Minnesota Press, 1957), 33.

3. Phillip Knightley, *The First Casualty: The War Correspondent as Hero and Myth-Maker from the Crimea to Iraq* (Baltimore: Johns Hopkins University Press, 2004), 2, 44.

4. Robert W. Desmond, *The Information Process: World News Reporting to the Twentieth Century* (Iowa City: University of Iowa Press, 1978), 177–80; Robert W. Desmond, *The Press and World Affairs* (New York: D. Appleton-Century, 1937), 21; Knightley, *The First Casualty*, 15.

5. Knightley, *The First Casualty*, 2.

6. Linda S. Hudson, *Mistress of Manifest Destiny: A Biography of Jane McManus Storm Cazneau, 1807–1878* (Austin: Texas State Historical Association, 2001); and Tom Reilly, "Jane McManus Storms: Letters from the Mexican War, 1846–1848," *Southwestern Historical Quarterly* 85 (July 1981): 21–44. See also, "Cora Montgomery," *(Cleveland, Ohio) Plain Dealer*, April 6, 1854.

7. Maurine Beasley and Sheila Jean Gibbons, *Taking Their Place: A Documentary History of Women and Journalism* (State College, PA: Strata Publishing, 2003), 9; Joyce Hoffmann, *On Their Own: Women Journalists and the American Experience in Vietnam* (New York: Da Capo Press, 2008), 3; and Mathews, *Reporting the Wars*, 54.

8. See, for examples of the many claims of "first in history" women war correspondents who reported on war up to one hundred years after Fuller and Cazneau: David A. Copeland, *Greenwood Library of American War Reporting: The Indian Wars & the Spanish-American War* (Westport, CT: Greenwood Press, 2005); Jane Eldridge Miller, *Who's Who in Contemporary Women's Writing* (New York: Routledge, 2001), 104; and Jan Whitt, *Women in American Journalism: A New History* (Urbana: University of Illinois Press, 2008), 28. Newspaper articles, especially obituaries, have regularly made such claims; see, for example, "Reporter, Writer for Movies," *The Washington Post*, May 15, 1973.

9. Knightley, *The First Casualty*, 43; Mathews, *Reporting the Wars*, 242.

10. Knightley, *The First Casualty*, 44; Barbara Korte, *Represented Reporters: Images of War Correspondents in Memoirs and Fiction* (New Brunswick, NJ: Transaction Publishers, 2009).

11. Frederic Hudson, *Journalism in the United States, 1690–1872* (New York: Harper & Brothers, 1873), 715.

12. Ibid., 25–27; Mathews, *Reporting the Wars*, 81–86.

13. Grace Farrell, *Lillie Devereux Blake: Retracing a Life Erased* (Amherst: University of Massachusetts Press, 2002): 80–90; Frances E. Willard and Mary A. Livermore, ed., *A Woman of the Century: Fourteen Hundred Biographical Sketches Accompanied by Portraits of Leading American Women in All Walks of Life* (Buffalo, NY: Charles Wells Moulton, 1893), 638; and "Queries and Answers," *New York Times*, September 8, 1900, about Laura Redden.

14. See, for example, "A Heroine in Petticoats: Remarkable Experiences of a Pittsburg Lady during the War—Adventures in Field and Prison Pen," *The Pittsburg Dispatch*, May 4, 1889, about Lottie Bengough; "Oldest House in Washington Occupied by Oldest Woman Correspondent," *The Washington Post*, November 15, 1908, about Emily Edson Briggs; and "Susan E. Dickinson Dead," *Middletown Daily Times-Press*, November 17, 1913.

15. Charles F. McGovern, *Sold American: Consumption and Citizenship, 1890–1945* (Chapel Hill: University of North Carolina Press, 2006), 36; Frank Luther Mott, *American Journalism* (New York: Macmillan, 1962), 598–99; and Edwin Llewellyn Shuman, *Steps into Journalism: Helps and Hints for Young Writers* (Evanston, IL: Evanston Press Co., 1894), 149–51.

16. Frederic Hudson, *Journalism in the United States, 1690–1872* (New York: Harper & Brothers, 1873), 504.

17. Margaret H. Welch, "Is Newspaper Work Healthful for Women?" *Journal of Social Science* 32 (1894), 113. Welch concluded "women are equal, physically, to newspaper work when they rid themselves of some of the handicaps of their own making. Two serious ones are improper dressing and unhygienic eating," she wrote, explaining that women cannot maintain good health wearing tight corsets, heavy skirts, and "thin kid shoes" as they work long hours

without a decent meal. "We women must equip ourselves better, physically, for the opportunities that are before us," ibid., 114–15.

18. Shuman, *Steps into Journalism*, 149.

19. Ibid., 154.

20. Ibid., 154. Fannie Brigham Ward wrote for the *Times Picayune*, *Los Angeles Times*, *Philadelphia Record*, and other publications in the late nineteenth and early twentieth centuries. See Fannie B. Ward, "The Chilean War: A Correspondent Who Sides With Balmaceda," *Los Angeles Times*, July 12, 1891; Fannie Brigham Ward, "Horrors of War: Past and Present Sufferings in Santiago de Cuba," *Los Angeles Times*, September 2, 1898; and "Mrs. F.B. Ward Dead: Prominent Newspaper Writer, Traveler, and Lecturer," *Washington Post*, October 6, 1913.

21. See, for example, Fannie B. Ward, "Red Cross In Cuba," *Los Angeles Times*, March 21, 1898; "A Woman War Correspondent," *Kansas City Journal*, May 29, 1899, about Kit Blake Watkins; and "The Fifth's Transfer," *(Baltimore) Sun*, June 1, 1898, about Nora O'Malley.

22. Teresa Patten lived with her parents at age eighteen, according to the 1870 census, and married Albert Dean in 1872, according to a marriage license on file with the State Historical Society of Wisconsin. Newspaper articles indicate that Teresa Dean divorced Albert Dean in 1888, married Lewis Tallman in 1892, divorced Tallman in 1896, and then resumed calling herself Teresa Dean. A letter dated January 9, 1942, from her son, Warren Dean, to historian Carlin Treat gives a timeline for Teresa Dean's life and includes the fact that she was twice married and twice divorced. See "Frontiersmen—Teresa Howard and Col. Warren Dean," Elmo Scott Watson Papers, The Newberry Library, Chicago.

23. "The Ways of Woman Fair," *(New York) World*, March 12, 1891.

24. Ibid.

25. Teresa Dean, "Memories of the Widow," in Teresa Dean Papers, 1899–1931, box #4 folder #5, "Drafts of Memoirs," Charles Deering McCormick Library of Special Collections, Northwestern University, Evanston, Illinois.

26. Ibid.

27. Teresa Dean, "He Was a Daring Man," *Chicago Herald*, February 5, 1891.

28. Teresa Dean, "Memories of the Widow," in Teresa Dean Papers, box #4 folder #5, "Drafts of Memoirs," Deering Library.

29. Thomas Henry Tibbles, *Buckskin and Blanket Days* (London: Oldbourne Book Co., Ltd., 1958), 275–76.

30. "Big Foot Caught, All Other Indians Surrender, and the Cruel War Is Over," *The Hillsboro (Ohio) Herald*, January 1, 1890.

31. Josephine Miles married Orlando Woodward in 1881, and the census places them in Cincinnati with their two sons, Ralph and Donald, in June 1900. Her U.S. passport application signed March 28, 1896, lists her birthdate as November 20, 1860, and her occupation as "journalism."

32. "A Clever Correspondent," *The Fourth Estate*, April 9, 1896.

33. "To Send Society Editor to Cuba," *Chicago Daily Tribune*, March 29, 1896.

34. "Neither Tells the Truth; Spaniards and Cubans Both Lie About the Situation in Cuba," *Sioux City (Iowa) Journal,* April 19, 1896; and "Shot in Morro Castle. Execution of Prisoners in Havana Made Great Occasions," *Philadelphia Inquirer*, April 20, 1896.

35. W. Joseph Campbell, *Yellow Journalism: Puncturing the Myths, Defining the Legacies* (Westport, CT: 2001), 96–123.

36. Mott, *American Journalism*, 533–34.

37. Anna Northend Benjamin's "War Correspondent's Pass No. 226," William Dummer Northend family papers, Stuart A. Rose Manuscript Archives and Rare Book Library, Emory University.

38. See, for examples of brief items claiming that individual reporters who covered the Spanish-American War in Cuba were the only women war correspondents, "A Blessing Disguise," *Los Angeles Times*, July 31, 1898; David MacGowan, "Poisoned by Army Ration: Private Gibbons, Fifth Illinois, Eats Corned Beef and Dies," *Chicago Daily Tribune*, May 27, 1898; "Girl Who Went to the Front: Elsie Reasoner," *St. Paul Globe*, September 4, 1898; "Glory of War Correspondents," *Galveston Daily News*, September 18, 1898, which profiled

war correspondents in Cuba and noted that only one woman was at the front, Marguerite Arlina Hamm; and "She's at the Front: Mrs. [Clara] Colby the Only Woman War Correspondent In Cuba," *Newark (New Jersey) Daily Advocate*, August 10, 1898.

39. See, for example, "Off for Cuba: First Salt Lake Girl to Go There," *Salt Lake Herald*, June 27, 1898; "Margherita Arlina Hamm," *Newark (New Jersey) Daily Advocate*, June 28, 1896; "She's At The Front: Mrs. Colby the Only Woman War Correspondent In Cuba," *Newark (New Jersey) Daily Advocate*, August 10, 1898; Eliza Archard Conner, "Women's World in Paragraphs," *Arizona Republican*, April 17, 1891; and David MacGowan, "Poisoned by Army Ration," *Chicago Daily Tribune*, May 27, 1898.

40. See, for example, Bessie Dow Bates, "Plucky Woman War Correspondent, Eliza Archard Connor Who Is Carrying a Typewriter around the World," *Daily (Wisconsin) Gazette*, June 20, 1899; Robert B. Cramer, "Little Stories of the War," *Atlanta Constitution*, September 3, 1898; "Woman War Correspondent," *Kansas City Journal*, March 29, 1899; and "Women Playing Part in War in the Balkans," *The (Baltimore) Sun*, November 17, 1912.

41. See, for example, Bates, "Plucky Woman War Correspondent"; "The Romance of the Only Woman War Correspondent," *St. Paul Globe*, June 1, 1904; and "Cora Montgomery," *(Cleveland, Ohio) Plain Dealer*, April 6, 1854.

42. See, for example, "Girl Who Went to the Front," *St. Paul Globe*, September 4, 1898; and "Miss Elsie Reasoner," *Kansas City Journal*, August 8, 1898.

43. "The Romance of the Only Woman War Correspondent," *St. Paul (Minnesota) Globe*, June 19, 1904.

44. Teresa Dean, "Memories of the Widow," in Teresa Dean Papers, box #4 folder #5, "Drafts of Memoirs," Deering Library.

45. From *The London (Ontario) Mail*, "Mrs. Blake Watkins: And How She Proved Herself One of the Boys at Tampa," *New York Times*, July 3, 1898.

46. Ibid.

47. "Skedaddled for Safety: London Telegraph's Woman War Correspondent Couldn't Stand Fire," *San Antonio Express*, November 20, 1899.

48. Ibid.

49. Ibid.

50. See, for example, Margherita Arlina Hamm, "Brown and Blue Boys: Soldier Life as Seen by a Woman Inspector. The Lighter Side of the War," *Washington Post*, July 31, 1898.

51. See, for example, Muriel Bailey, "At Home With Aguinaldo," *Overland Monthly*, March 1899; Eliza Archard Conner, "Our Boys in Luzon: Eliza Archard Conner Praises the American Soldier," *Akron (Ohio) Tribune*, June 19, 1899; Emma Paddock Telford, "Warships in Suda Bay: The First Sight of Crete to an American Passenger on the Way to Athens," *New York Times*, May 9, 1897; and "A War-Correspondent on Crutches," *Outlook*, January 14, 1899, about Mary Krout.

52. See, for example, Imogene Carter, "Soldiers Amazed to See a Woman on the Battlefield," *Chicago Daily Tribune*, May 10, 1897. Imogene Carter was a pseudonym used by Cora Taylor Crane.

53. "Our War Correspondent Creates Consternation," *(Richmond) Times Dispatch*, May 5, 1905.

54. Ibid.

55. *Army and Navy Journal*, April 2, 1910, 899.

56. Ibid.

57. Ibid.

58. "Women Will Jump at the Chance," *New York Times*, April 6, 1910.

Chapter Three

"Conditions of Acceptance," 1911–1939

A permit is a permit and while the Italian officers; who had stormed and captured these Austrian trenches only a few hours before, may have been surprised to see a woman appear, they accepted Mrs. Kirtland's credentials and showed her every inch of the battle-field.

—*Frank Leslie's Weekly*, 1918.[1]

Despite the *Army and Navy Journal*'s cautionary plea in 1910, the War Department published its field service regulations in 1914 without any mention of a person's sex as a factor for accrediting or governing war correspondents.[2] The department confined itself to discussing the relationship between the military and the press in times of war and to outlining ways in which the military would permit, accommodate, and regulate war correspondents. The press has the "dual and delicate position" of needing to present accurate news of war to the public while preventing the disclosure of information that could benefit the enemy, the regulations explained. "It is perfectly apparent to everyone who considers the question that these important functions can not be trusted to irresponsible people and can only be properly performed under reasonable rules and regulations with respect thereto."[3] These regulations provided the government's first official definition of a war correspondent and the first official guidance for military regulation of these individuals.[4] Neither the definition nor the guidance revealed any basis for preventing women from accreditation or restricting women in their work as war correspondents. Yet, the regulations left considerable room for the discretion of military officials—in their assessment of which individuals could be trusted as responsible people, for example. Furthermore, the new accreditation process was so prohibitive it excluded most reporters from gaining access to military officials or troops in action.

422. Conditions of Acceptance.—Each applicant shall present to the Secretary of War credentials from the owner or owners, managing editor, or responsible manager of the publication or publications he represents, giving a brief account of his career, stating exactly the nature of the work he is expected to do at the front, certifying to his trustworthiness as working member of his profession, and his personal fitness to accompany the army. His employer or employers shall give a bond for his good conduct in the field, which, in case of the withdrawal of his pass for infraction of any of the regulations shall be forfeited to any charity which the Secretary of War may name. He shall take an oath of loyalty of the usual military form and shall agree to abide in letter and spirit by all the regulations laid down for his guidance. [5]

These conditions also stipulated that accreditation would not be granted to those "with a view to adventure rather than serious work as correspondents." [6] The War Department required correspondents seeking accreditation to handwrite an autobiographical essay about their integrity and qualifications, as well as their specific plans for covering the war; they also had to pay $1,000 upfront for military travel and accommodations. [7] Additionally, as a means of ensuring as well as insuring their loyalty, correspondents had to swear their intentions in person to the Secretary of War or his representative and back up their promises with a $10,000 bond. [8] Finally, the War Department would only accept one correspondent to represent each newspaper or syndicate and required each correspondent to present proof of previous experience as a war correspondent—in the form of a letter from a military official who could vouch for the correspondent. [9] The hurdles posed by these regulations meant that just thirty-six "regularly accredited correspondents" traveled with armed forces and enjoyed "full liberty" to observe operations and visit American Expeditionary Forces unaccompanied during World War I. [10] While these requirements were extreme, they reflected the prevailing attitude of military officials at that time. The military's top priorities did not include communicating with the public or accommodating the press, and it would not be until the United States entered World War II that the War Department developed a public relations division. "Prior to 1939 the Army had been content to carry on quietly at its posts, a rather clannish society to which few people paid attention," noted Colonel Barney Oldfield in a memoir he published about his work as an information officer. "In almost any emergency the policy was to play dead or dumb, or both." [11]

These impressions aside, the Army did recognize the importance of conveying news to the public, but it also recognized its own limitations. In January 1918, Second Lieutenant Mark Watson sent a memo to the Intelligence Section commander, Colonel Denis E. Nolan, to address whether the Army should increase the number of accredited correspondents.

We recognise the desirability of having as many correspondents here as can be handled and furnishing them, when more motor equipment, etc., is available, with better facilities than can now be afforded. At the same time the number must be restricted because of the insufficiency of cable equipment. As an example it took 48 hours to complete the sending of the eight cables concerned with our occupation of the trenches two months ago. There has been no improvement in the service since then, and the situation, because of increasing official cables, undoubtedly will become worse before it becomes better.

Watson went on to acknowledge the fact that these limitations meant that many newspaper editors and reporters would see the military's actions as discriminatory. "Admitting this to be the case and admitting that this is unfortunate, we must take the position, temporarily at least, that it cannot be helped and that if we permit any other correspondents to be attached to our force, it will simply hamper still further the already difficult task of getting news to the United States."[12] Throughout the war, the military upheld this decision to strictly limit the number of correspondents it accommodated—to thirty-one attached to Army units and twelve accredited as correspondents.[13] And yet the military also reported that, by war's end, the number of visiting correspondents who had official access to armed forces and war fronts approached one thousand.[14] Interestingly, though numerous books and articles that address the subject of women war correspondents name Peggy Hull as the first and only woman to be accredited as a war correspondent during World War I, military records show that Hull was not alone. While neither Hull nor any other woman was listed among the Army's final tally of just thirty-six accredited correspondents who covered World War I, the Army's 1918 list of ninety-two visiting correspondents included Hull and seventeen other women.[15] In its final list of the sixteen visiting war correspondents of longest service, the AEF lists the names of fourteen men and two women: Elizabeth Frazier, who was accredited as a war correspondent for the *Saturday Evening Post*, and Cecil Dorrian, who was accredited as a war correspondent for the *Newark Evening News*.[16] A preliminary draft of the same document, dated February 11, 1919, has an additional woman's name, handwritten below the list of typed names of visiting correspondents of longest service: May Birkhead for the *New York Herald*.[17] In a military memorandum March 3, 1919, information officer Captain Arthur Hartzell provided descriptions of forty-seven war correspondents who had been accredited as visiting or Army correspondents. Hartzell explained, "There are no records showing the correspondents' personal history so I am giving you what I know about them from personal contact before the war and since their arrival in France." Hartzell included three women in these descriptions, writing that Elizabeth Frazier was in Paris for the *Saturday Evening Post* and had been in France for "some months," having "devoted her attention particularly to the various activities of the S.O.S. although she has visited the battlefields." He noted that May Birkhead, of the *New York Herald*, who "since early last spring" was a visiting correspondent with the Army, had "travelled over practically the entire Army area" writing stories for readers in New York and Paris, and that "her trips to the active front have been very few although since the signing of the armistice she has visited several battlefields."[18] Hartzell had more to say about Dorrian, a 1905 Barnard alumna who worked as a playwright and theater critic before becoming a European correspondent for the *Newark Evening News* in 1914.

> MISS CECILE [*sic*] DORRIAN wrote more intelligently about the operations of the Army than any other woman correspondent, if one judges her writing from a military viewpoint. Miss Dorrian came over here late last spring and visited the battlefields at various times. Her work is well known throughout the Eastern part of the United States. Miss Dorrian is in Paris.[19]

Figure 3.1. *Newark Evening News* **war correspondent Cecil Dorrian, second from left, poses with Red Cross and YMCA workers at a celebration to honor American troops July 4, 1918, in Alsace, Germany.**
Source: **Signal Corps, U.S.A., National Archives.**

At the end of the biographical descriptions that Hartzell wrote for each of the forty-four male and three female visiting war correspondents for whom he could account personally, he added:

> 2. It will be seen from the above that only a very few of the correspondents were qualified to write intelligently about the war but due to the fact that they were successful newspapermen in the United States they soon gained some knowledge of military operations and also, that efforts were made by G.2. to instruct these men, their dispatches were clear and intelligent accounts of what the American Army did in France. Judging them as war correspondents, I would say that all but a very few were rather reporters of the war than war correspondents such as those men who have made themselves famous in previous wars. [20]

Dorrian's war reporting often appeared as front page news in the *Newark Evening News* with her byline as a war correspondent. In October 1918, however, Dorrian herself made headlines nationally when she and a small group of correspondents were visiting reoccupied territory near the Western Front. At the battlefield of Mont de Bligny, French press officer Germaine de la Valette picked up a cylindrical object that turned out to be a "potato masher," or stick grenade. Valette carried the object a short while before it exploded in her hand, killing her instantly and badly injuring a military officer as well as Elizabeth Shepley Sergeant, correspondent for the *New Republic*.[21] Another correspondent, Eunice Tietjens, who wrote for the *Chicago Daily News*, was walking with Valette when she picked up the stick grenade. Tietjens later recalled that Dorrian had saved her life by calling her over to see the view, just after Valette had asked her about the mysterious object, which had white strings attached.

> Afterwards I learned that Mademoiselle went to the lieutenant and asked him the same question she had asked me. He replied, terror-stricken, "Put it down, mademoiselle, put it down quickly!" She leaned down to do so, but in some fashion she must have pulled one of the strings, or set it down too roughly in her confusion, for it exploded, killing her instantly, tearing off an arm of the lieutenant, and wounding Elizabeth Sergeant in the legs. As for me, I was by this time standing some paces away, my back to them, looking out over the wide and desolate view, and my thoughts were far away. Suddenly there was a sharp explosion, and Miss Dorrian and I wheeled about. We were scarcely farther off than Miss Sergeant but the explosion had gone the other way.
>
> When I turned I saw my friend's body, which had been leaning forward, straighten up from the waist and fall over on her back. The long Red Cross nurse's veil she wore had been blown so far away or into such little bits that, though we searched later, we could not find any trace of it. Her long hair was standing straight up from her head, her body from the waist up was quite naked. Her right hand was missing. She had been, as the French say, completely *éventrée*, and for some seconds after she fell all her entrails boiled up

through the broken abdominal walls like some hideous fountain. The lieutenant began to scream, a high piercing scream of agony like a woman's. Elizabeth Sergeant made no sound, only sank slowly to the ground, her eyes, which caught mine, curiously unveiled in the way in which eyes become in the face of death.[22]

Military officials saw this tragedy as reinforcing the argument that women did not belong at the front, but newspapers downplayed its significance, reporting the incident as a news brief that ran nationally. News accounts describing war correspondents during World War I were less concerned with the sex of the individuals than with the practice of war correspondence as a whole, especially in terms of the military's attempts to control the press. War correspondent Reginald Wright Kauffman noted in 1918 the limitations of the field service regulations, upon which "is declaredly built the entire structure of the Army's relations with the press; against it exists but one legitimate criticism: it never has been, and, in the present organization of our censorship never can be, adhered to."[23] Kauffman's employer had risked, and lost, thousands of dollars after the military revoked his credentials in retaliation for Kauffman's articles criticizing military operations. Yet, Kauffman noted, "Flocks of unaccredited correspondents appearing and receiving news-gathering facilities" benefitted from similar access and accommodation. "The only privilege accorded the accredited was that of forfeiting their bonds if they offended, whereas the unaccredited risked no financial loss at all."[24] The privileges for the unaccredited also included greater freedom to work and travel, by avoiding censors and other military officials. War correspondent Harry Carr, who in 1916 called the military's handling of the news "almost unbelievably stupid, unsatisfactory, and inefficient," noted another advantage to observing war from a distance, while unaccredited and separate from the troops: "Battles are now so extensive that the nearer you get the less you see," he explained, recalling colleagues who witnessed battles firsthand but entirely missed the bigger story.[25]

American women and men wrote war news from wherever they lived or traveled long before, and long after, the United States began regulating war correspondents.[26] Anyone could call himself or herself "a war correspondent," yet, as the 1914 *Field Service Regulations* specified, no member of the press could travel with the United States military as a correspondent without official permission or credentials.[27] Freelance foreign correspondents whose stories touched upon war were often billed as war correspondents by publications seeking to promote their war-related essays or articles. A wide variety of women's writing was deemed "war correspondence" in the decades leading up to World War II. Women brought many perspectives to their reporting beyond the scope of weaponry, troops, and military strategy—and only rarely did they step inside the traditionally masculine realm of war.[28] Thus this "woman's angle" often meant a look beyond the battle for the effects of war and within the battle for supporting elements of war. These effects and supporting elements were consistent with the aspects of war that women had written about in previous decades: war's toll on women and children, the work of the Red Cross, the care and feeding of soldiers, or the personal experience of a woman surrounded by men.[29] The purpose of the woman's angle, for newspaper publishers if not the writers themselves, continued to be largely commercial. Newspapers sought to attract women readers, who would, in turn, attract advertisers. Most newspaper editors continued to rely upon woman's angle stories, written by women, as the best means—if not the only means—of attracting women readers. At a journalism symposium in 1914, journalist Elizabeth Gilmer, known then as Dorothy Dix, stressed that the woman's point of view had gained editors' respect not only because so many women chose which newspaper a household would buy, but because a newspaper that reached every woman could name its own price for advertising.[30] Dix also stressed the non-commercial benefit of newspapers presenting women's views, stating that even "the most foolish little girl reporter is born knowing things about other women that it takes a man psychologist like Munsterberg fifty years of steady study even to guess at."[31] She compared the need for women to have a voice in the newspaper to their need for a voice at the polls. Other journalists opposed newspapers' emphasis on a distinct female perspective. Blaming "sob sister" journalism on editors' acceptance of this notion, reporter Sarah Addington wrote in the *New-York Tribune* in 1918 that the woman's angle was "very often an obtuse angle," and warned against newspapers losing sight of their purpose.[32] Sharing a similar perspective, Washington State newspaper publisher Frank Dallam Jr. in 1918 criticized female war correspondents for romanticizing war, filling "so much space in our popular magazines with their personal sensations, experiences, and impressions, with incidental reference to the momentous events they are supposed to 'cover.'"[33]

At the start of World War I, *Saturday Evening Post* editor George Lorimer argued that the woman's angle of war was expansive and necessary. A feature article by reporter Ann Simonton about Lorimer and the *Post*'s four female war correspondents opened with the statement, "There never was in the world before such a job for women as war corresponding." Simonton quoted Lorimer as he explained his decision to send Maude Radford Warren, Mary Roberts Rinehart, Corra Harris, and Isabel Brush to Europe: "'The big story of the war is never at the front,' George Horace Lorimer, the man who sent them, told me. 'It is in the hospitals and in the homes.' . . . 'But,' says the man who reaches more men in a week than any other in America, 'war is largely a woman's affair and women, I think, best understand the little things that go to make up the big story.'"[34] Simonton praised the woman's angle of war for what she saw as its ability to foster peace. Women were more likely

to provide unglossed accounts of war, she wrote, and the present war might
have been prevented if more voices in past wars "had been lifted to speak of
the honor and glory of carnage as mankind's great mirage" or to describe
plainly "in such figures all might read" the true cost of mourning "heroes
made on battlefields."[35] As editor of the *Saturday Evening Post*, Lorimer had
hired the four women to report the following stories: Brush to learn "how
Prohibition took the Russian Empire by storm," Harris to travel in England
and France and visit the Soissons battlefields, Warren to get "the going away
story" of regiments headed to military training at Salisbury Plain and the
battle at Neufchatel, and Rinehart to drop "round for a call on Queen Mary of
England in wartime."[36] As the Great War progressed, Lorimer continued to
publish writings by women the *Post* billed as war correspondents, including
Eleanor Franklin Egan, who had reported on topics of war and foreign relations for two decades.[37] Ten years after Egan had first made headlines by
surprising Japanese officials as a female war correspondent, Egan made national headlines when the *Saturday Evening Post* published her firsthand
account of surviving a submarine attack.[38]

> Mrs. Eleanor Franklin Egan, the American writer, who returned yesterday on
> the steamship New York from Liverpool, after spending six months in south-
> ern Europe and the Orient, told a thrilling story of an attack on a British
> passenger ship in the Mediterranean by a submarine flying the Turkish flag. As
> a result of the attack, of which she was an eyewitness, twenty-five persons
> were drowned.[39]

While Egan's article was closer to an unglossed account of war than an
idealized personal narrative, most war accounts that Lorimer published by
women writers throughout the war did fit more closely with Dallam's portrayal: "personal sensations, experiences, and impressions, with incidental
reference to the momentous events."[40] These accounts, along with so many
accounts written about "women war correspondents," continued to rely
upon—and feed—the public imagination. The majority of articles billed as
women's war correspondence throughout World War I were travelogues and
personal essays that rarely mentioned military operations or required access
to military officials. While many authors of these works did not fit the military's definition of a war correspondent, they each wrote articles for publications who billed them as "woman war correspondent" or "war correspondent." Yet, even a decade later, newspapers continued to announce individual
women as the first or only woman war correspondent, sometimes just for a
particular battle, but more often the description was unqualified and implied
that no other female war correspondent existed.[41]

The nature of war itself poses the greatest challenge in locating the work
of early-twentieth-century women who served as war correspondents, versus
those whose publications promoted them as "women war correspondents."

Reporters often had to send breaking news as brief cables from war zones or remote locations; their editors would compile news reports without bylines. Thus, women who reported on the hard news stories of war often worked behind the scenes until they became the subject of the news themselves. For example, *The Sun* described Marguerite Harrison's work reporting on the Armistice in Berlin after she was charged with being an American spy.[42] Mildred Farwell, who wrote as a war correspondent for the *Chicago Tribune* for several years, drew attention nationally after she was held captive by Bulgarian troops as a "semi-prisoner of war" in 1915 and again when she found herself amid a "hailstorm of bullets" during a riot in Petrograd in 1917.[43] Peggy Hull reported on war extensively for the El Paso *Morning Times* on the Mexican border in 1916, at an artillery training camp in France in 1917, as well as in several locations in Russia and the Pacific in 1918. While her articles were lauded for accurately depicting military operations and scenes of combat, they were first-person accounts accompanied by head-lines that emphasized Hull, the "girl war reporter," as the focus.[44]

In the years after the Great War, exceptional women columnists and essayists wrote regularly about foreign relations. Even as their own country

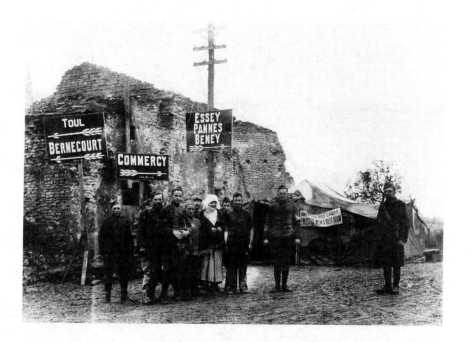

Figure 3.2. Mildred Farwell, who spent several years as a war correspondent for the *Chicago Tribune* before volunteering for the Red Cross, poses with American troops in France, October 22, 1918.
    Source: Signal Corps, U.S.A., National Archives.

Figure 3.3.   Peggy Hull covered World War I in France and Russia.
   Source: Reproduced with permission of Kenneth Spencer Research Library,
University of Kansas Libraries.

remained neutral, topics relating to war were unavoidable for most American writers stationed in Europe or Asia, and many of these women established a reputation for themselves as war correspondents. For example, in the 1920s, readers and editors heralded Dorothy Thompson for her work as a war correspondent with a "Richard Harding Davis reputation."[45] Before 1940, women made up less than 25 percent of the workforce. Working women were, for the most part, under thirty-five, single, non-white, and employed in domestic, clerical, sales, or service jobs.[46] Many women who had filled jobs during World War I either chose to return home or were forced to give up their jobs upon the soldiers' return. Even those women who needed or wanted to continue working found it difficult to find jobs during the Depression, when jobs were scarce and public sentiment grew more strongly opposed to women's employment. A 1936 Gallup poll revealed that 82 percent of Americans felt that women should not work if their husbands had jobs.[47] But during World War II, the number of jobs would soar and technological advances such as prefab-construction meant that much of the work in defense production, even ship-building, would be suitable for novice workers.[48] As the need for workers quickly outpaced supply, and as more men were conscripted for service, employers increasingly perceived the vast opportunity that so many women workers presented. Newspapers and magazines, as well as press associations and universities, regularly recognized women for their work writing about war in the years between the two world wars. Yet it wouldn't be until World War II that these writers would seek acceptance, once again, from the military and would have to work under the constraints of military supervision and regulation.

NOTES

1. Helen Johns Kirtland, "A Woman on the Battle Front," *Leslie's Weekly Newspaper*, August 24, 1918.
2. War Department Office of the Chief of Staff, *Field Service Regulations United States Army 1914: Text corrections through December 20, 1916: Changes No. 5* (New York: *Army and Navy Journal*, 1916), 165–69.
3. Ibid., 165.
4. Ibid., 165–69.
5. Ibid., 166–69.
6. Ibid., 166–69.
7. Phillip Knightley, *The First Casualty: The War Correspondent as Hero and Myth-Maker from the Crimea to Iraq* (Baltimore: Johns Hopkins University Press, 2004), 133. Knightley noted these requirements were so extreme they would "have to be read to be believed."
8. Ibid.
9. United States War Department Office of the Chief of Staff, *Field Service Regulations United States Army 1914: Text corrections through December 20, 1916: Changes No. 5* (New York: *Army and Navy Journal*, 1916), 166–69.

10. *United States Army in the World War 1917–1919: Reports of the Commander-in-Chief, Staff Sections and Services Volume 13* (Washington, D.C.: Center of Military History United States Army, 1991), 10.

11. Barney Oldfield, *Never a Shot in Anger* (New York: Duell, Sloan and Pearce, 1956), 5.

12. "Memorandum to Col. Nolan: Applications for Accrediting Correspondents," Mark Watson, Second Lieutenant, to Denis E. Nolan, Intelligence Section Commander, January 12, 1918; Lists of Correspondents, Accredited + Visiting; Correspondence and Other Records Relating to Press Correspondence in Territory Occupied by Allied Armies, 1917–19; Personnel, Miscellaneous; Record of the American Expeditionary Forces (World War I) General Headquarters; General Staff; G-2; Censorship and Press Division, Record Group 120, Box 6132 NM-91 Entry 228. National Archives at College Park, College Park, MD.

13. *United States Army in the World War 1917–1919*, 10.

14. Ibid.

15. "Lists of Correspondents, Accredited + Visiting; Correspondence and Other Records Relating to Press Correspondence in Territory Occupied by Allied Armies, 1917–19," Personnel, Miscellaneous, in REG 120: Record of the American Expeditionary Forces (World War I) General Headquarters; General Staff; G-2; Censorship and Press Division (G-2-D), Correspondence and Other Records Relating to Press Correspondence in Territory Occupied by Allied Armies, 1917–19, Personnel, Miscellaneous Box 6132 NM-91 Entry 228. National Archives at College Park, College Park, MD.

16. Ibid.

17. Ibid.

18. Arthur E. Hartzell, Captain, Inf., USA, G2D, GHQ, Am.E.F., to Colonel Moreno, March 3, 1919; "Lists of Correspondents, Accredited + Visiting," Correspondence and Other Records Relating to Press Correspondence in Territory Occupied by Allied Armies, 1917–19; Personnel, Miscellaneous; REG 120 Record of the American Expeditionary Forces (World War I) General Headquarters; General Staff; G-2; Censorship and Press Division (G-2-D) Correspondence and Other Records Relating to Press Correspondence in Territory Occupied by Allied Armies, 1917–19, Personnel, Miscellaneous Box 6132 NM-91 Entry 228. National Archives at College Park, College Park, MD.

19. Ibid.

20. Ibid.

21. "American Woman and a French Officer Are Wounded," *Washington Post*, October 22, 1918; Elizabeth Shepley Sergeant, *Shadow Shapes: The Journal of a Wounded Woman* (Boston: Houghton Mifflin Co., 1920), 15–21; and Eunice Tietjens, *The World at My Shoulder* (New York: MacMillan Company, 1938), 159–72.

22. Tietjens, *The World at My Shoulder*, 161.

23. Reginald Wright Kauffman, "The News Embargo," *North American Review,* 208, 757 (December 1918): 831. Kauffman's wife, Ruth Wright Kauffman, also worked as a war correspondent during World War I.

24. Ibid.

25. Harry Carr, "War Correspondents as an Army Problem," *Los Angeles Times*, August 4, 1916.

26. In addition to the preceding chapter in this book, see, for examples of the many reporters and foreign correspondents who wrote about war for American publications without being officially accredited, John Maxwell Hamilton, *Journalism's Roving Eye: A History of American Foreign Reporting* (Baton Rouge: Louisiana State University Press, 2009); Knightley, *The First Casualty*; Stephen R. and Oris Friesen Mackinnon, *China Reporting: An Oral History of American Journalism in the 1940s* (Berkeley: University of California Press, 1987); Joseph J. Mathews, *Reporting the Wars* (Minneapolis: University of Minnesota Press, 1957); and M. L. Stein, *Under Fire: The Story of American War Correspondents* (New York: J. Messner, 1968).

27. United States War Department, *Field Service Regulations United States Army 1914*, 168.

28. Jean Bethke Elshtain, *Women and War* (New York: Basic Books, 1987).

29. See, for example, "Does the Red Cross Prolong War?" *Outlook*, March 7, 1914; "Peggy Hull, War Correspondent, Drops Into City," *Chicago Daily Tribune*, December 22, 1917; Inez Milholland Boissevain, "France Shorn of Men to Work by Great War: Women and Boys Forced to Toil in the Fields," *Chicago Daily Tribune*, July 20, 1915; Rheta Childe Dorr, "A Soldier's Mother In France," *Chicago Daily Tribune*, June 2, 1918; and Ruth Wright Kauffman, "Back In an Empty," *Outlook*, July 3, 1918.

30. "Journalism Week, 1914. From Speeches by Newspaper Makers and Advertising Men at the University May 18–22, 1914," *The University of Missouri Bulletin*, 15, no. 20 (July 1914), 18.

31. Ibid., 17–18. Social psychologist Hugo Munsterberg wrote in his 1914 textbook, *Psychology: General and Applied* (New York: D. Appleton, 1914), that the female mind is "capricious, oversuggestible, often inclined to exaggeration, disinclined to abstract thought, unfit for mathematical reasoning, impulsive, overemotional" (p. 233).

32. Sarah Addington, "Sob Traitors," *New-York Tribune*, September 5, 1918. In an essay in which she spoke out against the sob sister trend, Addington commented briefly about the woman's angle, which she saw as providing a gateway for the many women reporters cluttering the pages of newspapers with their attempts to emulate reporter Nellie Bly.

33. Frank M. Dallam, Jr., "The American Fighting Man," *Goodwin's Weekly*, September 18, 1918. Dallam owned the *Oroville (Washington) Gazette*.

34. Ann Simonton, "Four American Women Who Have Been to the War," *New-York Tribune*, August 1, 1915.

35. Ibid.

36. Ibid.

37. See description of Eleanor Franklin (as her name appeared in bylines before marrying war correspondent Martin Egan) in the previous chapter.

38. "Our War Correspondent Creates Consternation," *(Richmond) Times Dispatch*, May 5, 1905; and "25 Drowned in Submarine Panic," *New York Times*, November 29, 1915.

39. "25 Drowned in Submarine Panic," *New York Times*.

40. Dallam, "The American Fighting Man."

41. See, for example, Rosemary Drachman, "Only Woman Correspondent on the Moroccan Front: Longworth's Sister as 'First Lady' of Fez," *Washington Post*, January 10, 1926.

42. "Mrs. Harrison Entered Russia As The Sun's Correspondent," *Baltimore Sun*, July 31, 1921.

43. "Chicago Woman in War Zone Searched For by Four Nations," *Chicago Daily Tribune*, November 21, 1915; Mildred Farwell, "Tribune Writer in Thick of the Riot at Petrograd," *Chicago Daily Tribune*, July 20, 1917; and John T. McCutcheon, "Mrs. [Mildred] Farwell Held Captive by Bulgars," *Chicago Daily Tribune*, December 21, 1915.

44. "Assignment to War Front Brings Fame to Miss Peggy Hull," *Wyoming State Tribune*, April 2, 1920; Emmet Crozier, *American Reporters on the Western Front, 1914–1918* (New York: Oxford University Press, 1959); "Girl Reporter Braves Terrors of Russia for the Evening Gazette," *Cedar Rapids Evening Gazette*, January 4, 1919; "Peggy Hull, War Correspondent, Drops Into City," *Chicago Daily Tribune*, December 22, 1917; and Wilda Smith and Eleanor Bogart, *The Wars of Peggy Hull: The Life and Times of a War Correspondent* (El Paso: Texas Western Press, 1991).

45. "The Press: Cartwheel Girl," *Time*, June 12, 1939.

46. Ibid., 66–69.

47. Ruth Milkman, *Gender at Work: The Dynamics of Job Segregation by Sex during World War II* (Urbana: University of Illinois Press, 1987), 28; and Rosalind Rosenberg, *Divided Lives: American Women in the Twentieth Century* (New York: Hill and Wang, 2008), 103.

48. William H. Chafe, *The Paradox of Change* (New York: Oxford University Press, 1991); Susan M. Hartmann, *The Home Front and Beyond* (Boston: Twayne Publishers, 1982); David M. Kennedy, *Freedom from Fear* (New York: Oxford University Press, 1999); Milkman, *Gender at Work*, 49, 60–64; and Rosenberg, *Divided Lives*, 103.

Chapter Four

"To Play Men's Rules," 1940–1942

When she was a guard on the girls' basketball team back in Syracuse, the girls played according to the girls' rules that made it an entirely different game from the basketball played by boys. But in the newspaper business there was no such thing as girls' rules. She had to play men's rules or not play at all. Dorothy [Thompson] was willing to play men's rules, for she asked no favors because she was a woman. But she demanded as fair treatment as a man.

—John McNamara[1]

In the early 1940s, newspaper reporting was still very much a male domain, though women who had proven themselves capable of playing by "men's rules" often found work as exceptional reporters whose editors and audiences could—and did—overlook their sex. Americans were reporting about aspects of war worldwide, but, as neutral correspondents, their access to these stories depended upon their own connections, creativity, and resources. Reporters who wrote about World War II in the years before the United States officially entered the war did not need United States military accreditation or recognition to cover the war, nor could they benefit from the resources, facilities, and access that such accreditation could provide.

Even before the United States entered the conflict, the War Department had begun paying more attention to the news industry and to the American reporters who were following the war overseas. When Germany invaded Poland in 1939, the American public was unprepared to enter another war. They were already fighting the Depression, and World War I was still fresh in many Americans' minds. The president and Congress were limited not only by public opposition to the war, but also by the United States Neutrality Act of 1937.[2] President Franklin Roosevelt called on Congress and the citizens of the United States to help America to become an "arsenal of democracy,"[3] with the quick and unprecedented production of "more ships, more

guns, more planes, more of everything."[4] Roosevelt continually pushed the
limits of his short-of-war strategy to shore up the nation's military and the
nation's allies. Through the Lend-Lease Act, the United States could "lease
or provide goods or services to any nation whose defense he thought vital to
the defense of the United States."[5] In September 1940, the United States
passed its first peacetime draft, the Selective Training and Service Act.[6]
Until the morning of December 7, 1941, when Japan's surprise attack on
Pearl Harbor claimed 4,575 casualties, 150 planes, and a half dozen battleships, many Americans "still thought it was not their war."[7]

At its essence, every war is based on the entangled notion "us against
them"—a group identity and a common cause for action, as well as a shared
perception of an enemy as different from the group. The strength of each of
these concepts affects the meaning and outcome of any battle—and thus
drove the desires and fears behind the government's control of media
throughout World War II.[8] The government needed Americans to feel united
and to believe that the Axis powers posed such a danger to the identity of
Americans that a war was inevitable, necessary, and achievable. Yet, democracy and freedom were integral to the identity of Americans, just as a lack of
democracy and freedom was integral to Americans' perception of the Axis
powers—and to the cause for war.[9] A democratic nation, by nature, fosters
opposing, diverse viewpoints that make unity more difficult to achieve.
Among these divergent viewpoints were many stereotypes, based on sex,
class, race, ethnicity, religion, and region, which had only been made worse
by the hard times most Americans had faced during the Depression.[10] The
United States was a nation of immigrants, but it was a patriarchal nation that
had yet to resolve its many racial and ethnic divisions. Thus the government
relied on propaganda and a generally cooperative fourth estate to develop and
sustain Americans' belief in a united (yet culturally diverse, economically
stratified, and racially segregated) citizenry, their belief in a just and crucial
war, and their belief in an evil, expendable enemy—all while ensuring that
no information reach the enemy that might hinder the chance of winning the
war.[11] Throughout the war, the government worked to balance its own interest and authority with the interests and rights of the press and the public,
while monitoring, producing, and regulating all kinds of communication relating to all segments of the nation's population—even, and often especially,
women.[12]

Much of the government's success or failure at balancing its interests and
authority with the interests and rights of a democratic nation depended upon
the "bureaucratization" of information control, as well as upon the individuals who were vested with that authority.[13] While the War Department sought
to influence public opinion and ready Americans for war, it also sought to
avoid repeating its Great War mistakes, such as overzealous censorship and
propaganda, to carry out its vision of a total war that would call upon every

citizen for assistance and support. This strategy included the creation of a department of public relations, in 1941, that would promote the war effort by working closely with journalists, rather than against them. [14] The War Department began by establishing the terms by which the military would both nurture and control this relationship, with a set of definitions and regulations that would grow and change throughout the war. The premise of these regulations was the mission of the public relations department, which the War Department defined as threefold:

1. To keep the people informed of the progress of war.
2. To give understanding of the Army to the people, and insure [*sic*] support and interest due to this active knowledge.
3. To aid in the maintenance of civilian morale, and incidentally, soldier morale, by the consistent release of hometown and general coverage stories about activities of men in the Army. [15]

The department further determined that it could best achieve its mission by accrediting civilian press representatives who could travel to military theaters and convey news of the war to the public. [16]

> As a method of providing news free from hint of propaganda, the principle has been accepted that civilian correspondents rather than public relations officers should prepare the news for the public. [17]

In January of 1942, just as the first American troops landed in England, the War Department's public relations division established its official procedures for accrediting, accommodating, and controlling war correspondents, along with establishing an official definition of the term "war correspondent." [18] These newly drafted regulations, published as a military field manual, affirmed that "correspondents perform an undoubted public function in the dissemination of news concerning the operations of the Army in time of war." [19] The field manual then noted that this function, which required accredited correspondents to truthfully convey facts without jeopardizing military strategy or morale, was delicate and therefore must be governed. The first regulation then defined the category of individuals who would be bound by these rules:

> The term "correspondent" as used in this manual includes journalists, feature writers, radio commentators, motion picture photographers, and still picture photographers accredited by the War Department to a theater of operations or a base command within or without the territorial limits of the United States in time of war. [20]

The War Department planned to limit the number of correspondents accredited from each publication or with each military group, requiring correspondents to rotate every thirty to ninety days, with preference "given to agencies representing the largest possible news or picture dissemination" as well as to "newspaper men with past military experience or past experience in the coverage of large maneuvers."[21] Reporters applying for military accreditation had to apply to the War Department Bureau of Public Relations Overseas Liaison Branch by completing a personnel security questionnaire and following instructions specific to war correspondents.[22] The form required the signature of the correspondent's employer and an accompanying letter from the news organization, specifying the theater requested and transportation required, along with two passport-size photos.[23]

A few months later, in April 1942, the Navy Department established procedures for correspondents seeking accreditation with the Navy, Marine Corps, or Coast Guard, with similar stipulations, definitions, and procedures.[24] The Navy regulations, however, noted that these units had limited capacity and posed additional complications, making the accreditation process more competitive, with the following clarification:

> Because of the inherent differences in Army and Navy conditions as regards accommodations, transportation, facilities, and the diverse character of naval activities and the composition of task forces, it is impracticable for the Navy to accredit war correspondents in the same number that the Army may find it possible to accommodate. Every effort will be made to give fair and just treatment to the assignment of correspondents, but the paramount consideration is the dissemination of trustworthy information to the maximum number of the public at large. Generally speaking, naval credentials will be confined to representatives of press associations and other publicity agencies having a national rather than a local or regional coverage.[25]

Before gaining accreditation from either the War Department or the Navy Department, war correspondents had to sign contracts vowing to abide by military rules, and to submit all of their writings to intelligence officers whose job it was to delete any portion of their work that they deemed objectionable.[26] How and when war correspondents' work was censored, however, was left to the discretion of military officials, which the War Department explained as follows:

> Correspondents, unless the occasion is unusual, will be permitted to see their dispatches after being censored in the event they desire to make a revision, or to note the objectionable portions for future avoidance, or to recheck on wordage for cable charges.[27]

No elaboration was provided for which circumstances might be deemed "unusual." Other regulations governing accredited war correspondents contained similarly vague language. War correspondents had to follow the provisions of the Selective Training and Service Act of 1940, remaining "under the control of the commander of the Army force which they accompany."[28] This stipulation also required war correspondents to dress and behave as members of the military, while offering them equal treatment—so long as such treatment was reasonable and within necessary limits, as noted in this 1942 field manual regulation: "Correspondents will be given the same privileges as commissioned officers in the matter of accommodations, transportation, and messing facilities. All courtesies extended them in such matters must be without expense to the Government." The manual further assured members of the press, while reminding members of the military, that "every reasonable facility and all possible assistance will be given correspondents to permit them to perform efficiently and intelligently their work of keeping the public informed of the activities of our forces within the limits dictated by military necessities."[29] Yet each officer was free to define reasonability and necessity, so this give and take was more ambiguous than the regulations conveyed. For example, the regulations also stated that so long as accredited correspondents did not interrupt troops at work or ask about anything "clearly secret," war correspondents could talk to troops about whatever they wanted, whenever they wanted—"subject to the approval of the officer present with the troops in question."[30]

When they were outside of the United States, all war correspondents— men and women alike—had to submit stories to United States censors before their material could be sent to their editors. Censors could strike out words, sentences, paragraphs, and whole stories they deemed objectionable. They sought to control information about strategy, weapons, technology, geographic locations and other information that might make the United States vulnerable or that might assist Axis forces.[31] Yet the government was equally concerned about information that might prove an even deadlier weapon against Americans—information that could divide Americans, make them question the war, or soften them toward their enemies.[32] A united front and a sustained fight depended upon engaging Americans in support of the war, developing their hatred for Germany and Japan, and sustaining their confidence in the military.[33] Instead, the government controlled the release of information and photographs, presenting the public and the media with a "sanitized war."[34] The standards of this sanitization evolved during the war. The military avoided releasing photos of slain or injured soldiers to prevent fear and anxiety among Americans, until 1943, when officials believed too many Americans were overconfident about the war's outcome.[35] The military also blocked the publication of photographs that depicted accidental or noncombat deaths, as well as photographs of soldiers who looked glib, drunk, weak, weary, grimy, or scared.[36] The military feared that images of black soldiers at ease or dying in combat might stir up racial tensions at home and thus often blocked these as well.[37] Reporters had to write carefully, with censors in mind, to avoid having their stories transmitted with large gaps in the text, which could render their work incoherent or insignificant. Thus the censors had a chilling effect on the stories journalists wrote. Author John Steinbeck contended that he and other World War II correspondents had "abetted" the war effort, often glossing over incidents and neglecting to report on anything that reflected badly on the war or the military.[38] "The foolish reporter who broke the rules would not be printed at home, and in addition would be put out of the theater by command," Steinbeck explained.[39]

War correspondent regulations stated that all accredited correspondents would remain under the control of military officials, who had the ultimate power to decide what correspondents could and could not do.[40] These regulations, from 1942 to 1944, also stipulated that the United States military must treat all accredited war correspondents equally, without specifying or limiting any category of correspondent. Thus, women who wrote as war correspondents in the first two years of World War II did so under the rules for men, and were therefore numbered among the most exceptional journalists—those whose publications trusted them enough to sponsor them for accreditation and relied upon them to cover the war for their readers.

Margaret Bourke-White, Helen Kirkpatrick, and Tania Long were among this group of exceptional women, and among the earliest groups of war correspondents the United States military accredited to cover the war. Bourke-White had covered the war for *Life* magazine in 1941 in Russia, where she photographed German bombing raids and interviewed Stalin.[41] In the spring of 1942, the United States Air Force accredited Bourke-White as a war photographer and she flew to England to cover the war for *Life* magazine from a "secret American bomber base," she recalled.[42]

My accreditation was a unique one, as war photographer directly assigned to the Air Force, with the Pentagon as well as *Life* using my pictures. I was allowed to do everything I required to build up my picture story: photograph the early dawn briefings, go on practice flights, whatever I needed except the one thing that really counted. I was not allowed to go on an actual combat mission. . . .

In the early weeks of my work with the heavy bombers, no one from the press was allowed to go on missions. Then the ban was lifted, as it obviously had to be. There was not a whisper of a double standard in the directive, but as though written in invisible ink, it was there for all the Air Force officers to read. Male correspondents who applied got permission. My requests got me nowhere. Yet I was fully qualified to cover a mission—perhaps more than they—not in the sense of woman against man, but because the Air Force was my explicit assignment, my special job and trust. I had to go on an actual combat mission. This was the heart and core of it all. On the first day the ban was lifted, two newspapermen flew the mission. They went in two different airplanes to the same target. Only one came back. This did not help my chances any.[43]

Figure 4.1.   Margaret Bourke-White, war correspondent for *Life* magazine.
   Source: **U.S. Army Signal Corps photograph, reproduced with permission of the Library of Virginia.**

Bourke-White decided to drop her request, however, when she learned of something "so spectacular, so tantalizing, that it overshadowed even the importance of going on a mission," which was the military's plan to invade the North African coast—"one of the best kept secrets of the entire war," she recalled. [44] Bourke-White asked to go along, even though it meant doing so quietly, without consulting her editors. Ironically, perhaps, she traveled by ship because "the high brass" thought it would be safer than traveling with them by air; her ship was torpedoed by Germans off the coast of North Africa and most of the six thousand people aboard escaped on lifeboats before being rescued by a destroyer. [45] As soon as Bourke-White was fully dry and rested, she had another surprise. The air officer who had been weighing her request to go on a combat mission in England told her that he would grant it because, as he explained to her: "'Well, you've been torpedoed. You might as well go through everything.'" [46] In January 1942, Bourke-White rode along on a successful combat mission, photographing the bombs they dropped as well as the bullets hitting their plane, and providing *Life* with a lead story that ran under the headline, "*Life*'s Bourke-White Goes Bombing." [47]

Much like Bourke-White, Helen Kirkpatrick had already built a reputation based on her reporting of war and international relations long before 1942. She had been working in England and Switzerland, writing as a foreign correspondent for four years, when the *Chicago Daily News* hired her as a full-time reporter in 1939, effectively ignoring (but not changing) its policy against hiring women reporters. [48] Two years later, the *Chicago Daily News* promoted its "famous war correspondents," in a series of advertisements syndicated to newspapers nationwide. These advertisements included Kirkpatrick's name, without noting that she was a woman or in any way different from her colleagues. For example, one such advertisement noted seven *Daily News* "ace correspondents," including Kirkpatrick, "who have been covering Europe with unparalleled brilliance," and further described their work in glowing terms. [49]

> Writing every day from the trouble spots of the world these tested foreign experts, augmenting these newspapers' great wire services, will present readers with the broadest possible coverage of history-making events. Noted for world scoops and brilliant, penetrating analyses of daily happenings on their world-wide beats, these correspondents have placed the *Daily News* foreign service in the front rank of world news-gathering forces. [50]

In July of 1942, four months after the United States military first accredited Kirkpatrick to cover the war in Europe, the *Boston Globe* reminded its readers that the *Chicago Daily News*, which it said offered the best foreign news, provided its war coverage. [51]

> Moving the group around and guessing where the news will break next is the job of Carroll Binder, a former war correspondent reluctantly turned editor. His staff, famed for their interpretive reporting, give him inside tips and private messages to keep the service up to its special standard. Helen Kirkpatrick, for instance, foretold the fall of France a week in advance, Edgar Mowrer the

deadlock with Germany several years ago, and A.T. Steele the Japanese aggression by 11 months. [52]

Few official records are available regarding individuals who were accredited as war correspondents before 1944. Media accounts, memoirs, personal correspondence, and other unofficial documents provide a limited picture of the process and experience of accreditation in these years. While most of these accounts list war correspondents who were men, several that describe war correspondents as early as March 1942 also reveal the names of women who were accredited. [53] Yet most news and government accounts of war correspondents, even some that named specific women as war correspondents, continued to discuss war correspondents as though they were a category entirely composed of men.

When the director of the Office of War Information, Elmer Davis, reported about the early activities of war correspondents, he noted that since the attack on Pearl Harbor the United States military had accredited more than six hundred correspondents, including "newspaper writers, radio commentators, and motion picture and still cameramen," and that about four hundred of these correspondents were "actively covering the news on the war fronts at all times." He also noted that thirteen of these correspondents had been killed, including Lea Burdette, a woman, whom he described as an accredited war correspondent for *PM* magazine. [54]

> "The gallantry of these reporters and photographers is akin to that of our fighting men, but it is also a thing apart," said Mr. Davis, "for they can't fight back when, as often happens, their own lives are jeopardized. Their mission is to mirror for us at home something of what our fighting men are doing for us. Whatever they may tell about themselves is but incidental to giving us the best understanding they can of those with whom they are joined. Their service is one to which we owe much; to which we will owe even more before we have achieved a victory based in part on the understanding they give to us. . . . In every corner of the world, these men are braving the rigors of climate and disease as well as the dangers from enemy high explosives." [55]

Editors who spoke publicly about war correspondents also described the group in terms that did not mention women and that might have seemed to apply only to men—if all of the individuals described had, in fact, been men. William Hutchinson, the bureau manager of International News Service, testified at a legislative hearing about the process of hiring war correspondents, beginning in 1942:

> At the start, we tried to take older men and send them abroad to the war fields in the belief in our organization—and I notice that the others did likewise— that it was sort of a patriotic feeling to take men above the draft age in order to use them as correspondents.

The result was that one after one they failed on the job, the work was just too tough for them, the experiences too exhausting, with the result that all of our older men, men over 40, have come home. That meant we had to send younger fellows, fellows who had the physical ability to stay up with the troops. [56]

The government also viewed the military's handling of press and war correspondents as a work in progress in 1942. In July, Davis announced the government's plan to restructure the Office of War Information. [57] The reorganized Office of War Information would consist of three branches, for policy development, domestic information, and overseas information operations, Davis explained, though periodic changes to this structure would be necessary. [58] By 1943, it was obvious to many war correspondents that the military's plans for public relations were also works in *need of* progress, though much of the challenge of regulating and accommodating such a role was inherent to the role itself. War correspondent Edmund Stevens, writing for the *Christian Science Monitor* in June of 1943, described the limitations of his job and the extent to which correspondents depended upon the cooperation of military officials, the whim of military censors, and the availability of military transportation.

> I defy anyone to watch a tank battle and obtain any accurate notion of what is happening, everything goes so fast, is so scrambled up and usually both sides are hidden from view by the mounting dust clouds in which the guns fire invisibly. To find out what really happened, you have to go back to a brigade or divisional headquarters, read the intelligence summary or listen while a staff officer explains the meaning of blue and red crayon marks on his map. But even after you have been "put into the picture," there is little you can do about it, for most of the stuff was off the record. [59]

While his readers imagined war correspondents as rushing everywhere "in one endless round of excitement," Stevens wrote, instead war was "tiresome and sordid," with long, boring stretches punctuated by brief moments of danger. [60] Military officials and their personnel, he wrote, were reluctant to help war correspondents and even more reluctant to tell them anything. "So, whether we got anywhere or picked up any stories beyond the official handouts depended on the individual contacts and ingenuity, especially as to the more narrow type of military mentality, a correspondent is at best a busybody and at worst a potential spy," he wrote. [61] War correspondents had to share jeeps with correspondents from competing publications, while sharing a conducting officer as "chaperone," as well. Even after an accredited correspondent managed to write a story worth sending to editors back home, Stevens noted, other challenges remained. [62]

In the stable periods, the Public Relations branch of the Eighth Army field headquarters to which I was accredited had its own dispatch rider service which used to pick up copy at regular points in the forward area and take it back to Eighth Army field headquarters whence it was sent by plane in a little red bag tagged "Urgent, Most Immediate" and, of course, "Secret."

But as soon as the front was on the move—and the African campaign was mainly a war of movement—the carefully organized dispatch rider system tended to break down. Thereafter, we sent our copy back whenever the opportunity presented itself or used the regular army liaison service when available. Consequently, the time it took stories to reach base was extremely elastic and often a later dispatch would arrive before the previous one. What the base censor did with your dispatches was strictly his own affair as you weren't there to wheedle and argue. And then finally to be datelined delayed. Under the circumstances, I used to marvel that anything ever got through at all. [63]

Problems that war correspondents and military officials described and addressed, publicly, in either news articles, memoirs, or official correspondence, rarely mentioned women in 1942 and 1943, most obviously because so few women were working as war correspondents at that time. These women were exceptions, and their employers and colleagues considered their work exceptional. At the annual conventions of the Associated Press and the American Newspaper Publishers Association, in April 1942, newspaper publisher William Allen White explained why he did not expect the war to have a significant effect on his hiring of women in the newsroom. [64]

The dean of America's country editors remarked, eyes twinkling, that he had not given too much thought to expected expansion of women into the newspaper field as a result of the war. "I hire women on ability," he said. "I give a woman the same salary as a man. If she's good she gets ahead just as fast. If she isn't she gets the gate just as quick." [65]

White's explanation seemed to imply and reflect the perceptions that were common among those who worked with women reporters at that time—it was the rare and exceptional woman, alone, who could be relied upon to do a newspaperman's work as well as a man. Raymond Daniell was a correspondent stationed in London for the *New York Times* when he first met the woman who would later become his wife, Tania Long. He recalled, somewhat sheepishly, his initial reaction when his friend Ed Angly first mentioned that Long would be joining him as a correspondent for the *New York Herald Tribune*.

He told me of the response his office had made to his request for reinforcements for the London bureau. He had told me they had offered to send a girl from Berlin, and I had snorted.

"Don't let them palm off any second-raters on you," I advised. "Besides, you don't want a girl. This is a man's job."

He agreed. And then Tania arrived. She proceeded to dig right into the job at hand and provided us with as much competition as any man in London. Before the war was eighteen months old she had won the prize of the New York Newspaper Women's Club for best reporting of the year. [66]

At a celebration to announce the award to which Daniell referred, Eleanor Roosevelt explained that the group had recognized Long "particularly for her stories on the bombing of London." She went on to list additional women who were working as war correspondents and whose work, she emphasized, was on par with that of their male colleagues. [67]

Among the coterie of women under fire, turning out their daily dispatches as competently as the men beside whom they work, we who envy their assignments and admire their achievements tonight honor Eleanor Packard of The United Press, in Rome; Helen Kirkpatrick of *The Chicago Daily News*, New York Post Service, and Tania Long of *The Herald Tribune*, both in London; Betty Wason on PM and Marie Marlin of The United Press, with the Greek forces in Albania. Also Sigrid Schultz, chief of *The Chicago Tribune* bureau in Berlin; Virginia Cowles, contributor to various papers, including *The New York Times*; Frances Davis, back from Spain and hospitalized in Boston; Mrs. Anne O'Hare McCormick, Sonia Tomara, Dorothy Thompson, and Hazel McDonald of *The Chicago Times,* all of whom are back again in this country. Here's a "bravo" to them all. They have done us proud.

Kirkpatrick, whose work Roosevelt referred to, above, in 1941, had returned to London by the time American troops first arrived, and her background made her an obvious choice for military accreditation at the start of the United States' involvement in World War II. She had graduated Phi Beta Kappa from Smith with a degree in history and had gained a strong background in foreign affairs after working in Geneva for several years, first as a secretary for the Students International Union and later as editor of *Geneva* magazine, while writing as a stringer for international newspapers and wire services. [68] Just as the *Chicago Daily News* had found her background exceptional enough to hire her despite its policy against hiring women reporters, her press colleagues had chosen her to represent them as a board member of the Association of American Correspondents. [69] In this role, she was one of two reporters to be named and quoted in a transcript of a press conference about war correspondents in July of 1942. General Dwight Eisenhower began the forum by acknowledging rumors that the military had fallen short with press relations. [70] Before addressing specific concerns, Eisenhower said he wanted to assure them all, again, of the following:

First, there is no doubt in my mind of the place of public opinion in winning the war. I think you can simplify it to this extent—that it's only public opinion that does win wars. It's only public opinion that translates into the soldier's

Figure 4.2.   Helen Kirkpatrick (left) and Mary Welsh (center) in England, 1942.
Source: Reproduced with permission of Sophia Smith Collection, Smith College.

mind the things to win wars with and makes them want to fight. So I have no
doubt in my mind of the place of the American newspaper and particularly en
masse over here and the service they've got to do toward winning this war. [71]

Speaking on behalf of the Association of War Correspondents, its president Raymond Daniell presented the war correspondents' main complaints,
most of which the association attributed to a lack of allocated resources and a
lack of cooperation on the part of the Press Relations Office. Eisenhower
read aloud the following passage, quoting from the association's list of concerns:

> "The attitude of the Press Relations Office is not conducive to good relations
> with the American correspondents. Their attitude is too often one of disdain to
> the jobs they are doing; instead of attempting to act as a liaison office between
> the Press and the Army, they have created the impression that their duty is to
> serve as obstacles between the correspondents and the services." [72]

Eisenhower then responded to these concerns by reiterating how much he
and all members of the military valued and depended upon the press, stating
that the appearance of anything else was unintentional and that he would
investigate any problem and "see that it gets corrected." [73] The war correspondents' other concerns included the time it took for their work to be
censored and the difficulty some correspondents had faced in accessing military sites, specifically facilities such as airdromes, right after an air raid.
Here, Eisenhower reacted with surprise, noting that accredited correspondents should already have such access. Kirkpatrick spoke up and contra-
dicted the association's complaint that some accredited correspondents had
been unable to access an airdrome after an air raid on July 4, 1942.

> Helen Kirkpatrick: "If it's a British airdrome, General Eisenhower, you can
> visit before the raid takes off, while it's going out, and while it's coming back
> and write your story afterward."
>
> General Eisenhower: I see now, I was just wondering in my own mind what
> could be the reason for any difficulty or why the question had to be asked.
>
> [Daniell:] "All operations taking place up to date have been from British
> airdromes."
>
> General Eisenhower: They wouldn't accept our correspondents you mean?
>
> Helen Kirkpatrick: "I've never had the slightest difficulty getting into British
> airdromes on any sort or kind of operations—never had the slightest trouble."

[Daniell:] "What we'd like to do is to guard against the recurrence of what happened on the Fourth of July, by being able to cover the thing ourselves rather than take the skeleton communique."[74]

Kirkpatrick's presence shows that she participated in an official military press conference. Her comments indicate that she wanted Eisenhower and her colleagues to know that a skilled war correspondent should not have trouble gaining access to military facilities. Here, the fact that she had not had difficulty should have been irrelevant: The correspondents' association had met to determine which complaints were valid and needed the military's attention; the correspondents' complaint was not that *no one* had access, but that the military should provide access to facilities more freely, to more correspondents. It is not possible to know Kirkpatrick's motivation in contradicting her colleagues here, but her statements and Eisenhower's response begin to illustrate that members of the military viewed and valued Kirkpatrick as a war correspondent—and not as a *woman* war correspondent, a category that would not be specified in military regulations for another two years.

NOTES

1. John McNamara, *Extra! U.S. War Correspondents in the Fighting Fronts* (Boston: Houghton Mifflin Company, 1945), 104.

2. David Kennedy, *Freedom from Fear* (New York: Oxford University Press, 1999), 3–8; and James Stokesbury, *A Short History of World War II* (New York: Morrow, 1980), 52–53, 117–22.

3. Michael S. Sherry, *In the Shadow of War: The United States Since the 1930s* (New Haven: Yale University Press, 1995), 45.

4. Kennedy, *Freedom from Fear*, 44.

5. Stokesbury, *A Short History of World War II*, 119.

6. Ibid.

7. Ibid., 122, 170–71.

8. See, for example, Gerd Horten, *Radio Goes to War: The Cultural Politics of Propaganda during World War II* (Berkeley: University of California Press, 2002); George H. Roeder, *The Censored War: American Visual Experience during World War Two* (New Haven: Yale University Press, 1993); Leila J. Rupp, *Mobilizing Women for War: German and American Propaganda, 1939–1945* (Princeton: Princeton University Press, 1978); and Barbara Savage, *Broadcasting Freedom: Radio, War, and the Politics of Race, 1938–1948* (Chapel Hill: University of North Carolina Press, 1999).

9. Horten, *Radio Goes to War*; and Savage, *Broadcasting Freedom*.

10. Savage, *Broadcasting Freedom*, 59.

11. See Horten, *Radio Goes to War*; Rupp, *Mobilizing Women for War*; Savage, *Broadcasting Freedom*; Jeffery Alan Smith, *War & Press Freedom: The Problem of Prerogative Power* (New York: Oxford University Press, 1999); Michael S. Sweeney, *The Military and the Press: An Uneasy Truce* (Evanston: Northwestern University Press, 2006); Michael S. Sweeney, *Secrets of Victory: The Office of Censorship and the American Press and Radio in World War II* (Chapel Hill: University of North Carolina Press, 2001); and Patrick Washburn, *The Office of Censorship's Attempt to Control Press Coverage of the Atomic Bomb during World War II* (Columbia, SC: Association for Education in Journalism and Mass Communication, 1990).

12. See Horten, *Radio Goes to War*; Rupp, *Mobilizing Women for War*; Savage, *Broadcasting Freedom*; and Sweeney, *Secrets of Victory*.

13. Horten, *Radio Goes to War*; Savage, *Broadcasting Freedom*; Sweeney, *Secrets of Victory*; Sweeney, *The Military and the Press*; Washburn, *The Office of Censorship's Attempt to Control Press Coverage*; and Betty Houchin Winfield, "Two Commanders-in-Chief: Free Expression's Most Severe Test" (Joan Shorenstein Barone Center, 1992), 1–22.

14. "July 1, 1941 to June 30, 1943," *Biennial Reports of the Chief of Staff of the United States Army to the Secretary of War, July 1, 1939–June 30, 1945* (Washington, D.C.: Center of Military History, United States Army, 1996), 49–50; and Joseph Mathews, *Reporting the Wars* (Minneapolis: University of Minnesota Press, 1957), 176–78.

15. 12th Army Group Publicity and Psychological Warfare Section, *Report of Operations (Final After Action Report)*, vol. 14 (1945): 22.

16. "July 1, 1941 to June 30, 1943," 93; and Mathews, *Reporting the Wars*, 176–78.

17. "July 1, 1941 to June 30, 1943," 93; and Mathews, *Reporting the Wars*, 176–78.

18. United States War Department, *Regulations for War Correspondents Accompanying United States Army Forces in the Field. Field Manual 30–26* (Washington, D.C.: Government Printing Office, January 21, 1942).

19. Ibid.

20. Ibid. (This definition changed after revisions in 1944 and 1945, which are described in chapter 8.)

21. Ibid. The term "newspaper men," as it is used here, did not necessarily indicate a person's sex; other official documents about accredited war correspondents published in the first two years of World War II (and referred to later in this chapter) use the term to describe reporters who are women.

22. "Instructions for Person Applying for Accreditation as a War Correspondent," War Department Bureau of Public Relations Overseas Liaison Branch, MC 572, in Caroline Iverson Ackerman Papers, 1927–2004, box #7, folder #6. Arthur and Elizabeth Schlesinger Library on the History of Women in America, Radcliffe Institute, Harvard University, Cambridge, MA.

23. Ibid.

24. United States Navy Department, "Directive for War Correspondents: U.S. Navy, U.S. Marine Corps, U.S. Coast Guard," April 28, 1942, Civilian Correspondence—General Directives and Procedures, Record Group 313: Records of Naval Operating Forces, 1849–1997, National Archives, College Park, MD.

25. Ibid.

26. Ibid.; and United States War Department, *Regulations for War Correspondents*, January 21, 1942.

27. United States War Department, *Regulations for War Correspondents*, January 21, 1942.

28. Ibid.

29. Ibid.

30. Ibid.

31. Sweeney, *Secrets of Victory*; Sweeney, *The Military and the Press*; and Washburn, "The Office of Censorship's Attempt."

32. Horten, *Radio Goes to War*; Savage, *Broadcasting Freedom*; Sweeney, *Secrets of Victory*; and Washburn, "The Office of Censorship's Attempt."

33. Horten, *Radio Goes to War*; Savage, *Broadcasting Freedom*; Sweeney, *Secrets of Victory*; and Washburn, "The Office of Censorship's Attempt."

34. Roeder, *The Censored War*.

35. Ibid.

36. Roeder, *The Censored War*.

37. Ibid., 57.

38. Paul Fussell, *Wartime: Understanding and Behavior in the Second World War* (New York: Oxford, 1989), 285–86.

39. Ibid., 286.

40. Ibid.; *FM 30–26 C 1 War Department Basic Field Manual Regulations for Correspondents Accompanying U.S. Army Forces in the Field, April 24, 1942*; *FM 30–26 C 2 War Department Basic Field Manual Regulations for Correspondents Accompanying U.S. Army*

Forces in the Field, July 25, 1942; and *FM 30–26 C 3 War Department Basic Field Manual Regulations for Correspondents Accompanying U.S. Army Forces in the Field, December 23, 1942.*

41. Margaret Bourke-White, *Portrait of Myself* (New York: Simon and Schuster, 1963), 174–202.

42. Ibid., 197–202.

43. Ibid., 202.

44. Ibid., 203.

45. Ibid., 203–16.

46. Ibid., 217.

47. Ibid., 228–32.

48. "Helen Kirkpatrick Milbank: Interview #1," Washington Press Club Foundation, April 3, 1990, in Williamsburg, VA, Anne Kasper, Interviewer.

49. "Biggest War News to Come: Starting Tomorrow in the *Herald-Journal*: Famous War Correspondents of the Chicago Daily News Foreign Service," *Syracuse Herald-Journal*, March 2, 1941.

50. Ibid.

51. "Great Staff of Foreign Correspondents," *Daily Boston Globe*, July 23, 1942.

52. Ibid.

53. See, for example, the biographies of sixty-five accredited Associated Press war correspondents, all of whom are men, published in Oliver Gramling, *Free Men Are Fighting: The Story of World War II* (New York: Farrar and Rinehart, Inc., 1942); as well as "A Letter from the Publisher," *Time*, August 3, 1942, which noted that Mary Welsh was accredited as a war correspondent; and "MacArthur Lauds Victims," *New York Times*, May 1, 1942, which described Annalee Jacoby, based in the Pacific, as "the only accredited woman war correspondent."

54. Associated Press, "Text of OWI Praise of Deeds of War Correspondents," *New York Times*, April 15, 1943. Lea Burdette, Davis noted, was "covering the British occupation of Iran" when she "was slain by Kurdisk bandits."

55. Associated Press, "Text of OWI Praise of Deeds of War Correspondents."

56. "Veteran's Legislation, Hearings Before a Subcommittee on the Committee on Finance," United States Senate, Seventy-Eighth Congress, First Session, March 1, 1943, 34–35.

57. Lewis Woods, "Full News of War Promised by Davis," *New York Times*, July 11, 1942.

58. Ibid.

59. Edmund Stevens, "War Correspondent: Thrills, Danger and Boredom," *Christian Science Monitor*, June 11, 1943.

60. Ibid.

61. Ibid.

62. Ibid.

63. Ibid.

64. "Women Publishers View War Changes," *New York Times*, April 21, 1942. White was a prolific author who, along with his wife, Mary Ann White, owned the *Emporia (Kansas) Gazette*.

65. "Women Publishers View War Changes."

66. Raymond Daniell, *Civilians Must Fight* (New York: Doubleday Doran, 1941), 69–70.

67. "Two News Women Honored for Work; Mrs. Roosevelt Presents $100 Prizes of Their Club at Front Page Ball; War Reporters Hailed," *New York Times*, February 15, 1941.

68. "Helen Kirkpatrick Milbank: Interview #1," Washington Press Club Foundation, April 3, 1990.

69. "U.S. Reporters in London Elect," *Christian Science Monitor*, May 7, 1942; and "Daniell Heads News Men: *Times* Correspondent Is Elected Head of London Association," *New York Times*, May 7, 1942.

70. "Press Conference, 4 PM, 14 July, 1942," in R. Ernest Dupuy Papers, 1943–1945, Wisconsin State Historical Society, Madison, Wisconsin.

71. Ibid.

72. Ibid.

73. Ibid.
74. Ibid., 5.

Chapter Five

"Women's Stuff and the Little Stories," 1942–1943

That is one reason I've stuck it out—to write the women's stuff and the little stories the heap big men won't be bothered with. I've learned through long experience that sometimes pays dividends!

—Ruth Cowan, war correspondent, Associated Press, 1943 [1]

The chief of the planning and liaison branch of the newly organized Bureau of Public Relations, Lieutenant Colonel R. Ernest Dupuy, recommended that the War Department establish a women's interest section of the bureau that would be directed by the executive vice president of the *Houston Post,* Oveta Culp Hobby. [2] Dupuy first suggested that Hobby would head the section, "either de facto or in an advisory capacity," and Hobby affirmed her interest in the role and arranged to meet with Dupuy the following month in Washington, D.C. [3] Hobby also attached a proposal for developing the section, declaring that the objective would be "to attune the women of the United States to constructive attitudes and efforts during the emergency," while keeping in mind the need to help women "overcome the peace talk of the last twenty years." [4] Hobby's plans to generate publicity included the dissemination of press releases to local newspapers about "routine Army news translated into terms of woman reader interest," "women's part in defense program," "news stressing health, disciplinary, recreational, and occupational training phases of military service," and "special assignments." [5] She also planned to invite women reporters who worked near military camps to act as liaisons between their newspapers and the public relations bureau "for army stories of special interest to women readers." [6] The War Department accepted her proposal and appointed Hobby "Expert Consultant to the Secretary of War" on July 28, 1941, with the official title of "Chief, Women's Interests Section,

Planning and Liaison Branch, Bureau of Public Relations."[7] Newspaper articles announcing her position described Hobby as a woman's interpreter of military news and emphasized her experience as a newspaper editor, wife, mother, and former first lady of Texas.

> She has learned much about "the women's viewpoint." Her selection to head the newly created women's division in the War Department's Bureau of Public Relations is viewed as a tacit recognition by men in the masculine profession of arms that there is such a viewpoint.[8]

Though Hobby did not have direct involvement in the accreditation of women war correspondents, her work launching the women's interest section and her newspaper background gave her a unique understanding of public relations, which she brought to bear in her later roles, developing and directing the Women's Army Auxiliary Corps and, as it was later established, the Women's Army Corps.[9] In congressional testimony to pave the way for programs such as the WAAC, Massachusetts Representative Edith Nourse Rogers had cited reporting by International News Service reporter Inez Robb to emphasize the importance of women's role in the war. Addressing the Speaker of the House, Rogers said: "Courageous Inez Robb saw the work of British women at first hand in England, and she reveals the remarkably fine job in the war that they are doing. They are a challenge to American women. We must do a better job."[10] The opening paragraph of the first article Rogers presented explained the purpose of Robb's series.

> Throughout America women anxious to do their part to win the war are asking, "What can I do to help?" To suggest an answer to the patriotic question being asked by so many American women, Inez Robb, star feature writer for International News Service and *New York Journal-American*, has made a detailed survey of Britain's women at war. In a series of illuminating articles, of which this is the first, Inez Robb reveals how the women of Britain have freed millions of additional men for the fighting forces and how their experience may prove of inestimable value to their sisters across the Atlantic.[11]

Beyond supporting the WAAC, the women's interest section, in reaching out to reporters and editors who covered women's news, sought to promote the idea of a woman's angle of war among members of the press, the military, and the public. Dupuy, writing to his wife in 1944, called the women's interest section that he and Hobby had developed "the most vital method of moulding the opinion of women of the U.S. solidly back of the Army."[12] When Hobby left the women's interest section for the WAAC in May 1942, news articles noted that the division would carry on "but with a vastly modified program. The new objectives of the war department's distaff side were explained today by WID's new chief, Mrs. Emily Newell Blair, and her assistant, Mrs. Lily Shepard. One of the main goals, they said, is to make our army a 'personalized' one."[13] Blair and Shepard also stressed that the division had changed its focus and that the syrupy tone of its communications, which Dorothy Thompson had once criticized in her column, were an example of the division's work before Pearl Harbor.[14] The women's interest section was charged with producing news releases, cartoons, and tip sheets, working closely with newspaper editors at more than two thousand publications nationwide, to ensure a continuous supply of women's interest stories in support of the war effort.[15]

When the Women's Army Auxiliary Corps made plans, in June 1942, to schedule its first training sessions in Des Moines, Iowa, newspaper editors requested permission for reporters to cover the new recruits firsthand.[16] The War Department refused initial requests, noting that the WAAC director felt it "unwise to have the light of minute-by-minute publicity shining down on these girls at the very first of their training."[17] But Genevieve Herrick, director of public relations for the WAAC and a former newspaper reporter, indicated that the department might be open to accrediting correspondents to cover WAAC activities in the future, when she responded to the International News Service's request to allow Robb, one of its top reporters, to cover the training.[18]

> This is to acknowledge your letter of June 4 in which you ask that your staff correspondent and my very good friend, Miss Inez Robb, be accredited to go to the new W.A.A.C. School at Fort Des Moines, Iowa, during its first days of operation. Your request and that of other editors is being given careful consideration by the War Department's Bureau of Public Relations. As soon as the definite plans and policies have been worked out, I shall let you know. You may be sure that Miss Robb will receive the same opportunities that any correspondent will have.[19]

Ultimately the War Department decision held, and reporters were not allowed to observe the WAAC's first training that summer. Although it is not clear whether it was Herrick's idea or her own, by September 1, 1942, Robb had set her sights on a larger goal, applying for accreditation to travel with the WAAC on its first trip overseas—and for the chance, as Robb explained in a letter to her managing editor, to become (what she believed to be) the first woman war correspondent.[20]

> This is the first time in the Army or the nation's history that it has ever sent a woman, whose status is that of a civilian, out attached to a task force.
> Army and Navy nurses and Red Cross workers have gone, but never before a woman newspaper reporter. My credentials, granted by the War Department and accrediting me to a task force as of Oct. 17, 1942, are the first such ever issued to a woman.[21]

Chapter 5

As Robb was readying herself to travel with the WAAC as an accredited correspondent, another reporter was setting the same goal. Associated Press reporter Ruth Cowan, after hearing about so many people who were heading

Figure 5.1.   Inez Robb, International News Service war correspondent.
   Source: Reproduced with permission of Robert E. Smylie Archives, College of Idaho.

off to war, was growing restless. "'Covering the woman's angle' in Washington, for the AP, became to me suddenly not enough," Cowan recalled. She was sitting with a fellow reporter when she realized what she had to do.[22]

> "Christine, let's go to war," I said to the girl with whom I had dined.
>
> "Fine, but how?" replied Christine Sadler, of the *Washington Post*.
>
> I leaned forward. "Why can't we be women war correspondents with the First Feminine American Expeditionary Force? That's what it is going to be—that first unit of WAACs to be sent overseas."
>
> I was referring to the already disclosed intention of the war department to send to England a detachment of several hundred members of the Women's Army Auxiliary Corps. . . .
>
> That November night in 1942 in the Ladies' Dining Room in the National Press Club, Christine replied: "All right, let us go to war."
>
> But Christine was not to go. Casey Jones, managing editor of the *Washington Post*, couldn't see it.
>
> I, however, struck pay dirt. Paul Miller, chief of the Washington Bureau of The Associated Press, and Bill Beale, the news editor, approved and sent their approval on to the AP headquarters in New York. Bill Beale, bearish on "women's stories" as they came across his editorial desk and who if he lost his glasses couldn't tell enemy from friend on the other side of the room, saw clearly into the future.[23]

Shortly after that dinner, Cowan ran the idea by her editors and then, while attending a WAAC news conference November 13, 1942, slipped a note to Colonel Hobby that read, "How about my going over as a war correspondent with that first detachment?"[24] In the end, Cowan's editors and Hobby all approved her request, and by December Cowan was well on her way to gaining official accreditation alongside Robb. Where else they might be headed was still a mystery. Though Hobby had publicly announced that WAACs could travel anywhere the United States military needed their service, Robb and Cowan first believed, as did their editors, that the military had accredited them as war correspondents to accompany the WAACs to England.[25] Their orders were confidential, but when the military outfitted them with gear best suited for a warmer climate, such as mosquito netting, the two reporters realized they might get a closer look at the war than anyone had suspected, a fact that made Cowan uneasy when she talked about her trip with her editor, John Evans, a conversation she described in an unpublished memoir she completed after the war.[26]

> "But Mr. Evans, suppose, just suppose, the ship doesn't go to England."
>
> Mr. Evans smiled reassuringly.
>
> "Of course, you are going to England. You don't think the war department is sending WAACs to North Africa, do you? They're fighting down there."
>
> I gulped. I remembered that mosquito netting hidden in my room. Now was the time to speak up—say what I suspected, what I almost knew. But

could I be sure? "There must not be a slip through a woman—" Would that refrain never cease? I was in the horrible position of seeming to deceive my office. But this was war. My first allegiance, my first loyalty, to whom did it belong? The AP or my country.[27]

While Robb's and Cowan's experiences are well documented in articles and other unofficial documents, little remains in government documents to show how or why the military decided to accredit these two women as war correspondents to cover the WAAC during "Operation Torch," the Allied Invasion in North Africa. However, both women often wrote first-person articles, from which a timeline and basic understanding of their experience can be drawn. These articles also show that newspaper editors nationwide viewed their presence in the theater as newsworthy in itself—with the words "woman war correspondent" or "girl reporter" displayed prominently, along with depictions of Robb or Cowan in photographs or cartoon illustrations, such as a line drawing of a woman in uniform applying makeup as she looks in a mirror.[28] Each woman described the challenges she faced adjusting to life in the midst of war, as well as life so far from home, in the middle of North Africa. But neither woman mentioned publicly the battles fought behind the scenes, with male journalists and military officers already stationed in the theater.

Just as the women did not know where they were headed until they disembarked January 2, 1942, several military officials themselves were caught off guard.[29] Brigadier General Robert McClure, Army chief of staff for the European Theater, reported that the two women's arrival was "totally unexpected and disrupting," and Eisenhower referenced McClure's cable as he expressed his own surprise and disapproval in the following message he sent to Major General Alexander Surles, Army director of public relations:[30]

I am informed by Ruth Cowan and Inez Robb that they were authorized by the War Department to remain here with the mission of covering WAAC and women activities. If this represents the desires of the War Department, I can make provision for their retention as additional to maximum previously fixed regardless of representations made in message referred to above. I have no information on subject and these two women are not repeat not accredited to this theater. In this connection the local heads of the newspaper services which these two girls represent did not repeat not have prior warning of their arrival. Please let me know your intentions and, above all, give me warning the next time you dispatch special newspaper representatives to this theater.[31]

It's unclear whether Surles responded to these cables, and the public relations bureau did not permit any "specialized attention" to the WAAC, which may have limited official records relating to Robb's and Cowan's accreditation.[32] Cowan's friend Lily Shepard, writing from her War Department post in the women's interest section, explained to Cowan that the misunderstanding was "just one of those things."[33]

> Colonel Fitzgerald says all the formalities of telling the European Theater of your expected arrival, were observed. A message was sent back from the European Theater that you would be welcome. At that time, North Africa was under the European Theater. But what the European Theater did not realize was that you were going to North Africa. It was thought at that time that your party (all of it) was going to England. So, no word was sent to North Africa for that reason.[34]

No word had reached Cowan's fellow Associated Press correspondent Wes Gallagher, either. Though Gallagher did not mention either woman in his detailed memoir of facing battles and bureaucracy throughout the North African campaign, Cowan's letters report that he openly fought the presence of a woman assigned to his theater.[35]

> Humiliating as was Mr. Gallagher's inhospitality—hostility is the more precise word—on my arrival, that is not the main point. The latter is that I came here on a definite assignment as an Associated Press reporter, and as such I feel that I had a right to help and co-operation from a fellow staff member.
>
> The way in which my copy went through should show how little such help I got. Yes, Mr. Gallagher is busy—but I've observed he has spare time. However, I got my copy off as best I could with the aid of censors, army press relations officers and other reporters. Russ Landstrum, although ill, gave me my first lessons on cablese. He did not want to leave on my account. He is tops.
>
> I was exhausted the night I arrived and was in the censors' office trying to file my story before the men reporters were got onto the fact that the WAACs had arrived when Mr. Gallagher, whom I had never seen before, came in. His greeting was that I could not stay in Africa. I spent the next three days, when I should have been writing stories, fighting to stay on the job.[36]

In Cowan's letters, her complaints centered around her perception of Gallagher as insensitive, impolite, and unhelpful—traits that might not have surprised nor offended Gallagher or other "rough-and-ready" war correspondents who took pride in being efficient, if not competitive and combative. For example, Cowan reported that Gallagher never checked on her or asked how she was doing, she explained, even after she had survived bombings and blackouts.[37] She said she had been "deeply hurt and confused" by his attitude toward her, which had "handicapped" her as she tried to do her job.[38] Cowan's boss, Edward Kennedy, recalled later that Cowan had first believed she was fighting to protect much more than her career.[39]

> I was faced by a serious administrative problem a few days after I reached Algiers: a charge of attempted murder against Wes Gallagher was brought by a

high-strung woman correspondent who alleged—not to prosecuting authorities but to all who would listen—that Gallagher had placed her where he knew she was sure to be bombed. In reality, Gallagher had merely found quarters for her in the overcrowded city. DeLuce and I eventually persuaded her that Wes had not sought her doom.[40]

Robb did not publicly report having encountered discrimination or hostility during her work in North Africa, nor did the memoirs of men who worked with Robb at that time mention any such conflict.[41] Cowan reported that Robb's colleagues at International News Service had been entirely welcoming and helpful, to both women.[42] Robb was dissatisfied with her interactions with military officials, however. In a letter to General Eisenhower in March 1943, she expressed outrage at the notion that the military should confine her to reporting solely on "woman's angle" topics.[43] In a three-page letter, Robb reminded General Eisenhower that she had written about women's activities, including extensive coverage of the WAACs and the Ninth Evacuation Hospital, but that she had been assured before her trip that she would have the same freedom to cover news stories as any accredited war correspondent. When Robb first arrived in Algiers, she noted, General Robert McClure had also assured her that Eisenhower would not tolerate any discrimination on the basis of race, creed, or sex. Robb had hesitated to burden Eisenhower with her problem, she wrote, but four futile weeks of negotiating with the Army Press Relations Office convinced her that she had no other option.

> Forty-eight hours ago, the P.R.O. ruled that I could write only stories that dealt with women. If this rule is enforced, it means that I must leave North Africa as soon as possible.
>
> Sir, I am one of the most respected newspaper reporters and magazine writers in the United States. For several years I have been a foreign correspondent for extended periods. I came here armed with every possible credential issued by the United States War Department. Yet since my arrival, I have been thwarted in everything I have attempted to do. . . .
>
> When my credentials were issued by the War Department in Washington, I was assured that as soon as my assignment with the WAACs had concluded, I would be released by the commanding officers and permitted to do a good reporting job in other fields.
>
> I have never asked to go into the front lines, I do not now ask to go into the front lines. All I ask now is permission to do feature stories in this area. Only 48-hours ago, I was refused permission by Col. Phillips, acting for Gen. McClure, to do a series of stories on the flying fortress crews. . . .
>
> Major Max Boyd had arranged for me to be based in Constantine and to drive out by day to visit the crews. The Twelfth Air Force Command, according to Maj. Floyd, was most eager for such a series. Undoubtedly, Maj. Gen. Spaatz would have approved, too, yet my request was flatly turned down by Col. Phillips and Gen. McClure on the ground I could write only about women!

(It seems to me that even crews of flying fortresses are the sons and the husbands of women, if technicalities are called for.)

If it is true that I am to be restricted to writing only about women, then I must request transportation home. No one in the United States is interested solely in women stories out of North Africa at a time like this. The arrival of the WAACs here was not a woman's story, Sir. It was a news story. But there is a saturation point to WAAC stories. [44]

Robb's letter indicates that she had understood that she was free to cover any topics she found newsworthy in her travels as an accredited correspondent with the WAACs. In 1942 and 1943, military officials and reporters might have made informal arrangements for women to cover the woman's angle of war, yet the existence of an official arrangement before June of 1944 is unclear from extant government records. A few personal documents, including communications from military officials and editors, state that the women were accredited to cover WAACs and "women's activities," but United States military regulations for war correspondents during World War II did not stipulate suitable topics of news coverage. Robb's attachment to a military unit was a rare privilege for any war correspondent at that time, and Robb had secured her place by agreeing to accompany, and cover, the WAACs. At the time Robb and Cowan were in North Africa, competition among war correspondents was fierce. Edward Kennedy recalled the "highly capable" Associated Press war correspondents chosen to cover the Allied Forces in North Africa—excluding Cowan as he did so by naming the twelve men to whom his comment referred. [45]

I believe this staff was the best group of reporters ever assembled; I was extremely pleased to be the head of it. . . . For the enormity of the story which we were covering, the staff was small. It was limited by a rigid quota system imposed by Army Public Relations; it took long arguments and cajolings to get each new man into the Theater. The home appetite for news from North Africa seemed insatiable. We were sending up to 20,000 words a day. There was the headquarters story, purporting to give an overall picture of the campaign each day, first-hand accounts by members of the staff at the front, countless "features," and reams of regional interest containing a never-ending flow of names of soldiers, their exploits, experiences and thoughts. [46]

Kennedy's and other editors' descriptions of war correspondents at the Tunisian front reveal that they did not fully consider Cowan and Robb among their peers at the time. Military officials, too, seemed to place Cowan and Robb in a category of their own, as women war correspondents. After their return, one Army public relations officer published a feature for *Editor and Publisher* about the two women—without mentioning any of the dozens of other war correspondents who had been working in North Africa at the time. The PRO noted that both women had completed a recent five-day tour of "rear lines on the fighting Tunisian front," earning recognition among the troops as "good soldiers," despite their lack of military knowledge. The article noted that Cowan's and Robb's days had been filled with blackout driving in a command car over mountains, hiking through a dusty African city, riding in the back of a weapon's carrier, a rough flight in an army transport, and another rough ride in a two-and-one-half-ton truck.[47]

> Put five such days together and it is obvious that claiming the girls were not tired would be foolish. They had filed by the time of their return one story. There was plenty of material for more. Inez had worn out four pencils taking notes. Ruth had filled three notebooks. In other words, they interviewed tirelessly and completely, giving out only when everybody went to bed or the story was done.
>
> Even in military "savoir faire," the women stood up well. It is true that Miss Cowan thought a stack of egg-shaped airplane auxiliary gas tanks were bombs and that neither of them knew who has the higher rank, a major general or a lieutenant general. But in such things they were not interested.[48]

Cowan and Robb wrote more than a dozen articles each as they covered the WAACs and the North African campaign. Cowan indicated in her letters that the lack of cooperation she faced as a woman had delayed her stories; her feature articles, such as those on WAAC housekeeping and entertainment, did have datelines indicating delays of up to three days.[49] And yet these datelines were typical for feature articles sent by courier from remote locations, because the cost of sending stories by "wireless" meant that most publications reserved its use for breaking or urgent news. Robb, one of International News Service's highest paid feature writers at the time, had nearly all of her articles labeled "delayed," with many appearing in print several weeks later.[50] While Robb's feature articles did include profiles of military officials and other stories unrelated to women's activities, both women tended to write around military strategy or operations, with a greater focus on news about women, such as WAACs, nurses, or civilians, or about aspects of the war that related to women's traditional roles, such as food preparation, laundry, children, fashion, and health.[51]

The fluid front of North Africa meant that, with or without military permission, the women found themselves in the midst of battle and in harm's way. And yet, each of their articles had an upbeat, promotional tone that did not reflect the gravity of the military's mission in Algiers or even the risks they often faced traveling in a war zone.[52] In a detailed account of their day-to-day routine, Cowan explained that the WAACs "are becoming aware that war is not a tea party," before providing several paragraphs that might suggest otherwise. "They rave about the charm and quaintness of the city in which they are stationed. 'It's wonderful!' says WAAC Auxiliary Frances Carland of Woodstock, Ill." Robb's article appeared just below and beside

Figure 5.2.   Ruth Cowan, Associated Press war correspondent.
   Source: Associated Press Photo/U.S. Army. Reproduced with permission of
Associated Press.

Cowan's, set together as a story package despite their competing organizations, profiling "the prettiest supply sergeant in this or any other army," Anne Bradley, who Robb said was "destined to live in Army clover so long as strong men in the supply service can buy, beg, borrow, or steal in hope of a smile."[53] Cowan and Robb seemed to be writing as much to entertain readers as to inform, a strategy that military officials seemed to appreciate. One commander who praised the Associated Press for sending Cowan to cover troops in North Africa saw her work as a service to her country.

> She wrote a flock of home town stories, just the right tales for mothers and relatives who want to know about those important facts of living, which most male reporters never see. I think that Ruth and AP can do more for this base and the families back home than any other writer I've met to date.[54]

Despite Eisenhower's immediate reaction to the presence in his theater of two women who were sent to report on WAACs, in later months Eisenhower would publicly support the accreditation of women war correspondents. In a letter to the editor of "Overseas Woman," Eisenhower explained that "in total war, women must bear their full share of the burden."[55] As military officials recognized the importance of gaining women's support and service, they increasingly recognized the need to keep women's share of the burden separate from men's. As the next chapter will show, the military's accreditation of female correspondents to cover the "woman's angle" of war meant that the military, the media, and the public began to value female war correspondents for their sex, and therefore for their expertise in matters relating to their sex, rather than for their expertise in matters of foreign relations or military operations. The military's perceptions and the media's portrayal of these women, in turn, began to overshadow the work of women whose exceptional backgrounds and relevant expertise had earned them their roles as accredited war correspondents.

NOTES

1. Letter from Ruth Cowan Nash to Hazel White (Reavis) MC 417 119 Personal Correspondence. July 28, 1943, in Ruth Cowan Nash Papers, 1905–1990, MC 417, Arthur and Elizabeth Schlesinger Library on the History of Women in America, Radcliffe Institute, Harvard University, Cambridge, MA.

2. Lt. Colonel R. Ernest Dupuy, unpublished journal entry, no date, R. Ernest Dupuy Papers, 1943–1945, unprocessed collection, Wisconsin State Historical Society, Madison, Wisconsin; Lt. Colonel R. Ernest Dupuy to Oveta Hobby, June 8, 1941, Oveta Culp Hobby Papers, Manuscript Collection, Library of Congress, Washington, D.C.

3. Oveta Hobby to Lt. Colonel R. Ernest Dupuy, July 12, 1941, Oveta Culp Hobby Papers, Manuscript Collection, Library of Congress, Washington, D.C.; and "Outline of Suggested Plan for Women's Branch of Bureau of Public Relations," Oveta Culp Hobby Papers, Manuscript Collection, Library of Congress, Washington, D.C.

4. "Outline of Suggested Plan for Women's Branch of Bureau of Public Relations," Oveta Culp Hobby Papers, Manuscript Collection, Library of Congress, Washington, D.C.

5. Ibid.

6. Ibid.

7. "Oveta C. Hobby is hereby appointed Expert Consultant to the Secretary of War," July 28, 1941, in Oveta Culp Hobby Papers, Manuscript Division, Library of Congress, Washington, D.C.

8. Eleanor Ragsdale, "Feminine Chapeau Pops Up Among Army Brass Hats," 1941, NEA Service, in Oveta Culp Hobby Papers, Manuscript Division, Library of Congress, Washington, D.C.

9. Oveta Culp Hobby, Chief, Woman's Interest Section, to The Director, Bureau of Public Relations, "Resignation," May 15, 1942, in Oveta Culp Hobby Papers, Manuscript Division, Library of Congress, Washington, D.C.; and Ann Allen, "The News Media and the Women's Army Auxiliary Corps: Protagonists for a Cause," *Military Affairs* 50, no. 2 (April, 1986): 77–83.

10. "What British Women Are Doing to Help: Extension of Remarks of Hon. Edith Nourse Rogers of Massachusetts in the House of Representatives, Thursday, March 5, 1942," Appendix to the Congressional Record, 88 Cong. Rec. A842 1942. Rogers presented two articles that Robb had published in *New York Journal-American* on January 12, 1942.

11. Inez Robb, "Blood and Toil of British Women Free Millions of Men for War Jobs," *New York Journal-American*, January 12, 1942.

12. Ernest Dupuy to Laura Dupuy, letter, April 28, 1944, R. Ernest Dupuy Papers, 1943–1945, unprocessed collection, Wisconsin State Historical Society, Madison, Wisconsin.

13. "WID Carries ON; 'Personalizing' Army Is Its Job. 'Turquoise Era' Ends; No More Sirupy [*sic*] Pamphlets," *Chicago Daily Tribune*, May 23, 1942.

14. Ibid.

15. "Woman's Page, 1942–1944: Scrapbook of Press Coverage," Record Group 208: Entry 194. Oversize box; and boxes 1034–36, National Archives at College Park, College Park, MD.

16. Brian Bell, Associated Press, to Genevieve Forbes Herrick, May 27, 1942, Oveta Culp Hobby Papers, Library of Congress; and Seymour Berkson, International News Service, to Genevieve Forbes Herrick, June 4, 1942, Oveta Culp Hobby Papers, Library of Congress.

17. Genevieve Forbes Herrick, Public Relations Headquarters, to Brian Bell, Associated Press, June 1, 1942, Oveta Culp Hobby Papers, Library of Congress.

18. Carolyn Edy, "Juggernaut in Kid Gloves: Inez Callaway Robb, 1901–1979," *American Journalism* 27, no. 4 (Fall 2010): 83–103. See, for example, Inez Robb, "Hard Winter but English 'Can Take It': Public Never Grouches Over War's Hardships, Correspondent Finds," *Syracuse Herald Journal*, February 10, 1942; and Inez Robb, "600 WAACs Will Make Up America's First Female AEF: 600 WAACs to Get Duty in England," *Washington Post*, August 25, 1942.

19. Genevieve Forbes Herrick, Public Relations Headquarters, to Seymour Berkson, Managing Editor, International News Service, June 8, 1942, Oveta Culp Hobby Papers, Library of Congress.

20. Inez Robb Letter to Seymour Berkson, Managing Editor of International News Service, undated, from unprocessed papers, Inez Callaway Robb, The Robert E. Smylie Archives, The College of Idaho, Caldwell, Idaho. Robb recounts the process of accreditation for her editor and indicates that she was writing sometime in early January 1943.

21. Ibid.

22. Ruth Cowan, "Why Go to War," an unpublished manuscript, Ruth Cowan Nash Papers, Schlesinger Library, 18–19.

23. Ruth Cowan, "Why Go to War," 18–19 and 28–29. This account, which Cowan wrote in May 1945, differs from the story Cowan tells years later, which has been repeated in many places since: In 1990 Cowan, forgetting that Robb was accredited in October 1942, tells an interviewer that when Robb heard that Cowan was going overseas, "she just went to work right now, trying to go, too. I felt that it didn't bother me that there would be another woman in the thing or anything like that, whether I would go alone or she would be with me, or anything else. So we sort of joined forces to get this ball rolling." See Interview with Ruth Cowan Nash by

Margot H. Knight, Women in Journalism oral history project of the Washington Press Club Foundation, September 26, 1987, page 23, in the Oral History Collection of Columbia University and other repositories.

24. Ruth Cowan, "Why Go to War," 18–19.

25. "WAACs Soon to Be Seen in Country's Major Centers: Graduates of Ft. Des Moines Scheduled for Assignment," *Los Angeles Times*, August 9, 1942; "4 WAAC Units Going to British Zone This Year," *Chicago Daily Tribune*, September 9, 1942; and Ruth Cowan, "Why Go to War," unpublished manuscript, Ruth Cowan Nash Papers, 1905–1990, MC 417, Schlesinger Library.

26. Ruth Cowan, "Why Go to War," unpublished manuscript, Ruth Cowan Nash Papers, Schlesinger Library, 87.

27. Ibid.

28. See, for example, Associated Press Photo, "Ready for War: She's Equipped," *Washington Post*, January 29, 1943; Ruth Cowan, "Girl Reporter in North African Battle Area Rides a Tank to Check Upon Musicians," *Washington Post*, March 14, 1943; Ruth Cowan, "Women Reporters Hitchhike to Escape Advance of Nazis," *Ironwood (Michigan) Daily Globe*, February 26, 1943; Inez Robb, "War Fails to Spoil Midwinter Cruise on Mediterranean," *Atlanta Constitution*, March 10, 1943; and Inez Robb, "Woman War Correspondent," *Washington Post*, a series of articles that ran daily from May 11 to May 15, 1943.

29. Ruth Cowan, "Why Go to War," unpublished manuscript, Ruth Cowan Nash Papers, Schlesinger Library, 78; and Inez Robb, "Inez Robb Finally Gets Answer To Transport's $64 Question," *Atlanta Constitution*, March 13, 1943.

30. McClure to Surles, "Cable #8006," January 30, 1943 (CM-IN 14082, OPD Message File); and Eisenhower to Surles, "Cable #8095," January 30, 1943, in Arthur D. Chandler, ed., *The Papers of Dwight D. Eisenhower: The War Years* (Baltimore: Johns Hopkins University Press, 1970), 933.

31. Ibid.

32. Ibid. A footnote from the editor states that no response had been found; Mattie Treadwell, *The Women's Army Corps* (Washington, D.C.: United States War Department, 1942), 374.

33. Lily Shepard to Ruth Cowan, November 2, 1943. Ruth Cowan Nash Papers, Schlesinger Library. Shepard was assistant to Emily Newell Blair, the director who took over the women's interest division after Oveta Hobby left for the WAACs. See "WID Carries On; 'Personalizing' Army Is Its Job: 'Turquoise Era Ends; No More Sirupy [*sic*] Pamphlets," *Chicago Daily Tribune*, May 23, 1942.

34. Lily Shepard to Ruth Cowan, November 2, 1943. Ruth Cowan Nash Papers, Schlesinger Library.

35. Wes Gallagher, *Back Door to Berlin: The Full Story of the American Coup in North Africa* (New York: Doubleday, 1943).

36. Ruth Cowan Letter to Robert Bunnelle, AP London, February 13, 1943, cc Mr. Hackler and Mr. Evans. Ruth Cowan Nash Papers, Schlesinger Library.

37. Ibid.

38. Ibid.

39. Edward Kennedy and Julia Kennedy Cochran, *Ed Kennedy's War: V-E Day, Censorship, and the Associated Press* (Baton Rouge: Louisiana State University Press, 2012), 106–7. Kennedy's daughter, Cochran, edited and published *Ed Kennedy's War* in 2012, more than sixty years after Kennedy had set the manuscript aside.

40. Kennedy and Kennedy Cochran, *Ed Kennedy's War*, 106–7.

41. Edy, "Juggernaut in Kid Gloves: Inez Callaway Robb, 1901–1979."

42. Ruth Cowan Letter to Robert Bunnelle, AP London, February 13, 1943, cc Mr. Hackler and Mr. Evans. Ruth Cowan Nash Papers, Schlesinger Library.

43. From Inez Robb to General Dwight Eisenhower, Commanding Allied Forces, North Africa, March 1, 1943, from unprocessed papers, Inez Callaway Robb, The Robert E. Smylie Archives, The College of Idaho, Caldwell, Idaho. No other records relating to this request have been found.

44. Ibid.

45. Kennedy and Kennedy Cochran, *Ed Kennedy's War*, 105.

46. Kennedy and Kennedy Cochran, *Ed Kennedy's War*, 104–5. Kennedy wrote that this group of AP reporters included Wes Gallagher, Noland Norgaard, Hal Boyle, Bill King, Dan DeLuce, Don Whitehead, George Tucker, and Paul Lee, who were joined later by Joe Morton, Kenneth Dixon, Lynn Heinzerling, and Joe Dynan.

47. Lieutenant Colonel Joseph B. Phillips, "Women Correspondents Called Good Soldiers in North Africa," *Editor & Publisher*, 1943.

48. Ibid.

49. See, for example, Ruth Cowan to Robert Bunnelle, February 13, 1943, Ruth Cowan Nash Papers, Schlesinger Library; Ruth Cowan, "WAACs Arrive in Africa Headed by a Boston Woman," January 31, 1943, *Daily Boston Globe*; Ruth Cowan, "Feminine AEF Greeted by Air Raid in Africa," *Washington Post*, February 3, 1943; and Ruth Cowan, "WAACs Who Drive Jeeps Win Eisenhower's Praise," *Los Angeles Times*, February 7, 1943—the dateline read "Allied Headquarters North Africa, February 6."

50. Edy, "Juggernaut in Kid Gloves: Inez Callaway Robb, 1901–1979"; many of Robb's articles ran in newspapers throughout the month of May, more than a month after her return, see, for example, Inez Robb, "Inez Robb Learns to Like Food While Stationed on African Front," *Atlanta Constitution*, May 15, 1943.

51. Ruth Cowan, "Folks Still Dress for Evening in Africa," *Washington Post*, February 9, 1943; Ruth Cowan, "Women's AEF Head Is Still Quite Feminine," *Washington Post*, January 31, 1943; Ruth Cowan, "N.E. Ambulance Drivers Among Unsung Heroes of Fighting in Tunisia," *Daily Boston Globe*, March 5, 1943; Inez Robb, "Gunner from Flatbush Riddles Own Plane Downing 2d Nazi," *Atlanta Constitution*, March 17, 1943; Inez Robb, "Tooth Brush Is Pressing Need for Soldiers in War Hospital," *Atlanta Constitution*, March 1, 1943; Ruth Cowan, "First WAACs to Join A.E.F. Sing Thru Sea Danger: Sleep in Blankets; How 'Eyes' Won Crew," *Chicago Tribune*, January 31, 1943; and Inez Robb, "Mail Arrival Brings Joy to WAACs Abroad," *Lima (Ohio) News*, February 2, 1943.

52. Cowan, "Folks Still Dress for Evening in Africa"; Cowan, "Women's AEF Head Is Still Quite Feminine"; Cowan, "N.E. Ambulance Drivers Among Unsung Heroes of Fighting in Tunisia"; Robb, "Gunner from Flatbush Riddles Own Plane Downing 2d Nazi"; Robb, "Tooth Brush Is Pressing Need for Soldiers in War Hospital"; Cowan, "First WAACs to Join A.E.F. Sing Thru Sea Danger: Sleep in Blankets; How 'Eyes' Won Crew"; and Robb, "Mail Arrival Brings Joy to WAACs Abroad."

53. Ruth Cowan, "War No Tea Party, WAACs Find in Africa," *Washington Post*, February 13, 1943; and Inez Robb, "Sergeant Is Glamour Girl of Africa," *Washington Post*, February 13, 1943.

54. Commander Bob Brown to Commander Barry Bingham, as quoted in a letter from Robert Bunnelle to Claude Jaggers, August 28, 1944. Ruth Cowan Nash Papers. Schlesinger Library.

55. Eisenhower to Arthur Good Friend, February 15, 1945, in Chandler, ed., *The Papers of Dwight Eisenhower*, 2479–80.

Chapter Six

"As Epitomes of All the Rest," 1943–1944

It was a nice thing for journalism that General George C. Marshall and General Eisenhower allowed girl correspondents to go along with the armies. To tell the story; tell it well. And to stand out themselves as epitomes of all the rest.

—Jack Oestreicher, International News Service [1]

Whether women followed "men's rules" in their reporting or committed themselves to covering the woman's angle, media often portrayed all female war correspondents as though they lived by a separate set of ideals and concerns. While Mary Welsh's wartime reports (in cables to her editors at *Time*) covered United States diplomacy in Africa, labor regulations, and censorship, when *Time* described Welsh's work to her readers, its focus was Welsh's "feminine" viewpoint and her coverage of fashions in Paris. [2] The Associated Press news brief announcing the military accreditation of Welsh and Helen Kirkpatrick did not mention either woman's expertise as foreign correspondents but, instead, highlighted their presence in wartime London and their wardrobe concerns. [3]

Two American women reporters who lived in London through its worst air attacks became today the first women correspondents formally accredited to the United States Army. They are Helen Kirkpatrick, of the *Chicago Daily News*, and Mary Welsh, of *Time* and *Life* magazines. They turned their attention at once to what kind of uniforms they would wear. The Army said they probably will be issued the same dress as women drivers attached to the U.S. embassy—an adaptation of an officer's uniform. [4]

Another news brief ran nationwide after the United States Army ordered that the uniform for female war correspondents would include a beige beret that

Figure 6.1. Women war correspondents in England. Working in the Press Room at Army Headquarters in London in November 1943 are, from left, war correspondents Betty Gaskill, Lady Margaret Stewart, Sally Reston, Ruth Cowan, Dixie Tighe, Mary Welsh, and Peggy Diggins, along with WAC private Mary Jane Nevel.
Source: **U.S. Army/International News Service photograph, reproduced with permission of Associated Press Corporate Archives.**

the women had chosen themselves—because, as ETO commander Lieutenant General Jacob Devers explained, "if eight women can agree on any one hat, they ought to have it."[5] Articles about women working as war correspondents often portrayed, humorously, the plight of male military officials who had to chaperone or otherwise handle the needs of female war correspondents. The article "Six Girls, No Chow, No Beds," described SHAEF facilities officer Major Charles Madary "after dark on a rainy night," stranded in Luxembourg as a chaperone for "six—count them—six beautiful female war correspondents."[6] The article featured the names of eighteen female war correspondents but provided no information about their backgrounds. Madary explained that he handled facilities for all war correspondents, "male and female," and that female war correspondents worked hard and were not "much trouble." Yet the reporter presented anecdotes throughout the article to show ways in which these women, with their restlessness and whimsical notions, continually challenged Madary. For example, in Paris the female correspondents "were distracted for a few days by the fall style shows; they got ants in their slacks again and pressed Major Madary to hit the open road."[7] Here and elsewhere the article implied that ignorance and frivolity—not courage or commitment—were behind women's desire to work as war correspondents. In describing his duties as a chaperone, Madary recounted the day he had been ordered to find and escort war correspondent Lee Miller to safety.

> "When I found her she was up on the rampart of an old fort making pictures of the shelling of the effort on the Isle de Cezezemore [*sic*]," the major said. "There was a flock of hens beside her taking a dust bath and an unexploded German hand grenade. She didn't want to leave."[8]

As quoted, Major Madary speaks of "making pictures" as though Miller's photography was a pastime and he implies that perhaps the hens in the dust bath had caught her eye and prevented her from noticing the unexploded grenade. This article was dated October 17, 1943, but the reporter was either unaware or unconcerned that the October issue of *Vogue* featured Miller's gruesome eleven-page account of the devastation she had witnessed at St. Malo, including detached body parts and the swollen corpses of a horse and an American soldier.[9]

The reporter disregarded the war reporting of other female war correspondents, as well, as he described Madary's supposed rescue of Catherine Coyne, of the *Boston Herald*, and Marjorie Avery, of the *Detroit Free-Press*. The two women were working as war correspondents in Antwerp when military officials notified Madary that the city was too dangerous. "The gals, who had been walking around the streets eating ice cream, protested that nobody else appeared frightened and insisted upon seeing Antwerp Cathedral, whence the British brigadier finally hustled them out of town."[10]

Similarly, when women wrote about surviving battles or witnessing violence in their work as accredited war correspondents, newspaper editors and other reporters often made light of these dangers, focusing instead on threats to their femininity. For instance, Cowan revealed in later years that she had vomited in her helmet after surviving her first air raid and her correspondence with her Associated Press editors indicates that she suffered an extended illness after enduring months of anxiety in North Africa.[11] Yet one newspaper introduced an article by Cowan as "her exciting story of fighting in North Africa, where, as anywhere else she worried most about being caught in an air raid shelter with a shiny nose."[12]

Martha Gellhorn, an experienced foreign correspondent who had covered the Spanish Civil War and other conflicts, had long blamed women themselves for these portrayals and for societal perceptions that often diminished their work and their potential. In a letter to Eleanor Roosevelt, Gellhorn wrote that it's "awful, when women go feminine publicly, especially about a good trade like writing, a trade that's as sound and practical as plumbing."[13] As veteran "woman's angle" reporters, Ruth Cowan, Caroline Iverson, and Inez Robb were all examples of accredited war correspondents regularly promoted by media as exceptional women, rather than as exceptional reporters. They are also examples of women who had gone "feminine publicly," by emphasizing their femininity in their articles, with self-deprecating anecdotes about having to overcome a fear of being seen in slacks or sans makeup, or having to go months without visiting a beauty parlor.[14] Iverson's expertise in aviation and engineering seemed lost on the reporters who wrote about her work, as *Life* magazine's aviation editor, as an exception—"the only woman the War Department has allowed on a military or nonmilitary mission aboard a bomber"—and the rule.[15] But Iverson, as she was quoted, appeared to play along.

> When you're the only girl—and pretty, at that—flying along on a mission in an Army bomber with a crew of eight handsome war heroes, you yearn for lipstick and powder but your better side tells you to wear those darn coveralls and like it. . . . In one zip, however, Miss Iverson divested herself of the coveralls and stood five-feet-three of femininity. A licensed pilot herself, Miss Iverson confessed, however, that flying with a crew of Army fliers "is a thrill any girl would like to have."[16]

In their personal letters Iverson and Cowan confessed to emotions and behaviors that they blamed on feminine traits. After Iverson read a military official's comment that Welsh could grasp "the full air picture" more readily than anyone he had ever known, Iverson replied: "I must confess that I was woman enough to pounce on your mention of Mary Welsh more than anything else in your long letter to Charlie. Do I envy her the chance to cover the war—so very ably—and visit with you for discussion of Chinese philosophers et al! What a break!"[17] Robb wrote about beauty regimen challenges at the front and downplayed her real fears, even as she imagined Rommel so close she could feel his breath on her neck, while writing openly about her fear of lice.[18] Cowan similarly joked that she would rather be hit by a bomb than have to share a foxhole with a spider.[19] In letters to her male editors, Cowan often cushioned her complaints with statements of self-blame, such as lamenting her "trusting spirit" or dismissing her anger toward Associated Press correspondent Edward Kennedy as a symptom of a possible mutual attraction that neither had acknowledged.[20] During and after the war, when Cowan wrote or spoke about her work as a war correspondent, she often described, at length, the challenge she faced trying to keep her brown hair blond on various battlefronts.[21]

Why any woman who is dependent upon an experienced beauty parlor to keep her blonde hair looking "so natural"—or even blonde at all—should want to go to war of her own accord is something I'll never understand.

But go to war I did, and I stayed in it two years and four months to come out of it on the eve of the last shot in Berlin—still a blonde. But they should have had some place in a hospital casualty list to record "Vanity."[22]

These anecdotes reflected the acceptance, among these women, their editors, and their readers, of traits and roles society ascribed to them as women—but their statements were also strategic. Robb's and Cowan's articles from North Africa ran under headlines such as "Girl Reporter at the Front" or "Woman War Correspondent," often without regard to the content of the article, revealing that the concept of female-at-the-front itself was still newsworthy.[23] In 1944 and 1945, nearly every article that accredited war correspondents Catherine Coyne and Iris Carpenter wrote, for the *Boston Herald* and *Boston Globe* respectively, featured their portraits and included the label "Girl" or "Woman" war correspondent.[24] Accredited female war correspondents remained a novelty in news coverage through the end of World War II. Articles continued to treat the presence and work of female war correspondents as record-setting achievements, as in the following excerpt from a 1944 *New York Times* article, which overlooked the fact that women correspondents had filed Navy news from the Pacific as early as 1942.

Journalistic history was made at Admiral Chester W. Nimitz's headquarters here today when Barbara Finch, Reuter [*sic*] correspondent, set up her typewriter in the public relations office and wrote the first Navy story to be filed from the Pacific area by a woman.[25]

One month later, the *New York Times* noted that "so far" four women had been accredited to the Pacific as war correspondents: Shelley Mydans, Peggy Hull, Barbara Finch, and Eleanor Packard.[26] The article was brief and did not mention the fact that Hull had worked as a war correspondent throughout World War I, or the fact that Mydans had been a prisoner of war in Japan— as had Gwen Dew, another woman accredited to the Pacific as a war correspondent but not mentioned in the article.[27] The article overlooked another woman accredited to the Pacific as well, Georgette "Dickey" Chapelle.[28]

When Chapelle first sought military accreditation in 1944 she was surprised to find that the process—from gaining the assignment to gaining the military credentials—was far easier than it had been the first time she applied, two years earlier. She started by approaching an editor at Fawcett Publications, publisher of *Women's Companion* and *Popular Mechanics*, where she had previously submitted articles and photographs of women working in war jobs. She recalled in her autobiography that she "had no reason to be really hopeful" and had sought any possible advantage to land the assignment. Before she had finished explaining to her editor why he should send her to cover the woman's angle in the Pacific, he told her, "We need somebody out there right now. Go ahead. Just be sure you're first someplace." The military processed Chapelle's application for accreditation "in an incredible forty-eight hours," she explained. "There was a clearinghouse for reporters' accreditation now, functioning like a well-oiled machine." While Chapelle became famous in later years for her war photography, in 1944 she still sought every advantage when military officers interviewed her before granting her accreditation.[29]

> "Now, let me see, Mrs. Chapelle," the lieutenant began, riffling the papers in his IN basket, "are you a writer or a photographer?" . . .
> I told him I'd be working as both reporter and photographer, since my magazines had no one else in the area.
> "You can't be both," he told me firmly. "On operations, you may use radio facilities if you are a writer, or your camera if you are a photographer. But only one."
> I didn't understand what he meant by "on operations." I was pretty sure the term in wartime usually meant "in combat." But certainly the Navy would never consent to a woman observer where there was any shooting! I wasn't willing, though, to ask the lieutenant any silly questions as long as he was taking my professional role so seriously.
> So I just looked thoughtful and asked, "How many accredited writers has the Navy sent out from San Francisco?"[30]

When the lieutenant replied that, as far as he knew, the Navy had accredited "a couple" women writers but no women photographers, Chapelle later recalled, "That settled it. Now anything I did, including breathing, west of where I sat was a scoop of some kind. 'I'm a photographer, then.'"[31] Similarly, Ruth Cowan appreciated the importance of "firsts" in her reporting, even if such a status relied on being first as a woman, rather than first with a news story or scoop. She wrote in a telegram in 1943 that she and Reuters correspondent Rena Billingham were applying for military permission to cross the English Channel with the ships that would bring back wounded soldiers when "suggestion was made that we go over on [a] Liberty ship—no women war correspondents had done that one. Sure, we jumped at it."[32]

Just as the woman's angle offered new material for editors who had to provide daily coverage of the war, many soldiers and officers believed that a woman's presence could brighten the monotony and drudgery of their service to the war. Lee Carson, war correspondent for International News Service, explained that the presence of any reporter made them feel like they were not "dying in anonymity. But the fact there was a dame around gave them something to talk about for weeks. And they thought, 'Well, if she's here, hell, it can't be too bad.'"[33] *Boston Globe* war correspondent Carlyle Holt, in an article about his colleague Iris Carpenter, explained that "every outfit is delighted if any woman who looks like home comes anywhere in their vicinity," even if her presence may be disruptive.[34]

> If there is one person that every member of a combat unit is happy to see, that person is a good-looking woman, including feminine war correspondents. There is nothing that a combat outfit will not do for them.
>
> Usually the gripe from the G.I.s and junior officers is that the senior officer pulls his rank and takes said female off in a corner somewhere so he can pour his story and that of his outfit into her pearly ears for as many hours as she can take it.
>
> Every outfit turns itself upside down to make her comfortable, get her anything and everything she can want, including especially all the stories that anybody can remember.[35]

Stand-alone photographs of female war correspondents ran with captions such as "The Gal Boosts Morale," for a photo of Associated Press correspondent Bonnie Wiley with wounded soldiers in Iwo Jima, and "Soldiers Greet Girl Reporter," which topped a photo of Inez Robb and described her as "fairly besieged by doughboys" in North Africa.[36] When female war correspondents visited military camps, newspapers, and even soldiers themselves often described the women's presence alone as a service to their country. In a letter to Cowan twenty-five years later, magazine writer Helena Huntington Smith recalled soldiers' reactions when she covered the war as an accredited correspondent for *Woman's Home Companion*.

> And did I take a lot of ribbing! Just the same, homesick GIs were glad to see anything in a skirt that talked American.
>
> When the battle of the Bulge had reached its declining phase I spent a short time up front as a guest of Major-General "Jim" Gavin of the 82d Airborne. General Gavin had seemed particularly pleased at having a woman visit his area.
>
> "The only reward these boys have," he said, "is to feel that people at home know what they're doing. So much the better that you're from *Woman's Home Companion*."[37]

Most female war correspondents recognized the advantages this novelty factor offered, in terms of access and attention. They also recognized their power in numbers, as women became more commonplace among war correspondents. Marguerite Higgins in 1944 was a young reporter for the *New York Herald Tribune* with a Columbia University degree in journalism when she first sought work as a war correspondent.[38]

> In arguing to be assigned to the Air Force junket, I had no idea of the adventure to which it would lead. I only knew that it seemed to offer the last best chance of getting to the war. Among those scheduled for the trip were Marga-

ret Bourke-White, of *Time* and *Life*, Lee Miller of *Vogue* magazine, and Helen Kirkpatrick. Their presence among the junketeers provided, it seemed to me, excellent ammunition for those of my bosses who were still saying that the front was no place for a woman.[39]

Yet, as Higgins noted, any advantage women gained through this attention just as easily served to disadvantage them. As a "beginner overseas," Higgins noted that her youth and her sex led to inevitable encounters with men in power who tried to brush her off "with the 'run-along-now-little-girl-I'm-a-busy-man' line."[40] As a reporter and as a war correspondent, Higgins said she had to prove herself continually to military officials and male colleagues who associated her "femininity and blond hair with either dumbness or slyness, or both."[41] Beyond the challenge for each individual who worked to overcome these preconceptions was an underlying awareness that one woman's actions often determined the ways in which military officials and professional colleagues treated all women. As Higgins explained, "Certainly unusual disadvantages face a woman war correspondent. One is the fact that since her presence is highly unusual anything she does, good or bad, is bound to be exaggerated and talked about."[42] This visibility could lead to greater problems. If military officials believed that the presence of one female war correspondent caused a problem, they could seek measures that hindered the work of all female war correspondents. Just months before the War Department drafted separate regulations for female correspondents, and months before Colonel Ernest Dupuy took over as head of public relations, Dupuy wrote to his wife about a tale that he found both humorous and cautionary.

> Heard an interesting story today. An officer who has WRENs and WACs in his establishment was visited by a succession of WREN officers, each proclaiming that the sanitary facilities were not suitable. The poor man sent squad after squad of soldiers into the toilets after hours and scrubbed and scrubbed and polished. Still the WREN ladies turned up indignant noses. It was not until a WAC officer came in and bluntly told him that he lacked receptacles for disposal of certain feminine monthly accessories that he tumbled! And yet we have women reporters who clamor to go to war. If they think we'll have special receptacles for them they are nuts. War is sure becoming hellier.[43]

Dupuy likely was aware of some hyperbole in the anecdote—and may even have embellished it himself, drawing out the confusion for its entertainment value. Yet his reaction illustrates the real concern that officers had about billeting and otherwise having to take responsibility for the "distaff side" in the midst of military operations. War correspondent Don Whitehead explained that while men "had only to pick up a shovel and walk over behind the nearest sandhill," military officials believed that women required "additional conveniences," such as latrines sheltered by canvas tarps.[44] But even makeshift facilities could not overcome the long-held prejudices of some military officials who refused to acknowledge women's right to cover the war. Cowan, writing years later, noted that the military's fixation on facilities was an alibi that "they always trotted out when they wanted to discourage women war correspondents," as well as an example of military prudishness.[45]

> Grown mature intelligent men know that it was women—their mothers, nurses, even sisters or maybe a bridge-playing friend—who put diapers on them. It was women teachers who taught Junior to say "May I be excused, please." Who better than women know that man and animal occasionally have to answer "the call of nature"?[46]

While some military officials hid behind the facilities alibi, others felt no need for excuses. Within the Eighth Army, for example, all women were "strictly taboo," Whitehead noted, because General Bernard Montgomery deemed them "an unnecessary nuisance." Veteran war correspondent Clare Hollingworth, who had been covering the war for British newspapers and scooping other correspondents since 1939, gained accreditation to the Supreme Headquarters, Allied Expeditionary Forces in February 1943. She "finagled" the long trip to Tripoli, Whitehead recalled, but "as soon as Montgomery heard about it, he was furious. 'I'll have no women correspondents with my army,' he said. 'Don't let her into Tripoli. Get rid of her.' So Clare did a quick return trip."[47] Hollingworth's own account of the ordeal shows "Monty," as she called him, to be even less reasonable. Hollingworth was no newcomer to North Africa nor to the Eighth Army and, back in 1941, *sans* Montgomery, had found "little difficulty visiting the 8th Army and attending official Press conferences and background briefings."[48] She had learned to fly in order to better understand warfare and had flown with the Royal Air Force on bombing operations. She covered war for the *Chicago Daily News* in Palestine, in Germany, and throughout the Middle East all before arranging a return trip to the Eighth Army, where Montgomery promptly demanded that she stay in Cairo. Instead of following Montgomery's orders, however, Hollingworth continued on from Cairo and joined U.S. operations as a war correspondent in Algiers.[49]

> Maybe no one told Monty that I was there but in any case I drew none of his usual wrath. By that time to his eternal credit, General Eisenhower insisted on having a few experienced women correspondents around, who—and this was vital—demanded no special treatment. It was essential to be able to go without washing, sleep in the open desert and live on bully-beef and biscuits for days on end. Many male correspondents got themselves sent back to Cairo because they could not take it.[50]

NOTES

1. J. C. Oestreicher, *The World Is Their Beat* (New York: Duell, Sloan and Pearce, 1945), 229.

2. Mary Welsh, "London Cable No. 6948, From Mary Welsh to David Hulburd—March 20, 1943 Re Winston Defending Randolph," Harvard Houghton Library; and Mary Welsh, "London Cable No. 6949, From Mary Welsh to David Hulburd—March 20, 1943 Re Giraud Cover," Harvard Houghton Library. See also "Foreign News: Retreat from Greatness," *Time*, March 29, 1943; and "Foreign News: Out of Boredom," *Time*, April 5, 1943.

3. Associated Press, "Two Women Reporters Accredited to Army," *Atlanta Constitution*, March 26, 1942.

4. Ibid.

5. By Cable to New York Times, "8 Women Agree on a Hat; to Devers That's News," *New York Times*, October 22, 1943.

6. Lee McCardell, "Six Girls, No Chow, No Beds," *(Baltimore) Sun*, October 17, 1944.

7. Ibid.

8. Ibid. It is likely that Madary was talking about the island of Cézembre.

9. Lee Miller, "France Free Again," *Vogue*, October 1944, 92–94, 129–34, 136, 143.

10. McCardell, "Six Girls, No Chow, No Beds."

11. Ruth Cowan to Jean E. Collins, 1979, Ruth Cowan Nash Papers, Arthur and Elizabeth Schlesinger Library on the History of Women in America, Radcliffe Institute, Harvard University, Cambridge, MA; and Ruth Cowan letter fragment, no date, Ruth Cowan Nash Papers, Schlesinger Library. Letters that Cowan's editors, Robert Bunnelle and Edward Kennedy, and friends sent to Cowan throughout 1944 also mention her illness.

12. "Woman War Correspondent Tells of Fight to the Front," *San Antonio Express*, August 2, 1943.

13. Martha Gellhorn to Eleanor Roosevelt, letter, November 11, 1936, in Caroline Moorehead, *Selected Letters of Martha Gellhorn* (New York: Henry Holt & Co., 2006), 42.

14. Ibid.; for examples in which Cowan and Robb had gone "feminine publicly," as Gellhorn described the tendency for some women to emphasize their femininity in their articles, see Ruth Cowan, "Adventure Seeker Finds It in Africa," *New York Times*, February 23, 1943; and Inez Robb, "Woman War Correspondent," *Washington Post*, May 14, 1943.

15. "Girl Reporter Makes Trip Here in Army Bomber," *Courier-Journal*, September 15, 1942.

16. Ibid.

17. Letter from Colonel Glen Williamson (GSC; O-17723, Hq. USSTAF, APO 633, NY NY), to Charlie Murphy, copy enclosed to Caroline Iverson (July 2, 1944). "Precision Bombing (Story and Support Material), 1943." Caroline Iverson Ackerman Papers, Schlesinger Library; and Letter from Caroline Iverson to Col. Williamson (August 1944). "Precision Bombing (Story and Support Material), 1943." Caroline Iverson Ackerman Papers, Schlesinger Library.

18. See, for example, Inez Robb, "Woman War Correspondent," *Washington Post*, May 11, 1943; Inez Robb, "Inez Robb Finds Beauty Shop—But No Soap in Hotel," *Atlanta Constitution*, May 12, 1943.

19. Helen M. Staunton, "Ruth Cowan Prefers Bombs to Spiders," *Editor & Publisher*, [no date, article fragment], Ruth Cowan Nash Papers, Schlesinger Library.

20. Ruth Cowan to Edward Kennedy, April 25, 1945, Ruth Cowan Nash Papers, Schlesinger Library.

21. Members of the Overseas Press Club of America, *Deadline Delayed* (New York: Dutton, 1947).

22. Cowan's manuscript submission to Overseas Press Club, undated, p. 2. Ruth Cowan Nash Papers, Schlesinger Library; and "American Girl Reporter Gets Taste of War," *Portsmouth (Ohio) Times*, August 8, 1944.

23. See, for example, Ruth Cowan, "Girl Reporter in North African Battle Area Rides a Tank to Check Upon Musicians," *Washington Post*, March 14, 1943.

24. See, for example, Iris Carpenter, "Nazis Won't Let Germans Quit, Says Surrendered Newsman," *Daily Boston Globe*, October 11, 1944; Catherine Coyne, "Fearing Air Raid, Writer Puts on Steel Helmet, Then Falls Asleep," *Boston Herald*, August 1944.

25. By Telephone to New York Times, "First Woman Reporter Files from Pacific Area," *New York Times*, October 10, 1944.

26. "Four Women Writers in Pacific," *New York Times*, November 15, 1944.

27. See Gwen Dew, "Repatriates Tell Stories of Jap Prisons: Talk to Internee of First Trade," *Chicago Daily Tribune*, December 3, 1943.

28. Dickey Chapelle, *What's a Woman Doing Here? A Reporter's Report on Herself* (New York: William Morrow & Co., 1962).

29. Ibid., 63–66.

30. Ibid.

31. Ibid.

32. Ruth Cowan to Associated Press, by telegram, June 1943, Ruth Cowan Nash Papers, Schlesinger Library.

33. Oestreicher, *The World Is Their Beat*, 221.

34. Carlyle Holt, "Even More Attractive Than Photo, Says Holt," *Daily Boston Globe*, April 29, 1945.

35. Ibid.

36. Associated Press, "Ready for War . . . She's Equipped," *Washington Post*, January 29, 1943; Associated Press, "The Gal Boosts Morale," *Atlanta Constitution*, March 12, 1945; and "Soldiers Greet Girl Reporter," *Wisconsin State Journal*, March 18, 1943.

37. Helena Huntington Smith to Ruth Cowan Nash, September 7, 1968, Ruth Cowan Nash Papers, Schlesinger Library.

38. Marguerite Higgins, *News Is a Singular Thing* (New York: Doubleday, 1955).

39. Ibid., 71–72.

40. Ibid., 56.

41. Ibid., 56.

42. Ibid., 213.

43. Ernest Dupuy to "Sweetheart" (Laura Dupuy), January 25, 1944. R. Ernest Dupuy Papers, 1943–1945, unprocessed collection, Wisconsin State Historical Society, Madison, Wisconsin.

44. John Romeiser, *Combat Reporter: Don Whitehead's World War II Diary and Memoirs* (New York: Fordham University Press, 2006), 66.

45. Ruth Cowan, "How to Get Into a War," unpublished manuscript, 40, Ruth Cowan Nash Papers, Schlesinger Library.

46. Ibid.

47. Romeiser, *Combat Reporter*, 66 and 114.

48. Clare Hollingworth, *Front Line* (London: Jonathan Cape, 1991), 124.

49. Ibid.

50. Ibid.

Chapter Seven

"A Matter of Special Facility," 1944

Women, no matter how rough and ready they claimed to be, continued all throughout the war to be the subject of a great debate. Every time allocations for space came up, someone was bound to suggest that the women stay with the field-hospital units where nurses were already provided or not go at all.

—Colonel Barney Oldfield [1]

The military did not officially address women as a group in war correspondent regulations until June 1944, several months after SHAEF (Supreme Headquarters, Allied Expeditionary Forces) officials sought to reassess, clarify, and improve military interactions with war correspondents. Before this date, neither the War Department nor the Navy Department had any official rules or regulations related to a war correspondent's sex. Instead, any differences in limitations, opportunities, or accommodations for women correspondents seemed to be, as Margaret Bourke-White once observed, "written in invisible ink," [2] which caused confusion for correspondents and officials alike. In April 1944, General Thomas Jefferson "T. J." Davis, head of public relations for SHAEF, requested General Dwight Eisenhower's assistance in calling upon all military personnel "to give correspondents and public relations officers complete access to the source of news," while reminding them of the importance of this role. [3]

In order to offer the general public current, complete and unabridged information, within military security limitations, war correspondents receive proper authoritative sanction or "accreditation" to accompany armed forces on military operations.

They are free to go wherever they choose in the legitimate pursuit of their profession, limited only by accommodation facilities. In order to perform their duties properly, commanders of all echelons must give them every assistance possible within military security. [4]

These ideas echoed the principles the War Department and the Navy Department had set forth in their 1942 regulations for accrediting war correspondents; the only reason Davis stated for asking Eisenhower to revisit them was "to forestall any disagreeable situation involving lack of understanding on the part of commanders with respect to public relations policies, security procedures, and treatment of war correspondents."[5] Yet Davis also emphasized to Eisenhower that SHAEF "must be prepared for heavy increases," noting that the list he had attached of correspondents accredited as of March 1944 was "not at all a heavy representation" and that Americans would continue to "demand more information about their men and their war" from the radio stations and newspapers they relied upon.[6] Other SHAEF officials sought to revisit accreditation policies, as well, while conveying an urgency that Davis did not reveal in his letters to Eisenhower. Colonel Justus "Jock" Lawrence notified Surles that the PRO had placed a hold on "further acceptance [of] War Correspondents here," until the following week when Major Edward Strode, the executive officer, would arrive to discuss "this and other subjects."[7] Lawrence ended his message with the explanation, "Problem requires reexamination and coordinated program."[8]

SHAEF reaccreditation of war correspondents included a new procedure to increase the number of accredited correspondents—while increasing SHAEF's control over their activities.[9] SHAEF also sought to ensure that only "bona fide war correspondents" would gain accreditation, and its reaccreditation process offered SHAEF the opportunity to "scrutinize" the background of each correspondent requesting reaccreditation.[10] Davis emphasized that this process would ensure that SHAEF did not accredit freelance correspondents, business representatives, and others who had previously gained accreditation despite regulations that should have prevented them from doing so.[11] The first step to gain the accreditation necessary to operate in any military theater was for news organizations to submit written approval for correspondents' accreditation.[12] SHAEF distributed a new form for editors and bureau chiefs to complete for their correspondents in fulfillment of this requirement. The form asked each employer to name its correspondents in order of priority, to indicate whether they would cover activities in London or overseas, and to indicate the specific service or location requested.[13] After processing these lists, SHAEF would hold "accreditation days" in the Public Relations Branch Information Room in London, assembling correspondents to hear a PRO official give a "brief talk." PRO officers then interviewed correspondents individually, reviewing their records, including proof of identification and personal histories, before reminding them of regulations governing their activities and obtaining their written promises to abide by these regulations.[14] The new process did not prove expeditious or uncomplicated, as Colonel Ernest Dupuy noted in the following diary entry dated April 28, 1944.

Tension is mounting here, and evidently in Germany. Our correspondent accrediting has been going on and the press-box building up, but have momentarily had to mark time since the higher-ups want to see the lists. It adds another difficulty to the job, since time is flying, and may also have some embarrassing elements, if anyone is arbitrarily withdrawn without definite cause. We'll see.[15]

Some war correspondents, such as A. J. Liebling, considered the lengthy reaccreditation process a "high point in *opera buffa* absurdity," with SHAEF operating "nine separate echelons of Public Relations in London at once."[16] Liebling argued that the process was a means of military censorship—forcing correspondents to mark time, instead of covering the war.[17] While gathered together in London in the spring of 1944, war correspondents campaigned for military recognition, such as campaign theater medals and ribbons for war correspondents "who have seen active and dangerous duty with the United States combat forces."[18] They wrote articles about biding their time between battles, about inadequate press facilities at the front, and about obstacles posed by accreditation and censorship.[19] Military officials similarly tended toward introspection during this waiting period. Lawrence wrote and distributed a pamphlet titled "Know Your War Correspondent," which targeted military officials but was picked up by newspapers nationwide.[20] SHAEF PRD officials planned communications for Operation Overlord (which now is better known as D-Day) and other operations, while they processed correspondents for accreditation. Initial plans for correspondents who would be accredited for Operation Overlord included a list of forty-three war correspondents, seven of whom were women.[21] SHAEF public relations officials also used this time to continue assessing regulations and policies. On May 15, 1944, Lawrence wrote to Dupuy and clarified SHAEF's position on war correspondents:

> Our fundamental policy is that, unless otherwise ordered, every publication in the U.S. is entitled to get an opportunity to report the doings of its men within the regulations outlined and as long as we can take care of the correspondents, we will do so. . . .
> There is every reason to believe that we are entering "the biggest show on earth" and that there will be use for every correspondent eventually. It is understandable that newspapers and services are trying to staff up their bureaux [*sic*] here to anticipate casualties and other hinderances [*sic*] which might arise in future.[22]

Correspondence and official documents in the months and weeks prior to Operation Overlord often referenced means of limiting the number of accredited correspondents and ensuring that only "bonafide war correspondents" gain reaccreditation.[23] While professional background, previous accreditation, and type of publication were all listed as means of differentiating correspondents, sex was not.

No mention of sex as a factor for accrediting or managing war correspondents appeared before June of 1944 in regulations published by the Navy Department (which governed correspondents attached to the Navy, Marine Corps, or Coast Guard) or by the War Department (which governed correspondents attached to SHAEF, including the Army and Air Force).[24] While it does not appear that the Navy Department formally reviewed or revised its policies to consider sex as a factor, one military official's memo reveals the unwritten policy that seemed to govern the Navy Department's treatment of war correspondents throughout much of World War II. The Commander in Chief of the U.S. Pacific Fleet wrote, in a letter to the Director of Public Relations for the Secretary of the Navy:

1. The inherent difficulties, such as housing facilities, which arise due to the presence of women in the forward areas naturally make their ready acceptance as Correspondents a problem. It is believed that sufficient male Correspondents are available to make it unnecessary to utilize women in these forward areas to cover spot news and technical subjects. It is recognized, however, that certain stories (such as those concerning Army or Navy nurses) can best be handled from a woman's point of view.
2. Accordingly, the Commander in Chief, U.S. Pacific Fleet, will accredit a small number of women Correspondents, each case to be judged upon its own merits.[25]

The Navy Department had far fewer opportunities and facilities for war correspondents than SHAEF and perhaps did not have the time, resources, or need to formally revise its policies for war correspondents to include this category of "women correspondents." At the same time, extant records do not explain what led SHAEF to review and revise its regulations to address female war correspondents. The first time sex appeared as a category in official war correspondent regulations and memoranda was the week after Operation Overlord. The SHAEF Public Relations Division policy dated June 11, 1944, stated, "Women correspondents are eligible to receive SHAEF endorsement within the assigned quotas. SHAEF endorsement will be affixed to credentials issued by Service Departments."[26] A few days later, an official memorandum specified that accredited women war correspondents could use information room facilities "on the same basis as a male correspondent accredited to SHAEF."[27] Yet these facilities would "normally be related to those arenas anywhere, within the overseas theatre in which women service personnel are on duty, provided prior approval is obtained from the command concerned."[28] That same week SHAEF published its revisions to the official uniform requirements for accredited correspondents—specifying differences for male and female correspondents.

(2) The proper uniform for accredited female correspondents, photographers, and broadcasters is similar to that for accredited male correspondents, as outlined in 1b (1) above, except that female correspondents will wear either skirts or (when in the field) slacks, if desired, and berets, to match the uniform and with a patch on the left side similar to that provided above for the garrison cap.[29]

This revision would not have had a direct bearing on accredited war correspondents because it specified the same uniform they had been wearing since 1942. Yet its timing further illustrates the military's official recognition, in 1944, of a new category for female war correspondents—and it may also illustrate the military's previous hesitation to mention female war correspondents in official documentation. Correspondence following these new policies continued to refer to "women war correspondents" or "female correspondents" as a separate category, such as the memo SHAEF sent on June 21, 1944, notifying the public relations officer of eleven "female War Correspondents" assigned to five hospitals in his command.[30] The SHAEF letter granting accreditation for Associated Press correspondent Ruth Cowan, in July 1944, described specific restrictions for her work and her access to facilities, required by her status as a female correspondent.[31]

1. The bearer of this letter Ruth Cowan–A.P. is a SHAEF accredited woman war correspondent and is to be attached to the 5th General hospital to do hospital and other stories.
2. Movements of the correspondent while attached to the hospital will be restricted except with prior approval of the commanding officer of the hospital and the Public Relations Officer of the command concerned.
3. Only courier press bag facilities of transmission will be provided and no demands will be made by the correspondent for electrical transmission facilities. The facility will extend for thirty days from date, subject to earlier termination by PRD SHAEF or on request for good reason by either the correspondent or the commanding officer of the hospital through PRO FUSA.[32]

The same month Cowan received her accreditation as a woman war correspondent, she wrote to the American War Correspondent Association, which in 1944 was headed by her editor Robert Bunnelle, to call the association's attention to the inconsistency of restrictions for women as war correspondents.[33] Elaborating upon a letter Martha Gellhorn had written to public relations officer Jock Lawrence, Cowan explained, "the position of wrangling and fighting into which we are forced in our efforts to do our jobs for the organizations that employ us is personally humiliating."[34] Yet SHAEF's new policy continued to restrict female correspondents' rights, as illustrated by an August 1944 official memorandum. This time, the focus of the memorandum was Helen Kirkpatrick and her goal "to cover French administrative activities in liberated area," with Dupuy's recommendation that Fitzgerald, of the Twelfth Army Group, assign Kirkpatrick to an evacuation hospital "as far forward as possible with understanding that movement from that station be only with permission of commanding officers concerned with liberal treatment within limits her safety and operations." The memorandum reminded Fitzgerald of the limitations that must apply to Kirkpatrick, as a woman correspondent:

> Presence of women correspondents in combat zones beyond forward limits in which women personnel are on duty will be matter of special facility which will be arranged unless commander concerned objects and within limits of facilities available. . . . Only press bag courier communications will be provided. This is in accordance with agreements signed by all other women correspondents on far shore.[35]

Kirkpatrick, who two years earlier had commanded Eisenhower's full attention when she vouched for war correspondent access to military facilities, now had her access deemed a "matter of special facility" dependent upon the

Figure 7.1.   War correspondents in France 1944, from left, Harold Denny, Helen Kirkpatrick, unidentified man, Jack Lieb, Bill Stringer, Lee Carson, and A. J. Liebling.
   Source: Reproduced with permission of CriticalPast.

approval of any "commander concerned." Even then, the policies would require her to settle for the hassle and delays of sending her stories by courier instead of wireless. Similarly, the directives SHAEF published on June 11, 1944, threatened Lee Miller's status as an accredited war correspondent— despite orders SHAEF distributed the same day to elevate her status. These orders confirmed the reassignments of accredited war correspondents to various theaters, listing these "men" by last name, including Therese "Bonney," Margaret "Bourke-White," and Helena "Pringle."[36] SHAEF then confirmed that Lee "Miller, of Conde Nast," would stay in the European theater "indefinitely as reward for strict adherence to pooling agreement and excellent coverage."[37] It is not clear when SHAEF's right hand caught up with its left, but the conflicting orders nearly cost Miller her war correspondent credentials. General Francis Fitzgerald, of the United States Twelfth Army Group, cabled Colonel Ernest Dupuy on August 7, 1944, to notify SHAEF PRD that Lee Miller, "female correspondent for *Vogue*," was present in a forward area and taking pictures of the fall of the citadel at Saint Malo.[38]

> Understand that she is accredited to Communications Zone for purpose of covering Civil Affairs and went into Combat Zone with permission of Public Relation Officer Communication Zone but without Army Group and Army approval. Strongly recommend no correspondent accredited to Communications Zone enter combat area without specific permission of Army Group in each case. Recommend that no female correspondent be permitted to enter forward area under any circumstances, that each one sign an agreement embodying this provision and that this Headquarters be furnished with copies of each agreement, irrespective of the assignment of the individual. Further recommend that credentials be promptly withdrawn for violation of agreement.[39]

Before these directives, Kirkpatrick and Miller had access to press facilities and privileges in accordance with their status as accredited war correspondents. Regulations and military correspondence give no reason as to why women needed to be identified as a separate category among war correspondents or why they should or should not be allowed to cover combat zones or areas not staffed by women personnel. Whatever circumstances led military officials to establish policies specific to female war correspondents, they remained undocumented, even after military officers sought further clarification, and fewer restrictions, for female correspondents assigned to their units. Less than a month after the first restrictions appeared, SHAEF investigated the "practicability" of easing its restrictions to allow female correspondents to visit the Far Shore.[40] Two days later, Lawrence replied: "ban on entry of women correspondents on Far Shore lifted by Supreme Commander," with no explanation in his cable nor the official communication he sent to elaborate on the change in policy.[41]

A sudden relaxation by SHAEF of the restrictions which hitherto have prevented women war correspondents from covering stories on the Far Shore will
enable at least 16 such correspondents to cross the Channel during the movement to France of the first group of WACs. A second group of ten women
correspondents will be enabled to participate in a limiting facility during the
comming [*sic*] week to cover the activities of field and evacuation hospitals on
the Far Shore. PRD, SHAEF is selecting the correspondents and arranging the
clearance in both of these facilities since PRO, ETOUSA is not, at this time,
undertaking to facilitate trips of correspondents on the Far Shore. Approval
has been received of a plan for a facility visit to observe the processing of
Prisoners of War which will occur during the coming week. [42]

If previous military regulations for war correspondents seemed to apply
to all correspondents, with no reference to a correspondent's sex, then the
War Department's 1944 revisions to those regulations made clear what was
self-evident all along: despite the assertion that the military would treat correspondents equally regardless of sex, race, or creed, the military had never
intended to consider the rights or responsibilities of correspondents who were
not men. Thus, as the military revised its press regulations to include specific
clauses for women, these revisions effectively excluded women from all
regulations that did not mention them—by creating two categories under
their jurisdiction: war correspondents and women war correspondents. This
official categorization, based upon sex, made it difficult for the military to
make exceptions for individuals who had gained military officials' respect as
war correspondents long before regulations redefined their role as "women
war correspondents." This exclusion, as the next chapter will demonstrate,
led women who previously identified as war correspondents to take on the
cause for all women war correspondents. As a *Boston Globe* article noted
about Iris Carpenter, "For months she was one of a small group of women
correspondents who fought for their right to use the press camps on the same
basis as the male correspondents, and she finally shared in the victory for
feminine rights. Since that victory she has stayed regularly with First
Army." [43]

NOTES

1. Barney Oldfield, *Never a Shot in Anger* (New York: Duell, Sloan and Pearce, 1956).
2. Margaret Bourke-White, *Portrait of Myself* (New York: Simon and Schuster, 1963),
202.
3. Gen. T. J. Davis to A C/S, G-6 SHAEF and Dep. C/S ETOUSA (for Deputy Theater
Commander), Subject: Accreditation of War Correspondents, April 4, 1944, 00074-1, 1-977,
Records of Allied Operational and Occupation Headquarters, World War II, 1907–1966, National Archives at College Park, College Park, MD.
4. Ibid.
5. Ibid.
6. Ibid.

7. Jock Lawrence to General Surles, 00074-1, Records of Allied Operational and Occupation Headquarters, World War II, 1907–1966, National Archives at College Park, College Park, MD.

8. Ibid.

9. SHAEF G-6 Publicity and Psychological Warfare Division, Proposed Plan and Procedure for Reaccreditation of Correspondents to SHAEF (Revised), April 12, 1944, 00074-1, 1-925 to 1-928, Records of Allied Operational and Occupation Headquarters, World War II, 1907–1966, National Archives at College Park, College Park, MD.

10. Ibid.

11. Jock Lawrence to Robert Bunnelle, April 11, 1944. SHAEF National Archives, 00074-1, 1-921, 00074-1, National Archives at College Park, College Park, MD.

12. From ETO Headquarters to Bureau Chiefs and Editors, Memorandum, "Pro Forma, Appendix A, April __, 1944 [template, has space to add date]," 00074-1, 1-928; 00074-1, 1-927, Records of Allied Operational and Occupation Headquarters, World War II, 1907–1966, National Archives at College Park, College Park, MD.

13. Ibid.

14. SHAEF G-6 Publicity and Psychological Warfare Division, Proposed Plan and Procedure for Reaccreditation of Correspondents to SHAEF (Revised), April 12, 1944, 00074-1, 1-925 to 1-928, Records of Allied Operational and Occupation Headquarters, World War II, 1907–1966, National Archives at College Park, College Park, MD.

15. Ernest Dupuy, diary entry, April 28, 1944. R. Ernest Dupuy Papers, 1943–1945, unprocessed collection, Wisconsin State Historical Society, Madison, Wisconsin.

16. A. J. Liebling, *The Wayward Pressman* (Garden City, NY: Doubleday, 1948), 125.

17. Ibid.

18. "Honor to Writers Urged: Colleagues Would Allow Ribbons for War Correspondents," *New York Times*, April 6, 1944.

19. See, for example, "The Office of Wordy Incompetence," *Chicago Daily Tribune*, April 22, 1944; "The OWI Promises Speedy News from Invasion Beachheads," *The (Baltimore) Sun*, April 23, 1944; Ernie Pyle, "London Filled with Reporters for Invasion," *Atlanta Constitution*, May 11, 1944.

20. To All Unit Commanders from R. B. Lord, Subject: "Know Your War Correspondent, an informal pamphlet" (May 22, 1944) File 1-1021, 000.74-1. Records of Allied Operational and Occupation Headquarters, World War II, 1907–1966, Record Group 331, National Archives at College Park, College Park, MD; and Associated Press, "Commanders Urged to Aid War Reporter: U. S. Headquarters Term Accurate Battle News Best Armor to Combat Axis Propaganda," *Christian Science Monitor*, May 23, 1944.

21. Memorandum for Chief of Staff from: T. J. Davis Subject: War Correspondents 00074-5, 1-1169 and 1-1170 (April 24, 1944). Records of Allied Operational and Occupation Headquarters, World War II, 1907–1966, National Archives at College Park, College Park, MD. The memorandum listed the following seven women, by last name and publication: [Ruth] "Cowan (Miss)" of Associated Press, [Marjorie] Avery of *Detroit Free-Press*, [Betty] Gaskill of *Liberty*, [Helen] Kirkpatrick of *Chicago Daily News*, [Rosette] "Hargrove (Miss)" of N.E.A., [Mary] "Welsh (Miss)" of *Time*, and Barbara Miller Browne of *Christian Science Monitor*. The use of "Miss" next to some women's names and not others is most likely a means of differentiating these four from male war correspondents who shared the same last name.

22. From PRO, ETO, J.B.L.L. ETOUSA 16 to Ch/PRD SHAEF, Attention: Ernest Dupuy (May 15, 1944) File 1-953, 00074-1, Record Group 331, Records of Allied Operational and Occupation Headquarters, World War II, 1907–1966, National Archives at College Park, College Park, MD.

23. See, for example, "Plan for Press Conference," 1-996. Records of Allied Operational and Occupation Headquarters, World War II, 1907–1966, National Archives at College Park, College Park, MD.

24. See previous discussion in chapter 4. Also see, for example, United States Navy Department, "Directive for War Correspondents: U.S. Navy, U.S. Marine Corps, U.S. Coast Guard," February 10, 1943, Civilian Correspondence—General Directives and Procedures, Record Group 313: Records of Naval Operating Forces, 1849–1997, National Archives, College Park,

MD; and United States Pacific Fleet, "Instructions for Correspondents Accredited to the Pacific Fleet," February 1, 1945, Civilian Correspondence—General Directives and Procedures, Record Group 313: Records of Naval Operating Forces, 1849–1997, National Archives, College Park, MD.

25. Commander in Chief of the U.S. Pacific Fleet to Director of Public Relations for the Secretary of the Navy, "Accreditation for Women Correspondents," November 30, 1944, Record Group 313: Records of Naval Operating Forces, 1849–1997, National Archives, College Park, MD.

26. SHAEF Public Relations Division Policy File, "Women Correspondents: SHAEF PRD Memo," June 11, 1944, Record Group 331, Records of Allied Operational and Occupation Headquarters, World War II, 1907–1966, National Archives at College Park, College Park, MD.

27. W. A. S. Turner to Director of Public Relations, War Office; Director of Public Relations Air Ministry; Deputy Director of Public Relations, C.M.H.Q., and Public Relations Officer ETOUSA, June 14, 1944; "Future Policies Regarding SHAEF Accreditation," page 3, File 1 1046; 1945:000.74-1 "Acceptance and Release, War Correspondents," ARC Identifier 615368, Series: General Correspondence, compiled 1944–1945; Records of Allied Operational and Occupation Headquarters, World War II, 1907–1966, Record Group 331, National Archives at College Park, College Park, MD.

28. Ibid.

29. From Headquarters European Theater of Operations United States Army to Commanding Generals, Forward Deputy Commander, Base Section Commanders, Commanding Officers, et al., "Subject: Prescribed Uniform for Civilians," APO 887, AG 421 OpGA, June 19, 1944, 3, Series: Decimal Files, Record Group 498, National Archives at College Park, College Park, MD.

30. PRO signed Lee to AD SEC COM Zone to Public Relations, June 21, 1944; File 1 1217, Declassified, 000.74-5 ARC Identifier 615368, Series: Decimal Files, Record Group 331, National Archives at College Park, College Park, MD. The message named the following eleven correspondents: Martha [Gellhorn] Hemingway, Marjorie Avery, Virginia Irwin, Erika Mann, Iris Carpenter, Anne Matheson, Dixie Tighe, Rose Hargraves [Rosette Hargrove], Ruth Cowan, Catherine Coyne, and Molly McGee.

31. Letter to Public Relations Officer, P&PW, FUSA, from Public Relations Division, SHAEF, July 26, 1944. Ruth Cowan Nash Papers, Arthur and Elizabeth Schlesinger Library on the History of Women in America, Radcliffe Institute, Harvard University, Cambridge, MA.

32. Ibid.

33. Ruth Cowan to Robert Bunnelle, president of the American Correspondents in London Association, July 1944, Ruth Cowan Nash Papers, Schlesinger Library.

34. Ibid.

35. To Fitzgerald from Dupuy, August 7, 1944, "REF NO S-57063. SHAEF Outgoing Message to Twelfth US Army Group for Fitzgerald from SHAEF FROM DUPUY SIGNED SCAEF," File 2-874; 1945:000.74-2 "Correspondents: Accreditations, Violations," ARC Identifier 613124, Series: General Correspondence, compiled 1944–1945; Records of Allied Operational and Occupation Headquarters, World War II, 1907–1966, Record Group 331, National Archives at College Park, College Park, MD.

36. To AGWAR for Surles for Mitchell and Ruby, from SHAEF Main, Signed Eisenhower, from Allen, from Newman, S-90785, June 11, 1944, File 3 849, Declassified, 000.74-1. Records of Allied Operational and Occupation Headquarters, World War II, 1907–1966, Record Group 331, National Archives at College Park, College Park, MD.

37. Ibid.

38. Twelfth Army Group from Fitzgerald Signed Army Group Commander to Public Relations Division, SHAEF, for Dupuy, Ref No Q-20550, August 19, 1944, File 2 880, Declassified, 000.74-2, Series: Decimal Files, Record Group 331, National Archives at College Park, College Park, MD.

39. Ibid.

40. Headquarters, ETOUSA, "Subject: Facility Visits," "Daily Journal of the Public Relations Office," APO 887, July 7, 1944, Record Group 498, National Archives at College Park, College Park, MD.

41. July 9, 1944. PR Section ETOUSA Staff Conf. Notes, Lt. Wylie for Col. Lawrence, Record Group 498, National Archives at College Park, College Park, MD.

42. Headquarters ETOUSA, "Daily Journal of the Public Relations Section," APO 887, July 8, 1944, Record Group 498, National Archives at College Park, College Park, MD.

43. Carlyle Holt, "Even More Attractive Than Photo, Says Holt," *Daily Boston Globe*, April 29, 1945.

Chapter Eight

"Outstanding and Conspicuous Service," 1945

IF CHANGES HOURLY ON THE HOUR SEEM CONFUSING TO YOU
THEIR INCEPTION THIS END HUNDRED TIMES MORE SO.

—Lee Carson, December 1944 [1]

As war correspondents and "good soldiers," Lee Carson and Iris Carpenter knew how and when to make the most of their surroundings—and when to move on. In the months after D-Day, when the War Department tied their accreditation to a willingness to cover women's activities, they wrote about women and wounded soldiers in France. [2] They used their reporting skills, and the military connections these skills had earned them, to find and break news stories so often that by March of 1945, their bylines appeared regularly beneath front-page headlines, nationally syndicated. [3] A SHAEF "Location Status" report from February 3, 1945, listed Carpenter and Carson, along with Helena Pringle, among the eighteen accredited war correspondents writing for American publications who were permanently attached to the First United States Army. [4] Despite War Department policies limiting female correspondents to the use of courier facilities, bylines on both women's articles revealed that their reports often traveled by wireless, appearing in print within twenty-four hours.

Other women did not have the same access or acceptance. After Ruth Cowan's stint covering the WAACs in North Africa, she continued to work as a war correspondent for the Associated Press, in England, Italy, and France. While Cowan spoke publicly about the value of the "woman's angle," she did not always agree with its interpretation. In letters to editors and military officials, she argued that she should be allowed to cover the repatriation of Marseilles and she expressed her resentment for their refusal. In a

105

Figure 8.1.   Lee Carson, war correspondent for International News Service.
Source: Reproduced with permission of George Peck Collection, San Diego Air
& Space Museum.

two-page letter, dated February 9, 1945, Cowan explained to editor Edward
Kennedy the medical stories she planned to write and the steps she had taken
to gain access to the Delta G-2 unit, before Major James Todd, in a manner
she recalled as "a touch threatening," had refused her.[5] Kennedy replied to
Cowan ten days later, in a tone echoing that of his previous letters to Cowan:
first admonishing her, and then trying to appease her.[6]

> I regret very much that despite your assurances to me that you would snap out
> of all this emotional business, you allowed yourself, on the basis of your letter,
> to get into a new tangle. Your assignment was not to cover repatriations, but to
> cover the Riviera. If there was a good repatriation story which fell your way,
> of course you should have tried to cover it—but not to the extent of getting all
> snarled up about it. . . .
>
>   On the Riviera you have just about the best assignment we have to offer in
> this bureau, and it is about the pleasantest place to stay at this time. There are
> plenty of stories there and I am sure you can get them. So I would say, please
> follow the lines of your assignment—which is to take it easy, get plenty of
> rest, don't get into emotional storms and do the fine job I know you can do if
> you follow this advice.[7]

Kennedy's suggestion for "plenty of rest" was an allusion to Cowan's previous letters informing her editors of an illness she had fought since North Africa, which she said her doctors had linked to the trauma, such as air raids, she had faced in North Africa, along with exhaustion. Yet Kennedy's advice did not sit well with Cowan, as her sarcastic response, typed beneath the words "THE ASSOCIATED PRESS Riviera Society Section," revealed.[8]

> Your letter clears up several things. I'm glad to get it straightened out just what my assignment is. It is simply the Riviera. I don't think we need to go into what I think about it. I'll do it because for the moment you've got me behind the eight ball. You've won this round.
> I'm sorry but I took you seriously when you suggested I operate as a sort of sub-bureau out of Marsailles [*sic*]. Remember?
> Certainly there are good stories here. But some of them are highly danger-ous. Some Americans are going to have pass-port difficulties, for example.[9]

Sometime during this written exchange with Kennedy, the public rela-tions division ordered that Cowan "proceed on 20 Feb 1945 from this hq to Hq Delta Base Section, on temporary duty for a period of approximately 90 days, for the purpose of carrying out instructions of the Theater Commander, and, upon completion of this duty will return to her proper station."[10] Though Cowan's orders and published articles indicate that she, the military, and her editors had reached a compromise, her illness worsened and she soon re-turned to New York.

A list of "SHAEF Accredited War Correspondents," as of February 10, 1945, showed thirty-two women among 298 Americans who were accredited as war correspondents.[11] One month later, SHAEF updated and corrected its listing to include 326 American correspondents, thirty-eight of whom were women.[12] On March 18, 1945, the public relations division wrote to all commanding generals requiring them to clarify their policies for accepting and accommodating female war correspondents. After reminding command-ers of the directive published in June 1944—which permitted female corre-spondents in areas where female service members were on duty, subject to commanders' approval—the letter explained the reason for the division's request.[13]

1. Some commanders maintain a more relaxed policy, giving facilities equal-ly to all correspondents, while others are more rigid in their interpretation.
2. In order for the Public Relations Division properly to assign and process women correspondents and efficiently carry out their public relations mis-sion, it is necessary to have the clearly defined policies of the Army and Air Force Commanders readily accessible.
3. A report will be submitted through the Adjutant General, this headquar-ters, outlining the established procedure of each Army and Air Force Com-mander with respect to the limitations placed on the assignment and subse-

quent freedom of movement of women correspondents within their command. [14]

Most commanders responded within days, conveying these relaxed to
rigid interpretations—and revealing just how little direction the directives
provided. Each general confirmed that his command followed the policies
from June 11, 1944, and a few did not elaborate further. [15] For example, the
Twenty-First Army Group had "no amendments or comments to make on the
present procedure which operates satisfactorily." [16] The most relaxed policy
was also the most straightforward: the First French Army Group's declara-
tion of equal treatment for all war correspondents. [17] The U.S. Strategic Air
Force and the Ninth U.S. Air Force also reported equal treatment for all war
correspondents, though neither command would allow women to accompany
combat missions. [18] Other responses were not as direct. The Third United
States Army Group had "no objection to arranging facility visits for women
war correspondents to such portions of the Army area as may be deemed
advisable," but also reported that accommodating women correspondents for
permanent assignment was "not considered practical." The Ninth United
States Army was similarly ambivalent: while its policy accommodated all
correspondents regardless of sex, the commander recommended "the number
of women correspondents sent to Ninth United States Army be kept to a
minimum." [19] The most detailed policy clarification, and the longest, served
to illustrate the directives' inherent challenge. The Sixth Army, which also
handled the Seventh Army's correspondents, responded twice within five
days. Its second letter sought to amend its first letter, which "was in error,"
by adding an item to its four-part response. [20]

1. Although in the 6th Army Group Area there is no official directive or
   policy governing accredited women war correspondents, other than
   SHAEF Directives, it is felt that the directives referred to in paragraph 1 of
   the basic communication are adequate and equitable.
2. The practice in connection with accredited women correspondents in this
   theater since D-Day is as follows:

   a. Women correspondents were informed at ROME on 1 August
      1944 that they would not be brought on the beaches but would be
      brought in by plane as soon as arrangements could be made, fol-
      lowing the landing of women army personnel (nurses). In accor-
      dance with this promise, women correspondents were flown into
      Southern France on D plus 7, the landing strip having been opened
      on the preceding day.
   b. Women correspondents were billeted at hospitals and permitted to
      live at hotels or with private families near press camp, if they so
      desired. Women correspondents have never been billeted in the
      American Press Camp. On the other hand, they are billeted in the

French Press Camp, where there are women employed as stenographers, drivers, etc.

3. Women correspondents have accompanied men correspondents on sorties without restriction other than the general safety and security of correspondents.
4. There has been no objection by the army, corps or divisional commanders in this area to accredited women correspondents accompanying men correspondents on sorties or to forward units. In case any commander should object, his desire should certainly govern the situation. [21]

Taken together, the collection of command responses revealed that the original directive's central problem, which no commander's clarification could resolve, was its reliance on the approval of commanding generals. This ambiguity allowed women to work freely as war correspondents in some commands but not others. Presumably, it also allowed commanders to provide access to *some* women war correspondents but not others. While a general could complain if an individual war correspondent's presence was disruptive or otherwise problematic, he could do little else if the correspondent was a man and had not broken any rules. On the other hand, generals could guard against a whole category of war correspondents just by declaring it impractical to accommodate women in their command. Even Carpenter, whose quality and quantity of war reports in 1945 might belie such hindrances, expressed frustration with the discord between military directives and the military mind-set.

Covering the war, under the "short-term facilities" which were SHAEF's compromise between the War Department ruling which stated that women could go to war to cover the war and the commanding attitude of mind which said, "Hell, they don't anywhere on my sector," turned life into a fantastic, beyond description, hodgepodge of flying or sailing between rocket-bombed London and shell-rocked Normandy. [22]

After the War Department's informal command survey of March 1945 to assess the consistency among commanders' policies for women war correspondents, the matter does not appear again in official documents or correspondence. Postwar field manuals and regulations, just as those prior to June 1944, do not mention sex as a category or condition of war correspondence. Military reports that provide detailed assessments of all aspects of communication also fail to mention sex as a category or condition, or even as a factor. Likewise, memoirs, diaries, correspondence, and other writings by men who served as war correspondents or public relations officers rarely—if ever— mention female war correspondents. In detailed, almost daily diary entries and letters home, Colonel Ernest Dupuy regularly described interactions with war correspondents and challenges they presented. He mentioned Helen

Kirkpatrick on a few occasions, speaking well of her work without any mention of her sex. [23] Otherwise, Dupuy did not mention female war correspondents by name nor did he mention specific challenges they presented. [24] The following remarks, from a 1946 WAC report on public relations activities during the war, offer some insight as to why military officials did not bother explaining the need for such limitations:

> While annoying, the difficulties encountered in accomplishing a well-rounded public relations program for the WACs in the ETO . . . were minor and never dangerously prejudicial to the Women's Army Corps. Among the chief headaches were:
> . . . Antagonisms between the Army male and the Army female. (Since this problem is self-evident, there's no reason for further discussion.) [25]

The problem might have seemed self-evident—within a society that defined and valued most aspects of war in masculine terms. Photographs, film clips, and descriptions of press camps illustrate some obvious challenges and inconveniences that the presence of a female war correspondent might have presented to her male counterparts at that time. One film clip of a press camp in the Mariana Islands shows several male war correspondents, some without shirts, some without pants, who are lounging on cots, playing cards, or typing their stories, with their laundry lying around and pinup posters hanging from the sides of their hut. [26] Another clip shows soldiers and war correspondents who, after having bathed for months with just their helmets to use as sinks, have thrown off their clothes and are jumping into a lake, where they are bathing nude, as well as swimming, splashing, and playing games in the water as they cool off. [27] War correspondent memoirs, too, depict the easy camaraderie in close quarters that, in the 1940s, seemed suitable only for men. [28] Don Whitehead, in his memoir, *Combat Reporter*, described traveling to Tripoli in February 1943 with fellow reporters Ned Russell, of United Press, and Jack Belden, of *Time*. Whitehead described the apparent discomfort of a YWCA woman who "steadfastly ignored" the fact that the plane's walls "had been plastered with pictures of nude women." [29]

Helen Kirkpatrick, speaking years later, recalled that the military restrictions for women were based on practical considerations, as well as personal prejudice and even ignorance. [30] On naval battleships, for instance, "men run around not fully dressed and the facilities are designed for men and not for women," she said. "If you have a whole bunch of men who have been in the army cut off from women and you put some young girl in their midst, this can cause certain problems." [31] Yet, Kirkpatrick said, the no-facilities-for-women claim was often made by public relations officials who "were really arm-chair characters" and did not understand life at the front. [32]

I said, "You don't know what you're talking about when you say, 'It poses problems for the commanding officers to have women there.' It doesn't pose problems at all. It poses fewer problems the nearer the front you get because life is very simple and very primitive."

"Well, you know the latrines."

I said, "Look, there aren't any latrines at the front, it is exactly like camping in the woods; it doesn't raise any problems."[33]

Kirkpatrick also noted that many of the restrictions the military imposed upon her were based on political concerns rather than discrimination and came from public relations officers and other military officials who were unhappy with her articles about de Gaulle and the Free French, topics that were not popular in Washington.[34] Military officials, editors, and even war correspondents themselves often discriminated against one another for reasons unrelated to an individual's sex. As hundreds of reporters were accredited toward the end of the war, news about them began to differentiate between the "war correspondent," who enjoyed the "softer" accommodations of hotel and press camp, and "combat correspondents," who slept in foxholes and faced the frontline assault.[35]

Those of us in the trade developed a snobbish pride in drawing a distinction between a "war" correspondent and a "combat" correspondent.

WE righteously considered our combat status a step higher in the correspondents' caste system and, consequently, we had the same clannish feeling that bound combat troops against the rear echelons who had never heard a shot fired in the war.[36]

Yet for all the categorizing in the last year of the war, when the War Department and the Navy Department officially recognized war correspondents for their service, in 1946, the honor reflected a broad definition of war correspondents that included all reporters whom the military had accredited to theaters of war. Campaign ribbons recognized accredited war correspondents for "outstanding and conspicuous service with the armed forces under difficult and hazardous combat conditions."[37] The War Department's original goal was to present one ribbon to a limited number of correspondents, no matter how many theaters they had served, but by the time commanders and public relations officers had all had their say, it seemed, the list of ribbons and medals had grown to include far more correspondents and, in many cases, several more awards.[38] For example, the War Department's original list, released in January 1945, presented "European-African-Middle Eastern Campaign" ribbons to 305 war correspondents, including twenty-seven women, and presented the same ribbon posthumously to eight war correspondents.[39] While the original list did not include Pacific-Asiatic Theater ribbons, it grew to 399 to represent all theaters by the time the War Department presented its awards at a dinner the following year—while noting that the department was still working through its records and expected to award additional ribbons and medals.[40] The full number of war correspondents, including those from Allied nations, that the War Department recognized with ribbons or medals totaled more than eight hundred, and some received as many as four awards, such as Noel Busch of *Time*, who had a Purple Heart and three campaign medals.[41] The discrepancies between official communications that outlined goals and criteria for recognizing war correspondents and the number and type of awards the War Department authorized likely was another symptom of the varying mind-sets among public relations officials who were charged with interpreting these directives. It is also likely that military officials found it easier to grant awards than to justify withholding them, especially because the war was behind them so, while their need to control correspondents had diminished, the desire for positive publicity had not.

The process by which officers chose Medal of Freedom candidates should have been simplified by the fact that it had fewer decision makers. The War Department had charged an ad hoc committee of five public relations officers with determining "appropriate decorations" for a proposed limit of just five war correspondents. The committee started by considering the full list of accredited war correspondents, including those from the United States and other Allied nations. "From this list, from the recommendations of the witnesses appearing before it, and from the considered personal opinion of the members of the Board, both [*sic*] of whom had wide personal knowledge of public relations operations during the late campaign in Western Europe," the board recommended twelve war correspondents as deserving of the Medal of Freedom, listing Helen Kirkpatrick third.[42] The paragraph that followed her name, to explain her nomination, did not describe Kirkpatrick as a woman war correspondent, nor did it mention whether she had covered women's activities or woman's angle topics.[43]

> Miss Helen Kirkpatrick, *Chicago Daily News*, attached to Supreme Headquarters also visited various armies in the field. Miss Kirkpatrick's objective interpretation of military operations and particularly of the renaissance of Occupied France not only contributed to understanding of the problem in the mind of the American public but also went far to promote good Allied relations. Miss Kirkpatrick never hesitated to face danger in the pursuance of her profession. As a member of the War Committee of the American Correspondents' Association, Miss Kirkpatrick was of outstanding assistance to Public Relations Division, SHAEF.[44]

While Kirkpatrick was the only woman among the correspondents the board recommended, official documents give no indication whether the board had considered sex as a factor in its assessment. The War Department approved the board's recommendations, but when the medals were announced in 1947, the list of twelve recipients had grown to nineteen, to include the names of seven additional men. [45]

NOTES

1. J. C. Oestreicher, *The World Is Their Beat* (New York: Duell, Sloan and Pearce, 1945), 217–18. Carson sent this message to editors by wireless from the United States First Army front in Belgium.

2. See, for example, Lee Carson, "French Women Chic Despite War Curbs: Art and Design of Gowns Disguise Poor Materials Brought On in Past Years," *New York Times*, August 29, 1944; Lee Carson, "Caring for Seriously Wounded Boys in Germany Is Told," *Tipton (Indiana) News*, December 3, 1944; Iris Carpenter, "Four Red Cross Girls Thumb Way Into Paris," *Daily Boston Globe*, September 3, 1944; and Iris Carpenter, "Captain with Moustache Cheers Sophie Who Is Ill," *Daily Boston Globe*, November 1, 1944.

3. See, for example, Iris Carpenter, "Thrilling Tank Brigade Charge Wrests Samree from Germans," *Atlanta Constitution*, January 13, 1945; Iris Carpenter, "Rhine Spanned in 10 Minutes," *Daily Boston Globe*, March 10, 1945; Lee Carson, "Second Infantry Division Blocked German Victory," *New Castle (Pennsylvania) News*, January 4, 1945; and Lee Carson, "Doughboys Suspect Healthy Young Cologne Civilians Are German Soldiers," *The Lowell Sun*, March 6, 1945.

4. "Location Status SHAEF War Correspondents as of 1200 Hours, 3 February 1945," Supreme Headquarters Allied Expeditionary Force, Public Relations Division, February 3, 1945. R. Ernest Dupuy Papers, 1943–1945, unprocessed collection, Wisconsin State Historical Society, Madison, Wisconsin. This list also included photographers and British war correspondents for a total of thirty-six correspondents attached to the First Army. The seven correspondents listed as having only facility passes, or temporary attachment, did not include women.

5. Letter from Ruth Cowan to Edward Kennedy, February 9, 1945. Ruth Cowan Nash Papers, Arthur and Elizabeth Schlesinger Library on the History of Women in America, Radcliffe Institute, Harvard University, Cambridge, MA.

6. Letter from Edward Kennedy to Ruth Cowan, February 19, 1945. Ruth Cowan Nash Papers, Schlesinger Library.

7. Ibid.

8. Letter from Ruth Cowan to Edward Kennedy, February 28, 1945. Ruth Cowan Nash Papers, Schlesinger Library.

9. Ibid.

10. To Ruth Cowan, From HQ ETO USA, By Command of General Eisenhower. Subject: Orders. February 19, 1945. Ruth Cowan Nash Papers, Schlesinger Library.

11. "List of SHAEF Accredited War Correspondents," Supreme Headquarters Allied Expeditionary Force, Public Relations Division, February 10, 1945, in R. Ernest Dupuy Papers, 1943–1945, unprocessed collection, Wisconsin State Historical Society, Madison, Wisconsin.

12. "Addendum Number 1 to Total Lists of War Correspondents Accredited to SHAEF, dated 10 February 1945," Supreme Headquarters Allied Expeditionary Force, Public Relations Division, March 10, 1945, in R. Ernest Dupuy Papers, 1943–1945, unprocessed collection, Wisconsin State Historical Society, Madison, Wisconsin. The list showed an additional six American women among correspondents who were "newly accredited or returned to the theater," and that two women (one of whom was not listed February 10) were among those "disaccredited or departed theatre, to be deleted from lists." Corrections to accreditation numbers or the spelling of war correspondent names included another woman who had not appeared on the February list.

13. To: Commanding Generals, From: H. H. Newman, Colonel, AGD, Assistant Adjutant General. PRD-AGM, "Subject: Facilities for Women War Correspondents" (March 18 1945) File 3-902 and 3-903, Declassified, 000.74-4, Records of Allied Operational and Occupation

Headquarters, World War II, 1907–1966, Record Group 331, National Archives at College Park, College Park, MD.

14. Ibid.

15. Responses that just restated or otherwise confirmed adherence to the directives, without elaboration, included the following letters: From Headquarters First U.S. Army; From Headquarters Fifteenth U.S. Army, A. Morris, Jr., Captain A.G.D., Asst Adjutant General. To: Commanding General, SHAEF, "Subject: Facilities for Women War Correspondents," File 3-914, Declassified, 000.74-4. Records of Allied Operational and Occupation Headquarters, World War II, 1907–1966, Record Group 331, National Archives at College Park, College Park, MD.

16. 21 Army Group to Supreme Commander AEF, March 29, 1945, File 3-910, Declassified, 000.74-4, "Facilities for Women War Correspondents," Records of Allied Operational and Occupation Headquarters, World War II, 1907–1966, Record Group 331, National Archives at College Park, College Park, MD.

17. From General De Lattre De Tassioni, to Colonel Newman, "Facilité Accordées Aux Femmes Correspondants de Guerre" (April 9, 1945) File 3-914, Declassified, "Facilities for Women War Correspondents," Records of Allied Operational and Occupation Headquarters, World War II, 1907–1966, Record Group 331, National Archives at College Park, College Park, MD. The response read: "Les femmes correspondantes de guerre bénéficient des même facilités que les hommes correspondants de guerre."

18. From Col. J. B. Gordon, HQ U.S. Strategic Air Forces in Europe, to Supreme Commander AEF (March 29, 1945) File 3-909, Declassified, 000.74-4, "Facilities for Women War Correspondents," Records of Allied Operational and Occupation Headquarters, World War II, 1907–1966, Record Group 331, National Archives at College Park, College Park, MD; From Lt. Col. F. H. Monahan HQ Ninth Air Force, to Supreme Commander AEF (March 23, 1945) File 3-911, Declassified, 000.74-4, "Facilities for Women War Correspondents," Records of Allied Operational and Occupation Headquarters, World War II, 1907–1966, Record Group 331, National Archives at College Park, College Park, MD.

19. From Col. John A. Klein, Adjutant General, "Subject: Facilities for Women War Correspondents," March 25, 1945, File 3 913 APO 339, Declassified, 000.74-4, "Facilities for Women War Correspondents," Records of Allied Operational and Occupation Headquarters, World War II, 1907–1966, Record Group 331, National Archives at College Park, College Park, MD.

20. From John E. Pederson, Headquarters Seventh Army, to Supreme Commander AEF, March 30, 1945 AG File 3-916 Declassified, 000.74-4, "Facilities for Women War Correspondents," Records of Allied Operational and Occupation Headquarters, World War II, 1907–1966, Record Group 331, National Archives at College Park, College Park, MD; From Headquarters 6th Army Group, Col. J. L. Tarr, To: Supreme Commander, AEF, File 3-904 Declassified, 000.74-4, "Facilities for Women War Correspondents," Records of Allied Operational and Occupation Headquarters, World War II, 1907–1966, Record Group 331, National Archives at College Park, College Park, MD; and From Headquarters 6th Army Group, Col. J. L. Tarr, To: Supreme Commander, AEF, 3-915 Declassified, 000.74-4, "Facilities for Women War Correspondents," Records of Allied Operational and Occupation Headquarters, World War II, 1907–1966, Record Group 331, National Archives at College Park, College Park, MD.

21. From Headquarters 6th Army Group, Col. J. L. Tarr, To: Supreme Commander, AEF, March 29, 1945, File 3-915, Declassified, 000.74-4, "Facilities for Women War Correspondents," Records of Allied Operational and Occupation Headquarters, World War II, 1907–1966, Record Group 331, National Archives at College Park, College Park, MD.

22. Iris Carpenter, *No Woman's World* (Boston: Houghton Mifflin Company, 1946), 35.

23. R. Ernest Dupuy Papers, 1943–1945, unprocessed collection, Wisconsin State Historical Society, Madison, Wisconsin.

24. From Headquarters, U.S. Forces European Theater, Public Relations Division to Theater WAC Staff Director, "Outline, WAC Public Relations Activities, European Theater of Operations, 4 July 1943–1 April 1946. ETO," November 23, 1945, 104–7. Records of Allied Operational and Occupation Headquarters, World War II, 1907–1966, Record Group 331, National Archives at College Park, College Park, MD.

25. Ibid.

26. Film clips on Critical Past: War Correspondents Typing Documents and Playing Cards in Their Hut on Saipan, Marianas Islands during World War II. Location: Saipan Mariana Islands Date: 1945 Duration: 32 sec. http://www.criticalpast.com.

27. Film clips on Critical Past: American Troops and War Correspondents at Mont Saint Michel and Saint Malo in France. Date: 1944 Duration: 6 min 11 sec. http://www.criticalpast.com/.

28. Wes Gallagher, *Back Door to Berlin: The Full Story of the American Coups in North Africa* (New York: Doubleday, 1943), 103–4.

29. John Romeiser, *Combat Reporter: Don Whitehead's World War II Diary and Memoirs* (New York: Fordham University Press, 2006), 114.

30. Helen Paull Kirkpatrick, Smith Centennial Study Oral History Project, 23–27, Helen Paull Kirkpatrick Papers, 1930–1998, Sophia Smith Collection, Smith College, Northampton, Massachusetts.

31. Ibid.

32. Ibid., 25.

33. Ibid.

34. Ibid.

35. See, for example, Romeiser, *Combat Reporter*, 47; Ernie Pyle, "Vet War Correspondents Scared," *Atlanta Constitution*, June 11, 1944.

36. Romeiser, *Combat Reporter*, 47.

37. "European-African-Middle Eastern Campaign Ribbon," Headquarters U.S. Forces, European Theater, November 26, 1945, R. Ernest Dupuy Papers, 1943–1945, unprocessed collection, Wisconsin State Historical Society, Madison, Wisconsin. The list noted that the ribbons had been authorized "under the provisions of War Department Cable WARX 29101, 30 January 1945."

38. "Awards to Accredited War Correspondents," R. Ernest Dupuy Papers, 1943–1945, unprocessed collection, Wisconsin State Historical Society, Madison, Wisconsin.

39. "European-African-Middle Eastern Campaign Ribbon," Headquarters U.S. Forces, European Theater, November 26, 1945, R. Ernest Dupuy Papers, 1943–1945, unprocessed collection, Wisconsin State Historical Society, Madison, Wisconsin. The list noted that the ribbons had been authorized "under the provisions of War Department Cable WARX 29101, 30 January 1945."

40. Ibid.

41. War Department, "War Correspondents—Decorations and Awards," 1-14, M.C. 417, folder 117, "Corr. U.S. War Dept., re: campaign ribbon, 1945–1946," Ruth Cowan Nash Papers, Schlesinger Library.

42. "Proceedings of a Board of Officers Convened in Accordance with the Following Orders: Special Orders No. 8," February 1, 1946, R. Ernest Dupuy Papers, 1943–1945, unprocessed collection, Wisconsin State Historical Society, Madison, Wisconsin. The board did not indicate whether the order in which correspondents were listed was significant, and the names were not in alphabetical order.

43. Ibid.

44. Ibid.

45. "Medal of Freedom Awarded by Army to 19 War Writers," *Chicago Daily Tribune*, September 27, 1947.

Chapter Nine

"Persona Non Grata," 1945 and Beyond

All I know is that when that dame presumes to tell me about the war, I don't just get mad—I explode. For war reporting is not a woman's province, though your readers would have it feminized to an immeasurable degree. They do not realize that, when a large society of persons is composed almost exclusively of man, the code of conduct is a masculine code, that the way of living is a masculine way. In such company a female is an undesirable alien and any attempt to crash into that world of men by apeing their ways only makes her "persona non grata."

—R., 1945[1]

In the spring of 1945, Iris Carpenter had been covering the war as an accredited correspondent for the *Boston Globe* for more than a year when a German woman, seeing Carpenter's uniform, "panted up one afternoon with an agonized expression and an urgent 'Soldier woman! Please come! You must come! You woman, you must help!'"[2] Carpenter heeded the German woman's call, and later wrote about the incident in her memoir:

I expected to find somebody badly wounded. Instead, a girl's screams came from behind a locked door and an American voice ordered gruffly, "Stop clawing, you little bitch, or I'm gonna break your bloody neck."

Banging and kicking, I bellowed an imperious "Hey, quit that and open the door!" Incredibly, the scuffling stopped and the door opened—just a chink—as a man about twenty-five peered out to demand, "What the hell do you mean, squawking orders at me?"

What I said I shall never know, any more than I shall never know what possessed me to stand there arguing with him instead of beating it to get somebody who could have thrown him out. At the time it seemed that it would be possible either to appeal to his sense of decency or else frighten him into leaving the girl alone. With a matter-of-fact brutality, which was more shocking than her sobbing, he told me, "I've got a pistol and there ain't nobody

117

going to stop me having her or any other German gal I want. And why not?
We won 'em didn't we? What the hell can they expect of an army that licked
'em?" Then he slammed the door. [3]

Realizing that she and the woman who had called her to the scene could
not save the young woman themselves, Carpenter left to find someone who
could.

> The officer we flagged set off to the rescue as though his jeep had been under
> fire, with a distressed "Hell! The most stinking part of this whole stinking war
> business is that there should be women anywhere near it." [4]

Carpenter didn't explain how the incident turned out, and she left it to the
reader to decide whether the officer meant to imply that the most "stinking
part" was the German woman's presence, for making the American soldier's
crime possible, or Carpenter's presence as an American woman witnessing
such a crime against another woman.

As this book has illustrated, both interpretations convey fears that the
military, the public, and the press struggled with as women entered the "inner
circle" of war. [5] Women's presence in war challenged gender roles in place at
that time, and even seemed, to some who opposed their presence, to threaten
the very outcome of the war as well as society's return to traditional values
after the war. [6] The military and the public perceived women as vulnerable, as
adding to men's physical and emotional responsibilities at the front. They
believed a woman's presence could also distract, tempt, or misguide soldiers
away from their duties. [7] Women at the front could bear witness to the worst
of humanity, which up close was rarely glorious, and portray their observa-
tions to the rest of the world, a role that outraged at least one *Boston Globe*
reader, who identified himself as "R." in letters to the editor declaring that
war was not a "woman's province." [8]

The fact that Carpenter described the incident in her memoir but not her
extensive war reporting further illustrates the precarious role of accredited
women war correspondents. All accredited World War II correspondents
faced conflicting motivations, as they weighed just how much truth they
could share without losing accreditation or access to their sources or, worse,
risking other people's lives and their own freedom. All war correspondents
also had to weigh just how much truth they could keep to themselves without
losing their readers, their reputations, or their jobs. But women, whose presence was controversial both in the office and at the front, had the added
pressure of proving themselves in two unwelcoming territories, while knowing their actions could be construed as representative of all women war
correspondents, and vice versa. They also had to live with what Carpenter
called a "fantastic, beyond description hodgepodge" of factors working for
and against them wherever they tried to do their jobs, with regulations per-

mitting women to cover war even while many military officials, editors, and others strictly forbade their presence.[9]

Public and private documents written by editors, reporters, and military officials also illustrate the precariousness of women's role as war correspondents, as well as the (perhaps perceived) precariousness of gender roles and relationships between the sexes throughout World War II. Military regulations, as well as public and private accounts of war correspondents, revealed at least two categories of war correspondents by the end of World War II: the war correspondent, who wrote primarily for and about men, and the *woman* war correspondent, who wrote primarily for and about women. Some writings reveal an acceptance among men of the press and the military for the exceptional women whose war reporting rivaled war reporting by their male colleagues. Others reveal an acceptance only for women who covered news for and about women, while still others reveal an opposition to women reporting on war in any capacity. Among women who worked as war correspondents, their interpretations and expectations for the role also varied— with some women wanting only to report alongside male reporters on hard news topics of war while resenting female reporters who were content to report on "woman's angle" topics of war—and vice versa.

This book has shown that American women have consistently made a place for themselves as war correspondents, but whether they worked beside men or among women, they remained outsiders, in one sense or another, through the end of World War II. Their acceptance by the military, their coworkers, and their audiences depended upon this outsider status—either standing apart from other women, as exceptions, or standing apart from other war correspondents, as women. It has also shown the roles the press and the military held in constructing the "woman war correspondent" as an outsider, or alien, among the public, the press, and the military. No matter how many women worked as war correspondents, writing about battles they witnessed firsthand or military strategy they gleaned from official interviews, members of the press and public were ready to label them "women war correspondents" and laud them for their novelty, their status as exceptions, often with no consideration of their work. The military first denied or ignored the presence of women among war correspondents. Official attempts to make a place for "women war correspondents," situating them outside the inner circle of war, ultimately helped more women find their way to the front.[10]

This book has outlined the early history of American women who worked as war correspondents, while demonstrating the ways in which the press and the military both promoted and prevented their access to war. As the first historical analysis considering the concepts of "woman war correspondent" and "war correspondent" as they were constructed by the press, the military, and women themselves, its value lies both in the answers it provides and the questions it presents. Previous works about women war correspondents have offered rich narratives about the experiences of individual women, while weaving a tale of heroic women challenging an army of chauvinistic editors and commanders. This book has drawn from a variety of sources, considering the roles and influences, positive and negative, not only of the women who worked as war correspondents but of the individuals and institutions surrounding them. The result is a more nuanced picture that reflects the reality many women faced as Americans balanced the need for women to work with the greater need for stability and social acceptance. The press' and the military's attempts during World War II to segregate war correspondents, by sex, are consistent with the wartime segregation in many occupations and industries, and with the ongoing segregation between the roles of newspapermen and "sob sisters" or "society girls" in journalism.[11] When the military invited women to work as war correspondents who would cover the woman's angle, the military created a new set of rules for all women, thus creating barriers that might otherwise be viewed as entry points.

Despite the concept of the "first and only" woman war correspondent, which continually resurfaced in newspaper articles throughout the nineteenth and early twentieth centuries, American women wrote about war whenever Americans participated in war. Just as the military and the press were navigating the goals and limitations of their early relationship with one another, the military and the press changed their definitions and expectations for war correspondents with each war. Whereas the term "war correspondent" had been loosely defined—used whenever and however it suited writers and editors to do so—the field regulations of 1914 offered an official definition for war correspondents, and official guidance for military officials who sought to regulate them. Despite the warnings of some military officials who called for regulations that would exclude women from working as war correspondents, the regulations instead stipulated criteria that were rigid enough to exclude most men and women, yet did not specify sex as a category or even a factor for consideration.

By the time the United States entered World War II in 1941, several women had already established themselves as exceptional reporters, whose coverage of war and foreign relations had helped them secure enough readers and professional connections to prove their worth to their employers. Likewise, military officials recognized the influence of exceptional reporters, whether they were male or female. The women who worked as foreign correspondents, covering war news from Europe and the Pacific, in the years before World War II, had developed a competing storyline to the sob-sister and society-girl categories. Most readers, editors, and military officials took seriously the writings by foreign correspondents, such as Sigrid Schultz and Anne O'Hare McCormick, whose expertise in their subject matter was exceptional among all reporters, male and female. At the start of World War II, these exceptional journalists had reason to believe the War Department's official communications, and Eisenhower's assurances, that all war correspondents would be treated equally. Most of them had already proven that rules for other women did not apply to them—by proving themselves the best man for the job.

In 1942 and 1943, however, the military began considering the best women for the job. In its commitment to total war, the War Department began a public relations campaign to encourage women's participation. Just as the new women's interest section worked with woman's angle reporters to promote the war effort domestically, it soon made sense to send women reporters, as accredited war correspondents, to cover the first WAACs stationed in North Africa. Yet their presence was an unwelcome surprise to the veteran war correspondents who had been reporting on Operation Torch since November 1942, as well as to many military officials who knew how to work with war correspondents but were unprepared for two "women war correspondents," who were similarly unprepared for the front and whose very presence was permitted because of their difference—the novelty and unique perspective offered by a female at the front. As the value of a woman's angle of war took hold, the military sought to accredit more women and editors sought to send more women. Many of these women had never traveled abroad, had never reported on politics or military strategy or anything close to war. Articles about them ran nearly as often as articles by them—stories that exaggerated their femininity against masculine surroundings.

The short-term effect of the presence of so many "women war correspondents" was to make life more difficult for women who had long worked as "war correspondents." While it might only have been a few, if any, female war correspondents whose presence was truly disruptive, news articles held up women war correspondents as "epitomes of all the rest." Those who saw themselves as war correspondents, whether they were men or women, often resented "women war correspondents" not only because these women competed for facilities, stories, and access, but because the attention they drew was capable of influencing the public's perception of "war correspondent"—as not necessarily a man's job—as well as the public's perception of a "woman war correspondent"—as not necessarily a war correspondent. Some of this resentment was likely territorial. Skilled war correspondents who knew their way around war and the military, and who had worked hard to secure their status and privilege, resented these newcomers. Yet it was also likely a reaction to the frivolous tone common to many woman's angle articles, and even more common in the headlines that editors plastered above these stories.

This tension is well illustrated in personal correspondence, if not in official documents or news stories. It is likely these conflicts are what led the War Department, in 1944, to officially recognize a new category for women war correspondents within its accreditation procedures, along with a separate set of directives to assist military officials in handling them. The War Department did not document the rationale behind the new policies, yet it is clear that many military officials would have welcomed the directive as a means of handling the many women who sought more serious assignments and greater access to the front, without losing sight of the military's goal to promote the war effort among all of its citizens. This strategy also stood to benefit the military as an indirect form of information control, if not propaganda. Accrediting more women as war correspondents, and limiting them to assignments related to women's activities, offered the military a way to increase news coverage while assuring a steady stream of stories that were least likely to assist the enemy and most likely to promote the military and boost morale.

The War Department also likely saw the directives as a means of reducing conflict: among war correspondents who were grappling for the limited accommodations at the front; among commanders who did not believe women belonged at the front; and among women who continually questioned why military officials were excluding them when regulations provided them the same rights as men. The military needed a way to justify its treatment of women, within a military culture that was traditionally masculine but comprised individuals from varying backgrounds, education levels, and beliefs, who had similarly varied opinions on women's rights. The military's reasons aside, its attempt to officially segregate the work of war correspondents by sex was consistent with workplace strategies in industries nationwide, throughout the war, to balance the need for more women workers with a greater societal need to ensure that women could step outside their roles without challenging society's accepted roles for men and women.

The folly of these partial directives became obvious immediately. The military had attempted to fit a diverse group of individuals—with varying backgrounds, ages, skills, and goals, among other differences—into the category of "woman war correspondent," revoking many of their privileges in the process. The directives not only discounted the differences among the women whom they described, they also failed to take into account the differences in the mind-sets of the military officials who would be charged with interpreting them. Clearly, the Public Relations Division would not have seen itself as the place, or the war as the time, to fight the equal rights battles society as a whole hadn't resolved. In that sense, allowing individual commanders to limit the work of female war correspondents might have seemed necessary. Not only did these commanders themselves represent a diverse group of Americans, with a range of backgrounds and levels of education, but the commands to which correspondents were assigned represented Allied nations—from Britain's blanket no-women-correspondents policy to France's all-correspondents policy. Instead, the military's attempt to navigate these attitudes, by creating a directive with no consequences but plenty of room for interpretation, just led to further confusion and conflict.

Figure 9.1.   Iris Carpenter, war correspondent for the *Boston Globe*.
Source: Reproduced with permission of Patricia Perry and Brian Scruby.

The directives appeared to have backfired on the military in other ways. The "exceptional" women, who had gained accreditation as war correspondents before losing ground as women war correspondents, began to challenge the military. Instead of working efficiently among men, separate from other women, they began to speak up for their rights, and therefore the rights of other women. They pointed out the overarching field regulations that stipulated equal treatment for all war correspondents, and found new ways to work around the flawed directives. Women who were exceptional reporters were by definition hardworking and resourceful; by 1945, many of them knew their way around a military command better than the public relations officials who sought to control them. Those whose bylines had become household names, who knew more about war, military strategy, and international affairs than most men, had connections to match their reputations. Military officials who had worked with Ann Stringer, Helen Kirkpatrick, Iris Carpenter, Lee Carson, and so many others, understood that it was not in the military's best interest to prevent these women from working as war correspondents. As more women found their way around the directives, and as more military officials relaxed their interpretations of the policies, female war correspondents, as a group, began to redefine the concept of "woman war correspondent." Stories by women who had started reporting as women war correspondents, such as Lee Carson and Iris Carpenter, appeared regularly as front-page news, with "war correspondent" bylines. When the government presented its theater campaign ribbons to war correspondents, in honor of their "outstanding and conspicuous service" in the face of danger, once again the only category the government recognized was "accredited war correspondent."

By the end of the war, many women who had fought to work alongside men as equals had earned that right. They had won a victory, having proven themselves equal to men in reporting abilities and having widened their path to war correspondence.[12] While outside the scope of this book, other works have shown that the ground these women gained as war correspondents soon shifted, just as the short-term gains of women in other professions had done after World War II.[13] Victorious or no, when the war ended, women war correspondents returned to safety—but not necessarily to security. Their personal risk had diminished drastically, but so had their professional potential. As Patricia Bradley noted, "the role of women correspondents in World War II did not clear the way for women in journalism," and these women returned from the war only to encounter the same working conditions they had faced before the war.[14] Women journalists faced the shared plight of all working women after the war: postwar propaganda beseeching women to step aside and return home so men could reclaim their jobs.[15] Most women turned or returned to traditional, full-time roles of marriage and motherhood or found jobs with women's magazines or women's pages at newspapers.[16] Even women whose work had all but guaranteed them lifelong respect and writing assignments faced challenges returning home, as they readjusted to life that was, as Martha Gellhorn described it, "tiresomely superficial" and tried to find work that they felt to be as "necessary" as the work they'd done during the war.[17] Nancy Caldwell Sorel noted that a number of women war correspondents, upon their return home, "joined the great post-war fraternity of the psychically displaced."[18]

The six years from 1939 to 1945 saw more death and destruction worldwide than arguably any other time since the battles and bubonic plague in the fourteenth century.[19] Of more than 70 million people who fought in World War II, about 17 million died, along with at least 20 million civilians.[20] Yet these six years were also a time of enormous growth and opportunity, a time unmatched in terms of the development of technology for communications, industry, transportation, and weaponry. As armies destroyed cities, towns, and villages throughout Europe and Asia, countries worked to mobilize their citizens to produce weapons, vehicles, and other matériel, and to develop ever faster and better ways of doing so. The United States' involvement in all stages of World War II saved Americans from the Depression—just as the Depression steeled Americans and, ultimately, helped save them from defeat in World War II.[21] The abundance of dormant factories and unemployed workers during the Depression, along with a growing acceptance of the need for individual restraint and government intervention, had conditioned and prepared the United States for wartime mobilization.[22] Roosevelt's early realization that winning the war would require a great amount of time, men, and matériel, and the ensuing national campaign, led to the prosperity that lifted the nation out of the Depression—and to the productivity that made room for more men and women to enter or move up in the nation's workforce.[23] But the United States' prosperity came at a great cost. While other countries suffered far greater losses than the United States, nonetheless World War II represented the greatest sacrifice Americans had ever made for a war, with three times as many Americans serving in the military and a death toll nearly four times higher than in World War I.[24] Between 1941 and 1946, the years of its official involvement in World War II, more than 16 million Americans served in the United States military for an average duration of thirty-three months; 300,000 died in battle, and more than 100,000 died from causes related to war.[25]

During World War II, three news agencies, three radio networks, several magazines, and ten daily newspapers in the United States employed international correspondents.[26] Working for these media were an estimated three-hundred international correspondents in the 1930s and more than 2,600 by the end of World War II.[27] The United States War Department accredited more than 1,500 war correspondents during World War II, less than 10 percent of whom were women.[28] The military provided accredited correspondents with facilities and transportation, and assigned them the rank of captain.[29] As uniformed captains, correspondents were thought to have greater leverage and protection if captured by the enemy and would be less likely to be mistaken for spies. The title and uniform particularly helped female correspondents, providing a professional appearance and status that was similar, if not equal, to that of men.[30] World War II was riskier for correspondents than previous wars because military advances, such as submarine and aircraft technologies, increased the threat of sudden attack away from the front.[31] The casualty rate for United States correspondents in Europe during World War II was reported to be 15 to 20 percent between September 1939 and the spring of 1943, dropping to about 5 percent in 1944–1945.[32] Close to fifty United States war correspondents lost their lives in combat during the war, all men.[33] No American women war correspondents died in combat-related incidents, although several were injured or confined to internment camps, and at least two who had worked with their husbands, as a reporting team, were widowed during the war.[34]

In January 1942, a government survey reported that employers expected to hire women to fill just 29 percent of available jobs in defense industries; within six months employers expected to hire women to fill 70 percent of available jobs.[35] Women had many incentives to work during the war, including the availability of better jobs, job training, and record-high wages, a desire for financial independence, and a need, for many of them, to supplement low government allowances from their military husbands.[36] Americans' acceptance of women's employment and women's role in the war effort, as Susan Hartmann has noted, was contingent upon three conditions that preserved the gender status quo: women must only work during the war; women must retain their femininity; and women must retain their primary motivation, caring for home and family.[37] Featured in ads, articles, or broadcast programming, these women displayed the ideals of femininity of their time, with slight frames, styled hair, fair skin, fashionable clothes, and plenty of lipstick. Mass-mediated messages in wartime compared women's work to tasks they had always done—for example, the housewife who can press orange juice has an easy time with a drill press.[38] Jobs open to women were described as requiring womanly abilities, such as an attention to detail, enthusiasm for the mundane or routine, and an ability to work with small parts.[39] For all the jobs and opportunities open to women, none came close to those available to men. While the government and industry actively engaged women's services and opinions, trying to sway them and trying to use them to sway others, women were rarely provided with positions of power.[40] For example, though women's union membership climbed to almost 20 percent, women rarely held supervisory roles within unions or the workforce.[41] The ways in which companies organized and managed their workforce to accommodate women conformed to the conditions that Hartmann noted, as well as the "double-helix effect"—the tendency of gender roles to vary by culture or circumstance while retaining the hierarchy that holds women subordinate to men.[42] Wages increased for all men and women, but for women less than men, and still for blacks less than whites.[43] Ruth Milkman, in her study showing the hierarchy of sex-segregated jobs in the electrical and automotive industries during World War II, observed that the types of jobs designated as men-only or women-only varied widely from one factory to another.[44] Yet managers insisted that such designations were essential and fixed, and companies paid more for the jobs held by men.[45] Milkman concluded that job segregation helped sustain male morale by constructing gendered meanings for jobs and by ensuring that women earned less than men.[46] Companies found it easy to get around government mandates or recommendations to pay women equal wages for equal work by hiring women to do jobs described as "light," and men to do jobs described as "heavy," though jobs considered heavy at one company were as likely to be considered light at another.[47] Despite reporting that they were highly satisfied with female workers overall during the war, companies continued to pay more to hire men for jobs that women could do and, after the war, often refused to hire women at all.[48]

Likewise, while some women reporters continued to work as foreign correspondents after the war, the few remaining posts were generally reserved for men. Women, such as May Craig, who sought access to military transport in 1947, once again faced exclusion from military officials who blamed inadequate facilities.[49] These arguments resurfaced in the Korean and Vietnam wars when the military sought to prevent all women, even veteran correspondents such as Marguerite Higgins and Dickey Chapelle, from gaining accreditation and access to war.[50] Writing in 1955, Higgins considered her work as a war correspondent in World War II and the Korean War, and her experience as a woman.

> And do I still think women correspondents should be allowed at the war fronts? Of course, if they are there to do a bona fide reporting job and if they have the common sense not to make nuisances or fools out of themselves. I have some pet dislikes in journalistic styles and high on the list is the story we used to call the "lookee here, I'm only a girl but look where I am."[51]

LIMITATIONS AND FUTURE STUDIES

As a starting point for this book, and not the focus, I explored the early conceptualization in the press, the public, and the military of the woman war correspondent and the woman's angle of war. In the years before World War I, the military did little to regulate war correspondents and lacked an official policy or even definition for the term. Within this "free-for-all" period of war correspondence, many women found work reporting on war as "specials," or stringers, and many publications promoted these women as war correspondents. The seventy-three American women (see Appendix 1) I have uncovered whose publications labeled them as war correspondents before 1920 far exceeds the numbers given in any previous work about the history of journalism. Whether historians simply overlooked these women, or whether historians intentionally excluded these women because they were writing woman's angle topics, is unclear. Electronic databases certainly make it easier to uncover the names and works of these women, which could account for some of the discrepancy, and yet the lists of names and the copies of censored articles have existed all along in military documents from World War I in the National Archives. I hope I have helped to correct the record and to bring historians' attention to many women whose war reporting has been hidden away for too long. This work, of mining the names and histories of early women war correspondents, has been rewarding but has also called for much self-restraint. I have been tempted to follow each woman's story from birth to death, to read every word each woman wrote about war and every other topic. Uncovering so much material and so many individuals is as exciting as it is daunting. I can only imagine how many more women's stories are buried in archives or newspaper morgues, or how many stories remain to be told about the ones I have already uncovered.

Similarly, the 181 women (see Appendix 2) whom the government recognized or accredited as war correspondents during World War II include many whose names do not appear in historical works about journalists or women of their time. Each one has a story worth telling, and many of these women's stories have not been told, such as Elizabeth Murphy Phillips, who appears to have been the only African-American woman to be accredited as a war correspondent before 1945. Black press newspapers nationwide ran standalone photographs and articles announcing Phillips' accreditation and her travels to England as the first and only black woman to be accredited as a war correspondent during World War II.[52] Phillips was a longtime reporter for the *Baltimore Afro-American* when she gained SHAEF accreditation, but she was hospitalized shortly after her arrival in London with a severe illness that left her partially paralyzed and forced her to return home.[53] She was one of just thirty African-American war correspondents who were accredited during World War II.[54]

As I researched each woman who was accredited as a war correspondent in World War II, I continued to identify errors in accounts of war correspondents that are cited repeatedly in other works. The list of 116 women who worked as war correspondents, published on the Library of Congress website within its "Women Come to the Front" exhibit, was drawn from the names of war correspondents Colonel Barney Oldfield listed as an appendix in his book, *Never a Shot in Anger*.[55] Each mention I have found about women war correspondents cites one of these two sources, or presents the same informa-

Figure 9.2.   Elizabeth Murphy Phillips, war correspondent for the *Baltimore Afro-American*.
     Source: Reproduced with permission of the Phillips Family Archives.

tion without any citation. Yet this list is missing the names of at least sixty-five women whom the United States accredited as war correspondents during World War II, including many whose work was well known and well respected by readers of their time, such as Iris Carpenter, Lee Carson, Lyn Crost, Dudley Ann Harmon, Inez Robb, and Dixie Tighe. At the same time, these lists recognize the names of several women who were not granted military accreditation. They also include several misspelled names, and one woman is listed twice: war correspondent Irina Skariatina is listed with her full maiden name in one place, but elsewhere the list includes her married name, Mrs. Blakeslee, as though the names represent two different women. It is easy to see how such errors were introduced; official listings of accredited correspondents contained such errors as well, and though the military began distributing lists on a near-monthly basis in 1944 and 1945, no list was comprehensive or entirely accurate. Individual military units, especially those outside the European Theater of Operations, often handled accreditation and regulation of war correspondents themselves and did not always report the names of these individuals to the War Department's or Navy Department's public relations divisions. Researching these lists, some seventy years later, requires a working knowledge of the many individual journalists, their spouses, and the organizations that hired them. For example, the lists most often listed just a last name and publication, and war correspondents often shared the same last name—sometimes because they were married to each other (couples such as the Stringers, Mydanses, Vandiverts, Jacobys, Packards, Brownes, Franks, Daniells, and Wertenbakers), and other times by coincidence, such as Hal Cowan and Ruth Cowan or even the Bill Stringer who died in action, whose widow, Ann Stringer, was a war correspondent, as was another, unrelated Bill Stringer who wrote for the *Christian Science Monitor*. While Lee Miller was the name of a man who wrote for International News Service, it also was the name of a woman who worked as a writer and photographer for Condé Nast publications. Thus, even as I conclude this study, I have introduced the possibilities for so many future inquiries, ranging in significance and scope: considerations of war correspondent couples, of bylined versus non-bylined articles, of the human-interest angle versus the woman's angle, as well as a more thorough consideration of correspondence between editors and the women they assigned as war correspondents. Future research could consider these concepts more broadly, situating them in the context of women's history, military history, or journalism history, and more deeply, considering, for instance, the concept of "woman war correspondent," within the concepts of stunt journalism, yellow journalism, or sob sisters.

As I researched the military's rationale for restricting women's access to war correspondence, I began to see that the military itself had not answered the question during World War II, and in fact had all but avoided the question in previous decades. I had hoped to find clear documentation illustrating the military's arguments for and against women as war correspondents, and the process by which regulations evolved for women war correspondents. I discovered that the volume of documents created by the Allied nations during World War II is nearly unmatched—except possibly by the number of documents that are missing or otherwise unavailable.[56] And yet I soon learned that the vast amount of documents belies a simple truth: clear and complete documentation by a multifaceted military during wartime is not a logical expectation. While at first I assumed that the challenge of locating documents was preventing me from answering my original question, as to how and why the military accepted and restricted women as war correspondents, I soon discovered the real challenge: throughout the war, the military had avoided this question as best it could. This finding ultimately helped strengthen my study by forcing me to find answers elsewhere, piecing together evidence from correspondence and memoranda—considering as significant what the military did not say, what was not in the documents, often as more significant than what was there. Here, too, I found challenges that became opportunities. Most of these challenges were typical of any historical study that relies upon primary documents. Letter fragments, government memoranda, and cabled messages can easily obscure or omit significant details. As I became more familiar with the names of the various public relations officials, who changed jobs throughout the war, as well as the various military units, battles, locations, editors, and war correspondents, and as I began to consider letters, diary entries, and government documents chronologically, suddenly a cable that read "I was misinformed, sorry," gained significance and meaning. It is both frustrating and exciting to think that if these documents, articles, and letters took on greater meaning each time I read them, the opportunity remains for the discovery of more evidence, significance, and meaning with future readings.

NOTES

1. R., "A Rebuttal from 'R,'" What People Talk About, *Daily Boston Globe*, April 3, 1945, 8. This rebuttal followed a series of letters to the editor in March 1945 that defended Iris Carpenter after "R.," an anonymous letter writer, wrote to complain about having to read war news written by a woman. See R., "Woman Has No Business Reporting War, He Says," What People Talk About, *Daily Boston Globe*, March 16, 1945.

2. Iris Carpenter, *No Woman's World* (Boston: Houghton Mifflin Company, 1946), 291–92.

3. Ibid., 291.

4. Ibid.

5. Jean Bethke Elshtain, *Women and War* (New York: Basic Books, 1987).

6. D'Ann Campbell, *Women at War with America: Private Lives in a Patriotic Era* (Cambridge: Harvard University Press, 1984), 223; and Susan M. Hartmann, *The Home Front and Beyond* (Boston: Twayne Publishers, 1982), 20–27.

7. "The Rhine Maidens," March 14, 1945, *Newsweek*. This article, about war correspondents Iris Carpenter, Ann Stringer, and Lee Carson, reported that in the Army's "Chesterfieldian view," women at the front distract soldiers.

8. R., "A Rebuttal from 'R,'" What People Talk About, *Daily Boston Globe*, April 3, 1945.

9. Carpenter, *No Woman's World*, 35.

10. See Elshtain, *Women and War*, 183, for a discussion of women and their presence in what Elshtain describes as a series of ever-widening circles surrounding an inner circle of war.

11. See, c.f., Karen Anderson, *Wartime Women: Sex Roles, Family Relations, and the Status of Women during World War II* (Westport, CT: Greenwood Press, 1981), 173; Campbell, *Women at War with America*, 223; Hartmann, *The Home Front and Beyond*, 20–27; Marion Marzolf, *Up from the Footnote: A History of Women Journalists* (New York: Hastings House, 1977); Margaret Randolph Higonnet, Jane Jenson, Sonya Michel, and Margaret Collins Weitz, eds., *Behind the Lines: Gender and the Two World Wars* (New Haven: Yale University Press, 1987).

12. Nancy Caldwell Sorel, *The Women Who Wrote the War* (New York: HarperCollins, 1999), 388–89.

13. Campbell, *Women at War with America*, 223; Hartmann, *The Home Front and Beyond*, 20–27; Marzolf, *Up from the Footnote*, 72; Joan W. Scott, "Re-Writing History," in eds. Higonnet, Jenson, Michel, and Weitz, *Behind the Lines*, 23–25; and Lilya Wagner, *Women War Correspondents of World War II* (New York: Greenwood Press, 1989), 5.

14. Patricia Bradley, *Women and the Press: The Struggle for Equality* (Evanston: Northwestern University Press, 2005), 221.

15. Anderson, *Wartime Women*, 161; Campbell, *Women at War with America*, 223; and Hartmann, *The Home Front and Beyond*, 20–27.

16. Marzolf, *Up from the Footnote*, 72; and Wagner, *Women War Correspondents of World War II*, 5. This renewed focus, postwar, on traditional roles and values was true for women in other professions as well; c.f., Campbell, *Women at War with America*, 223; and Hartmann, *The Home Front and Beyond*, 20–27.

17. Sorel, *The Women Who Wrote the War*, 38, 389.

18. Ibid.

19. James Stokesbury, *A Short History of World War II* (New York: Morrow, 1980), 377.

20. Ibid., 378.

21. David M. Kennedy, *Freedom from Fear* (New York: Oxford University Press, 1999), 191–92; Hartmann, *The Home Front and Beyond*, 1–27; and Gerhard Weinberg, *A World at Arms: A Global History of World War II* (Cambridge: Cambridge University Press, 1995), 914.

22. Kennedy, *Freedom from Fear*, 191–92.

23. Ibid.

24. Robert Goralski, *World War II Almanac 1931–1945* (New York: Bonanza Books, 1981); and "Table No. 523. Armed Forces Personnel—Summary of Major Conflicts," *United States Census Bureau, Statistical Abstract of the United States: 2003* (National Defense and Veterans Affairs), 348.

25. "Table No. 523. Armed Forces Personnel," 348.

26. Robert William Desmond, *Tides of War: World News Reporting, 1931–1945* (Iowa City: University of Iowa Press, 1984), 449.

27. Ibid. This number also includes reporters who were not accredited or stationed in war zones, as well as those who wrote for foreign newspapers, who may have written infrequently, and who may not have sought access to the military.

28. Wagner, *Women War Correspondents of World War II*, 159–62.

29. Ibid.

30. Sorel, *The Women Who Wrote the War*, 171–72.

31. Desmond, *Tides of War*, 451.

32. Ibid., 452–53.

33. Desmond, *Tides of War*, 451; and Sorel, *The Women Who Wrote the War*, 171–72.

34. Desmond, *Tides of War*, 451; and Sorel, *The Women Who Wrote the War*, 171–72.

35. William H. Chafe, *The Paradox of Change* (New York: Oxford University Press, 1991), 122–23; and Hartmann, *The Home Front and Beyond*, 54–55.

36. Anderson, *Wartime Women*; Campbell, *Women at War with America*, 191; and Chafe, *The Paradox of Change*, 128.

37. Hartmann, *The Home Front and Beyond*, 23.

38. Chafe, *The Paradox of Change*, 124; and Milkman, *Gender at Work*, 5.

39. Chafe, *The Paradox of Change*, 124; and Milkman, *Gender at Work*, 5.

40. Chafe, *The Paradox of Change*, 129, 135—36.

41. Chafe, *The Paradox of Change*, 129; and Milkman, *Gender at Work*, 85, 92, 97–98.

42. Hartmann, *The Home Front and Beyond*; and Higonnet et al., *Behind the Lines*.

43. Chafe, *The Paradox of Change*, 127–28; and Hartmann, *The Home Front and Beyond*, 94, 124–25.

44. Milkman, *Gender at Work*, 19.

45. Ibid., 19–26.

46. Ibid., 19–26.

47. Ibid., 71, 75.

48. Ibid., 118–23.

49. Doris Fleeson, "Who Banned Maine Woman Correspondent from Return from Rio on Missouri?" *Daily Boston Globe*, August 29, 1947.

50. Joyce Hoffmann, *On Their Own: Women Journalists and the American Experience in Vietnam* (New York: Da Capo Press, 2008).

51. Marguerite Higgins, *News Is a Singular Thing* (New York: Doubleday, 1955), 212.

52. See, for example, "Covers War," *Pittsburgh Courier,* October 28, 1944; *New Journal and Guide*, "And Now a Woman War Correspondent," November 4, 1944; *New York Amsterdam News*, "New War Correspondent," October 28, 1944; and *Philadelphia Tribune*, "War Correspondent," October 28, 1944; "War Correspondent," *Plaindealer* (Kansas City, KS), October 27, 1944.

53. Bettye Phillips, "Phillips' Hospital Room Is Meeting Place for Yanks," *(Baltimore) Afro-American*, January 13, 1945; Bettye Phillips, "Regains Use of Arm, Leg, but Doctors Still Check," *(Baltimore) Afro-American*, December 2, 1944; and *(Baltimore) Afro-American*, "Phillips Due Home Soon, Says Stewart," January 27, 1945.

54. Jinx Broussard, *African American Foreign Correspondents* (Baton Rouge: Louisiana State University Press), 107–9.

55. Barney Oldfield, *Never a Shot in Anger* (New York: Duell, Sloan and Pearce, 1956); "Women Come to the Front: Journalists, Photographers, and Broadcasters of World War II," Library of Congress. http://www.loc.gov/exhibits/wcf/wcf0005.html.

56. James E. O'Neill and Robert W. Krauskopf, eds., *World War II: An Account of Its Documents* (Washington, D.C.: Howard University Press, 1976), 72–83; and Timothy Mulligan, *World War II Guide to Records Relating to United States Military Participation,* Rebecca L. Collier, Judith Koucky, and Patrick R. Osborn, eds. (Washington, D.C.: National Archives and Records Administration, 2008).

Appendix 1

American Women War Correspondents
through World War I

American women war correspondents through World War I, by the earliest war in which American newspapers, magazines, or military described them as war correspondents.*

	Names (and pseudonyms)	Sponsoring Publications	Wars Reported	Home State	Lifetime	Spouse	Other Jobs
1	Jane Maria Eliza McManus **Cazneau** (Cora or Corrine Montgomery; Storms)	*New York Times, New York Sun, New-York Tribune*	Mexican War	NY	1807–1878	Allen Storm, William Cazneau	Author, diplomat
2	Margaret **Fuller** Ossoli	*New-York Tribune*	Roman Revolution	NY	1810–1850	Angelo Ossoli	Author
3	Lillie **Devereaux** Blake (Aesop, Essex)	*New York Evening Post*	Civil War	CT, DC, NJ	1833–1913	Frank Umstead, Grinfille Blake	Lecturer, novelist
4	Emily Pomona Edson **Briggs** (Olivia)	*Philadelphia Press, Washington Chronicle*	Civil War	DC	1830–1910	John Briggs	Teacher
5	Susan Elizabeth **Dickinson**	*New-York Tribune*	Civil War	PA	~1833–1915		Editor
6	Lottie **Bengough** McCaffrey		Civil War	PA		John Bengough,† Richard McCaffrey	Printer
7	Laura Catherine **Redden** Searing (Howard Glyndon)	*New York Times, New-York Tribune, New York Mail, Missouri Republican*	Civil War; Franco-Prussian War	MO	1839–1923	Edward Searing	Poet, novelist
8	Teresa Patten Howard **Dean**†† (Theo, The Widow)	*Chicago Tribune, Chicago Inter-Ocean*	Sioux Indian War, Spanish-American War, Boxer Rebellion, Philippine-American War, Mexican War	WI	~1859–1935	James Howard,† Albert Dean, Lewis Tallman	Novelist

#	Names (and pseudonyms)	Sponsoring Publications	Wars Reported	Home State	Lifetime	Spouse	Other Jobs
9	Bright Eyes, Susette **LaFlesche** Tibbles	Omaha World-Herald, Chicago Express	Sioux Indian War	NE	1854–1903	Thomas Tibbles[†]	Lecturer, author
10	Clara Dorothy Bewick **Colby**[††]	Woman's Tribune	Sioux- Indian War, Spanish-American War	NE	1846–1916	General Colby[†]	Editor, Latin and history professor
11	Mary Hannah **Krout**	Chicago Inter-Ocean, Chicago Tribune	Hawaiian Revolution	IL	1851–1927		Author, poet, teacher
12	Margherita Arlina **Hamm**	Boston Herald	Sino-Japanese War, Spanish-American War	ME	1867–1909	William Fales,[†] John McMahon[†]	Author
13	Cora Howorth Taylor **Crane** (Imogene Carter)	Chicago Tribune	Greco-Turkish War	NY	1865–1910	Stephen Crane,[†] Hammond, McNeil, others	Owned brothel
14	Emma Paddock **Telford**	New York Times, New-York Tribune	Greco-Turkish War	NY	1851–1920	William H. Telford	Teacher
15	Muriel Hannah **Bailey**	San Francisco Call	Philippine-American War	CA	1873–	Isaac Hull	
16	Anna Northend **Benjamin**[††]	Leslie's, New-York Tribune	Spanish-American War, Philippine-American War, Boxer Rebellion	MA	1874–1902		
17	Lily **Curry** Tyner (Miss Paul Rochester, Cecil Charles)	Hearst	Spanish-American War	NY	1867–	Paul Tyner	Translator
18	Mary C. **Francis**	New York Herald, Harper's Bazaar, Cincinnati	Spanish-American War	OH	~1860–		

#	Names (and pseudonyms)	Sponsoring Publications	Wars Reported	Home State	Lifetime	Spouse	Other Jobs
		Commercial Gazette					
19	Annabel **Lee**	*Outlook, Los Angeles Times*	Spanish-American War				
20	Catherine "Kate" Kelly **Masterson**	*New York American, New York Herald*	Spanish-American War	NY	~1864–1927	Masterson	Novelist
21	Sadie Kneller **Miller**	*Leslie's*	Spanish-American War, Balkan Wars, Rif War	MD	~1867–1920	Charles Robert Miller	Photographer
22	Nora **O'Malley**	*Indiana Woman*	Spanish-American War	IN	~1878–1971	Edmund Bingham	
23	Elsie **Reasoner** Ralph	*Chicago Tribune, McClure's, AP*	Spanish-American War	KS	1878–1913	Lester Ralph	Sculptor
24	Fannie Brigham **Ward**	*New Orleans Picayune, Phil. Record*	Spanish-American War	MI, OH	1843–1913	William Ward	U.S. Treasury
25	Katherine Short **White**	*Chicago Record*	Spanish-American War	KS	1869–	Trumball White†	
26	Josephine Miles **Woodward**††	*Cincinnati Commercial Gazette*	Spanish-American War	OH	1862–1932	Orlando J. Woodard	Society editor
27	Eliza Archard **Conner** (Zig)	*Cincinnati Commercial Gazette, Saturday Evening Post*	Philippine-American War	OH	~1850–1912	Conner	German/Latin teacher, novelist
28	Eugenie Magnus **Ingleton** (Midge)	Transvaal newspapers	South-African War	CA	~1886–1936	George Ingleton, Fred Hogue	Playwright, actress
29	Eleanor Franklin	*Atlanta*	Russo-Japanese	IN	-1925	Martin Egan	

	Names (and pseudonyms)	Sponsoring Publications	Wars Reported	Home State	Lifetime	Spouse	Other Jobs
30	Eleanor Henrietta "Peggy" **Hull** Goodnough Deuell[tt]	Cleveland Plain Dealer, El Paso Herald	Mexican War, WWI	KS	1890–1967	George Hull, John Kinley, Harvey Deuell	Author, radio host
31	Jean Cabell **O'Neill**	Brooklyn Eagle	Mexican War, WWI	NY, DC	~1873	Francis O'Neill, Joseph Herbert	
32	Alice Muriel Livingston **Williamson** (Alice Stuyvesant)	McClure's	Mexican War, WWI	NY	1869–1933	Charles Norris Wiliamson	Novelist, screenwriter
33	Harriet Chalmers **Adams**	Harper's, National Geographic	WWI	CA	1875–1937	Franklin Pierce Adams	Explorer, photographer
34	Esther **Andrews**[tt]	Adams Newspaper Service	WWI	IA	1880–1962	Canby Chambers	Seamstress
35	Gladys Weil **Axman**[tt]	Philadelphia Press	WWI	MA	1888–1968	Clarence Axman,[t] William Taylor	Opera singer
36	Bessie **Beatty**	San Francisco Chronicle	WWI	CA	1886–1947	William Sauter	Author, industrialist
37	May R. **Birkhead**[tt]	New York Herald	WWI	MO	1882–1941		Society writer
38	Elizabeth Jane Cochrane Seaman (Nellie **Bly**)	New York Evening Journal	WWI	PA	~1864–1922	Robert Seaman	
39	Mary Isabel **Brush** Williams	Chicago Tribune, New York Times, Saturday Evening Post	WWI	IN	1888–1944	Pierce Williams	
40	Anna Louisa Mohan, Louise **Bryant**[tt]	Philadelphia Public Ledger	WWI	NV	1885–1936	John Reed,[t] others	Author
41	Edith **Callahan**[tt]	Catholic Press	WWI	KY	1896–1983		
42	Harriet Inez Gray **Carberry**[tt]	Boston Post	WWI	MA	1876–1956	Clifton Carberry[t]	

	Names (and pseudonyms)	Sponsoring Publications	Wars Reported	Home State	Lifetime	Spouse	Other Jobs
43	Margaret Wade Campbell **Deland**	Woman's Home Companion	WWI	PA	1857–1945	Lorin Deland	Poet, novelist
44	Faith Hunter **Dodge**[tt]	La Prensa (New York)	WWI	IN	1886–1965		Language Teacher
45	Rheta Louise Childe **Dorr**[tt]	New York Evening Mail	WWI	NE	1866–1948	John Pixley Dorr	Author
46	Cecil Inslee **Dorrian**[tt]	Newark Evening News, New-York Tribune	WWI	NY	1882–1926		Playwright, theater critic
47	Mildred Williams **Farwell**	Chicago Tribune	WWI	DC	1880–1941	Walter Farwell	
48	Marion **Francis**	San Francisco Examiner	WWI	CA	~1887–1973	Fred Thomson, George Hill	Painter, actor, director
49	Elizabeth **Frazier**[tt]	Saturday Evening Post	WWI	CA	1877–1967		Editor
50	Corra May White **Harris**	Saturday Evening Post, Atlanta Constitution	WWI	GA	1869–1935	Lundy Harris	Novelist
51	Marguerite Elton Baker **Harrison**[tt]	Baltimore Sun	WWI	MD	1879–1967	Thomas Harrison	Society editor, filmmaker
52	Inez Haynes **Irwin**	McClure's	WWI	MA	~1873–1970	Rufus Gilmore, William Irwin[†]	Novelist
53	Frances Borgia **Jolliffe**[tt]	San Francisco Bulletin	WWI	CA	1873–1925		
54	Ruth Wright **Kauffman**	Outlook	WWI	NY	1883–1952	Reginald Wright Kauffman[†]	Novelist
55	Helen Johns **Kirtland**[tt]	Leslie's	WWI	NY	1890–1979	Lucien Swift Kirtland[†]	Photographer
56	Mary-Cécile "Marc" **Logé**[tt]	Christian Science Monitor	WWI	London (U.K.)	1887–1949	Henri Jean François Joseph Verne	Translator

#	Names (and pseudonyms)	Sponsoring Publications	Wars Reported	Home State	Lifetime	Spouse	Other Jobs
57	Gertrude **Lynch**††	New York Sun	WWI	CT	1863–1929		
58	Inez **Milholland**	McClure's, Harper's	WWI	NY	~1886–1916	Freda Eugene Boissevain	Lawyer, social reformer
59	Mary Heaton Vorse **O'Brien**††	Public Ledger	WWI	MA	1874–1966	Albert White Vorse; Joe O'Brien	
60	Mary Boyle **O'Reilly**	Newspaper Enterprise Association	WWI	MA	~1873–1939		Settlement house owner
61	Maude **Radford** Warren	Chicago Tribune, New York Times	WWI	IL	~1875–1934	Joseph Warren	Author, professor
62	Leonora Sheehan **Raines**††	New York Sun	WWI	GA	1871–1952	Robert Raines	Musician
63	Mary Roberts **Rinehart**††	Saturday Evening Post	WWI	PA	1876	Stanley Rinehart	Novelist, playwright
64	Alice **Rohe**	New York World, Denver Times, United Press	WWI	KS	1876–1957		Photographer
65	Esther Sayles **Root** Adams††	Independent	WWI	NY	1894–1981	Franklin P. Adams	
66	Clara **Savage** Littledale††	Good Housekeeping	WWI	MA	1891–1956		Editor, author
67	Elizabeth Shepley **Sergeant**††	New Republic	WWI	MA	1881–1965		Novelist
68	Grace Ellery Channing **Stetson**	Harper's, Saturday Evening Post	WWI	RI	1862–1937	Charles Walter Stetson	Playwright, author
69	Ida Minerva **Tarbell**††	Red Cross Magazine	WWI	PA	1857–1944		Teacher, editor, author
70	Eunice **Tietjens**††	Chicago Daily News	WWI	IL	1884–1944	Paul Tietjens, Cloyd Head	Poet, editor

	Names (and pseudonyms)	Sponsoring Publications	Wars Reported	Home State	Lifetime	Spouse	Other Jobs
71	Sophie **Treadwell**	*San Francisco Bulletin*	WWI	CA	1885–1970	William McGeehan	Playwright
72	Carolyn **Wilson**	*Chicago Daily Tribune*	WWI	MA	~1886–1960		
73	Evelina Orrick Bandel **Wilson**††	*Baltimore Evening News*	WWI	MD	1878–1967	John Glover Wilson	

*This table is not exhaustive, in terms of individuals, names, publications, battles, or other details. Where a cell is blank, the information was unconfirmed or unavailable. Where "~" appears, the date is unconfirmed and may be off by one year. Information for this table was drawn from Census documents, vital records, military records, biographies, and contemporaneous news and magazine articles, as well as biographical entries from contemporaneous works, such as social registries, town histories, and alumni publications.
†Spouse was a war correspondent or military official *during the time* his wife was described as a war correspondent.
††Records indicate the individual served as a war correspondent with official government permission or accreditation.

Appendix 2

Women War Correspondents during World War II

Women whom the U.S. military recognized or accredited as war correspondents during World War II.*

	All Names	*Accrediting Publications*
1	Gladys **Arnold**	Canadian Press
2	Oriana MacIlveen Torrey **Atkinson**	*New York Times*
3	Marjorie "Dot" **Avery** Bernhard	*Detroit Free-Press*
4	Honor Catherine Mary **Balfour**	Time-Life
5	Judy **Barden**	North American News Alliance, *New York Sun*
6	Nellie B. **Beeby**	*American Journal of Nursing*
7	Dorothy **Benyas**	*Honolulu Advertiser*
8	Dorothy **Bess**	*Saturday Evening Post*
9	Rena **Billingham**	Reuters
10	Therese **Bonney**	Duell, Sloan, Pearce
11	Edna Lee **Booker**	International News Service
12	Margaret **Bourke-White**	Time-Life, *Tomorrow*
13	Kay **Boyle** von Frankenstein	*New Yorker*
14	Virginia Lee Warren **Bracker**	*New York Times*
15	Mary H. **Bradley**	*Collier's*
16	Mary Marvin **Breckinridge** Patterson	NBC Radio
17	Anita **Brenner** Glusker	North American News Alliance
18	Julie **Bridgman**	*Liberty*

	All Names	**Accrediting Publications**
19	Olive **Brooks**	International News Service
20	Zenith Jones **Brown** (Leslie Ford)	*Saturday Evening Post*
21	Barbara P. Ellis **Browne**	*Christian Science Monitor*
22	Katharine Ingham **Brush** Winans	(Novelist)
23	Helen **Camp**	Associated Press
24	Iris **Carpenter** Akers	*Boston Globe*
25	Gladys Lee **Carson** Putnam Boudreau Reeves	International News Service
26	Georgette "Dickey" Meyer **Chapelle**	*Look*
27	Mina Fox **Chappelle** Klein	*American Home*
28	Katherine L. **Clark**	WCAU radio
29	Jacqueline **Cochran** (Bessie Lee Pittman)	*Liberty*
30	Mary Carter Carson **Cookman** Bass Gibson Newlin	*Ladies' Home Journal*
31	Anice Page **Cooper**	Whittlesey House
32	Ruth Baldwin **Cowan** Nash	Associated Press
33	Harriet Virginia Spencer **Cowles** Crawley	North American News Alliance
34	Catherine **Coyne**	*Boston Herald*
35	Elisabeth May **Craig**	Gannett Publishing
36	Kathryn **Cravens**	Mutual Broadcasting
37	Lyn **Crost**	*Honolulu Star Bulletin*
38	Annabel Lee **Damon**	*Honolulu Advertiser*
39	Elsie Florence Nicholas **Danenberg**	North American News Alliance
40	Tatiana "Tania" Long **Daniell**	*New York Times*
41	Gladys **Davis**	*Life*
42	Maxine **Davis**	Macmillan
43	Sylvia **de Bettencourt**	*Correio de Manha*
44	Anna **DeCormis** Mackenzie	*Fortune*
45	Gwen **Dew**	*Detroit News, Newsweek*
46	Margaret Mary "Peggy" **Diggins**	International News Service
47	Dorothy Cameron **Disney** MacKaye	*Saturday Evening Post, Ladies' Home Journal*
48	Katharine Zimmerman **Drake**	*Reader's Digest*
49	Eleanor **Draper**	Agence France-Presse
50	Margaret Peggy L. **Durdin**	*Time*

	All Names	Accrediting Publications
51	Charlotte **Ebener**	International News Service
52	Drucilla **Evans**	*New York Post*
53	Edna **Ferber**	North American News Alliance
54	Elizabeth "Betty" Sturges Field **Finan** LoSavio Allen	*Harper's Bazaar*
55	Barbara Miller **Finch**	Reuters
56	Janet **Flanner**	*New Yorker*
57	Doris **Fleeson**	*Woman's Home Companion*
58	Helen **Foster** Snow (Nym Wales)	(Novelist)
59	June Mickel **Frank**	*This Month*, Overseas News Agency
60	Pauline **Frederick**	Western Newspaper Union
61	Beatrice Oppenheim **Freeman**	*Magazine Digest, New York Herald Tribune*
62	Antoinette " Toni" **Frissell** Bacon	*Vogue, Harper's*
63	Betty Milton **Gaskill** Shinn	*Liberty*
64	Martha **Gellhorn**	*Collier's*
65	Helen **Gingrich**	Esquire-Coronet
66	Beatrice Blackmar **Gould**	*Ladies' Home Journal*
67	Janet **Green**	Trans-Radio Press
68	Alice Rogers **Hager**	*Skyways Magazine*
69	Edith Iglauer **Hamburger** Daly	*Cleveland Press*
70	Harriet C. **Hardesty**	United Press
71	Rosette **Hargrove**	Newspaper Enterprise Assoc., *New York World Telegram*
72	Dudley Ann **Harmon**	United Press
73	Kathleen **Harriman**	International News Service
74	Hazel **Hartzog**	United Press
75	Helen **Hiett** Waller	NBC Radio
76	Marguerite **Higgins**	*New York Herald Tribune*
77	Carol E. Denny **Hill** Brandt	*Collier's Redbook*
78	Clare **Hollingworth**	*Daily Telegraph*
79	Mary **Hornaday**	*Christian Science Monitor*
80	Rosemary **Howard**	*Newsweek*
81	Henrietta Eleanor "Peggy" Goodnough Kinley **Hull** Deuell	*Cleveland Plain Dealer*
82	Rita **Hume**	International News Service
83	Ann **Hunter** (Joan Rapoport)	WAIT Radio

	All Names	Accrediting Publications
84	Virginia **Irwin**	*St. Louis Post-Dispatch*
85	Caroline **Iverson** Ackerman	*Life*
86	Ann Loyd **Jacobs** Pakradooni	*Young America*
87	Annalee **Jacoby**	*Time*
88	Lucy **Jamieson**	Radio Station KGU
89	Elizabeth "Betty" Beaman **John**	*Cleveland News*
90	Carol L. **Johnson**	Newspaper Enterprise Association
91	Laura Margaret "Laurie" **Johnston**	*Newsweek, Honolulu Advertiser*
92	Leota **Kelly**	American Red Cross
93	Mary Jane **Kempner**	*Vogue*
94	Sally **Kirkland**	*Vogue*
95	Helen Paull **Kirkpatrick** Milbank	*Chicago Daily News*
96	Agnes Schjoldager **Knickerbocker** Walker	*New York Times*
97	Betty **Knox**	*London Evening News*
98	Irene **Kuhn**	NBC
99	Sara M. **Lamport** Azrael	*New York Post*
100	Ida B. **Landau**	Overseas News Agency
101	Elise **Lavelle**	National Catholic News Service
102	Martha Jansen-**Lecoutre**	*Tri-Color*
103	Flora **Lewis**	Associated Press
104	Rhona **Lloyd** Churchill	*Philadelphia Evening News*
105	Mary Patricia **Lochridge**	*Women's Home Companion*
106	Cynthia Coleman **Lowry**	Associated Press
107	Lenore Virginia Hippard Sandberg **Lucas**	Overseas News Agency
108	Isabel **MacCormac**	*New York Times*
109	Hedvig Rosa Marianne Thorburn **MacFarlane**	*Goteborgs-Posten*
110	Cathleen Sabine **Mann**, Marchioness of Queensbury	Time-Life
111	Erika **Mann**	*Liberty*
112	Cecilia Jackie Barber **Martin**	*Ladies' Home Journal*
113	Alice **Maslin** Junkin (Nancy Booth Craig)	Blue Network
114	Anne **Matheson**	Australian Consolidated Press
115	Francis **McCall**	NBC

	All Names	Accrediting Publications
116	Elizabeth Anne O'Hare **McCormick**	*New York Times*
117	Mary "Molly" V. P. **McGee**	*Toronto Globe & Mail*
118	Eleanor **McIlhenny**	Pan-American
119	Rose **McKee**	International News Service
120	Kathleen **McLaughlin**	*New York Times*
121	Dorothy **Melendez**	*Star Herald*
122	Jane **Meyer**	*Chicago Herald-American*
123	Elizabeth Lee **Miller**	Condé Nast
124	Lois Mattox Miller **Monahan**	*Reader's Digest*
125	Alice-Leone B. **Moats**	*Collier's*
126	Mary T. **Muller**	*Reader's Digest*
127	Barbara Mifflin Boyd **Murdoch**	*Philadelphia Bulletin*
128	Shelley Smith **Mydans**	*Life*
129	Mary H. **O'Brien**	Fawcett Publications
130	Philippa Gerry Whiting **Offner**	*Life*
131	Eleanor Newell Cryan **Packard**	United Press
132	Gretta Brooker **Palmer** Clark	*Liberty*
133	Mary Babcock **Palmer**	*Newsweek*
134	Margaret "Pegge" **Parker** Lyons Mackiernan Hlavacek	*American Weekly*
135	Alice Kelly **Perkins**	Fairchild
136	Martha Elizabeth "Bettye" Murphy **Phillips** Moss	*Afro-American News*
137	Mary Catherine **Phillips** Polk Hill	*Los Angeles News*
138	Peggy **Poor**	*New York Post*
139	Ruth **Portugal**	*Harper's Bazaar*
140	Virginia **Prewett**	*Chicago Sun*
141	Helena Huntington Smith **Pringle**	*Woman's Home Companion*
142	Eva B. **Putnam**	Trans-Radio Press
143	Eleanor Murray Jones **Ragsdale** Lovitt	Newspaper Enterprise Association
144	Margaret Elizabeth **Reeve**	Time-Life
145	Sarah Jane Sally Fulton **Reston**	*New York Times*
146	Martha Sawyers **Reusswig**	*Collier's*
147	Inez Callaway **Robb**	International News Service
148	Ruth A. **Robertson**	Press Syndicate

All Names	Accrediting Publications
149 Iona **Robinson**	*Saturday Review*
150 Ethel P. **Rocho**	*Collier's*
151 Nancy W. **Ross** Young	(Novelist)
152 Jaqueline **Saix**	Time-Life
153 Sigrid **Schultz**	*Chicago Tribune*
154 Margaret **Scripps**	*Honolulu Star Bulletin*
155 Marjorie **Severyns**	*Time*
156 Irina **Skariatina** Blakeslee	*New York Times*
157 Agnes **Smedley**	*Nation*
158 Beverly **Smith**	*Collier's*
159 Lady Margaret **Stewart**	Truth Newspapers
160 Hermione Monica **Stirling**	*Atlantic Monthly*
161 Elizabeth Ann **Stringer**	United Press
162 Elaine Fogg **Stroup**	*Honolulu Advertiser*
163 Lorraine **Stumm**	*London Daily Mirror*
164 Pauline Whittington **Tait**	*Chicago Sun*
165 Mary Molly Cogswell Van Rensselaer **Thayer**	International News Service
166 Dorothy **Thompson** Kopf	Bell Syndicate
167 Dixie **Tighe**	*New York Post*
168 Sonia **Tomara**	*New York Herald Tribune*
169 Kathleen "Kay" **Tremaine**	*Honolulu Advertiser*
170 Candace Baird Alig **Vanderlip**	International News Service
171 Margrethe "Rita" **Vandivert**	*Time*
172 Barbara **Wace**	Associated Press
173 Betty **Wason**	CBS
174 Mary **Welsh** Monks Hemingway	Time-Life
175 Lael Tucker **Wertenbaker**	*Time*
176 Betsey Maria Cushing Roosevelt **Whitney**	*Washington Times-Herald*
177 Bonnie **Wiley**	Associated Press
178 Betty Dablanc **Winkler**	Press Alliance
179 Mary Day **Winn**	*This Week*
180 Margaret Karch **Zaimes**	American Red Cross

All Names	Accrediting Publications
181 Leane **Zugsmith** Randau	*PM*

*This table is not exhaustive, in terms of individuals or their publications. The accreditation information was drawn from government documents within collections at the National Archives at College Park, the Library of Congress, Schlesinger Library, and the Wisconsin State Historical Society. Additional details about women's names and identities were drawn from biographical sources and newspaper articles.

Bibliography

MANUSCRIPT COLLECTIONS

Associated Press Corporate Archives, New York, New York.
   1. Edward Kennedy Papers.
   2. Subject Files, 1900–1967.

College of Idaho, Caldwell, Idaho.
   1. The Robert E. Smylie Archives.
      1.1. Inez Callaway Robb, unprocessed papers.

Emory University, Atlanta, Georgia.
   1. Stuart A. Rose Manuscript, Archives, and Rare Book Library.
      1.1. William Dummer Northend Family Papers.

Harvard University, Cambridge, Massachusetts.
   1. Arthur and Elizabeth Schlesinger Library on the History of Women in America.
      1.1. Caroline Iverson Ackerman Papers.
      1.2. Therese Bonney Papers.
      1.3. Catherine Coyne Papers.
      1.4. Grace Ellery Channing Stetson Papers.
      1.5. Ruth Cowan Nash Papers.
   2. Houghton Library
      2.1. Time Inc. collection.

Library of Congress, Washington, D.C.
   1. Oveta Culp Hobby papers.

National Archives at College Park, College Park, Maryland.
   1. Record Group 107: Records of the Office of the Secretary of War.
   2. Record Group 120: Records of the American Expeditionary Forces (World War I).
   3. Record Group 208: Records of the Office of War Information.
   4. Record Group 313: Records of Naval Operating Forces, 1849–1997.
   5. Record Group 331: Records of Allied Operational and Occupation Headquarters, World War II.

6. Record Group 337: Records of Headquarters Army Ground Forces.

7. Record Group 393: Records of United States Army Continental Commands, 1821–1920.

8. Record Group 498: Records of Headquarters, European Theater of Operations, United States Army (World War II).

Newberry Library, Chicago, Illinois.
1. Roger and Julie Baskes Department of Special Collections.
2. Robert J. Casey Papers.
3. Carroll Binder Papers.
4. Hazel MacDonald Papers.
5. Elmo Scott Watson Papers.

New York Public Library, New York, New York.
1. Manuscripts and Archives Division.
1.1. Anne O'Hare McCormick Papers.

Northwestern University, Evanston, Illinois.
1. Charles Deering McCormick Library of Special Collections.
1.1. Teresa Dean Papers.

Smith College, Northampton, Massachusetts.
1. Sophia Smith Collection.
1.1. Helen Paull Kirkpatrick Papers.

Stanford University, Stanford, California.
1. Hoover Institution Archives.
1.1. Cecil Dorrian Papers.

Syracuse University, Syracuse, New York.
1. Syracuse University Libraries Special Collections Research Center.
1.1. Margaret Bourke-White Papers.

University of Kansas Libraries, Lawrence, Kansas.
1. Kenneth Spencer Research Library.
1.1. Peggy Hull Deuell Papers.

Wisconsin Historical Society, Madison, Wisconsin.
1. R. Ernest Dupuy papers, unprocessed collection.

CONTEMPORANEOUS ARTICLES FROM NEWSPAPERS AND MAGAZINES

Addington, Sarah. "Sob Traitors." *New-York Tribune*, September 5, 1918.

Army and Navy Journal, April 2, 1910.

Associated Press. "Commanders Urged to Aid War Reporter: U.S. Headquarters Term Accurate Battle News Best Armor to Combat Axis Propaganda." *Christian Science Monitor*, May 23, 1944.

———. "The Gal Boosts Morale." *Atlanta Constitution*, March 12, 1945.

———. "Ready for War: She's Equipped." *Washington Post,* January 29, 1943.

———. "Text of OWI Praise of Deeds of War Correspondents." *New York Times*, April 15, 1943.

———. "Two Women Reporters Accredited to Army." *Atlanta Constitution*, March 26, 1942.

———. "Women Writers Observers in Carolina War Games En Route to the Front." *Knicker-bocker News* (Albany, New York), November 17, 1943.

Bailey, Muriel. "At Home with Aguinaldo." *Overland Monthly*, March 1899.

Bates, Bessie Dow. "Plucky Woman War Correspondent: Eliza Archard Connor Who Is Carrying a Typewriter around the World." *Daily (Wisconsin) Gazette*, June 20, 1899.

Boissevain, Inez Milholland. "France Shorn of Men to Work by Great War: Women and Boys Forced to Toil in the Fields." *Chicago Daily Tribune*, July 20, 1915.

By Cable to *New York Times*. "8 Women Agree on a Hat; to Devers That's News." *New York Times*, October 22, 1943.

By Telephone to *New York Times*. "First Woman Reporter Files from Pacific Area." *New York Times,* October 10, 1944.

Baltimore Sun. "The Fifth's Transfer." June 1, 1898.

———. "Mrs. Harrison Entered Russia as *The Sun's* Correspondent." July 31, 1921.

———. "The OWI Promises Speedy News from Invasion Beachheads." April 23, 1944.

———. "The Wreck of the Elizabeth." July 26, 1850.

———. "Women Playing Part in War in the Balkans." November 17, 1912.

Boston Daily Globe. "American Woman War Correspondent." August 19, 1926.

———. "American Woman War Correspondent." August 19, 1926.

Chicago Daily Tribune. "4 WAAC Units Going to British Zone This Year." September 9, 1942.

———. "Brussels Has Plenty of Food." August 14, 1914.

———. "Chicago Woman in War Zone Searched For by Four Nations." November 21, 1915.

———. "Medal of Freedom Awarded by Army to 19 War Writers." September 27, 1947.

———. "Peggy Hull, War Correspondent, Drops Into City." December 22, 1917.

———. "The Office of Wordy Incompetence." April 22, 1944.

———. "WID Carries ON; 'Personalizing' Army Is Its Job. 'Turquoise Era' Ends; No More Sirupy [*sic*] Pamphlets." May 23, 1942.

Christian Science Monitor. "U.S. Reporters in London Elect." May 7, 1942.

Courier-Journal. "Girl Reporter Makes Trip Here in Army Bomber." September 15, 1942.

Carpenter, Iris. "Four Red Cross Girls Thumb Way into Paris." *Daily Boston Globe*, September 3, 1944.

———. "Nazis Won't Let Germans Quit, Says Surrendered Newsman." *Daily Boston Globe*, October 11, 1944.

———. "Rhine Spanned in 10 Minutes." *Daily Boston Globe*, March 10, 1945.

———. "Thrilling Tank Brigade Charge Wrests Samree from Germans." *Atlanta Constitution,* January 13, 1945.

———. "Captain with Moustache Cheers Sophie Who Is Ill." *Daily Boston Globe*, November 1, 1944.

Carr, Harry. "War Correspondents as an Army Problem." *Los Angeles Times*, August 4, 1916.

Carson, Lee. "Doughboys Suspect Healthy Young Cologne Civilians Are German Soldiers." *The Lowell Sun*, March 6, 1945.

———. "Caring for Seriously Wounded Boys in Germany Is Told." *Tipton (Indiana) News*, December 3, 1944.

———. "French Women Chic Despite War Curbs: Art and Design of Gowns Disguise Poor Materials Brought On in Past Years." *New York Times*, August 29, 1944.

———. "Second Infantry Division Blocked German Victory." *New Castle (Pennsylvania) News*, January 4, 1945.

Carter, Imogene [Cora Taylor Crane]. "Soldiers Amazed to See a Woman on the Battlefield." *Chicago Daily Tribune,* May 10, 1897.

Cedar Rapids Evening Gazette. "Girl Reporter Braves Terrors of Russia for the Evening Gazette," January 4, 1919.

Conner, Eliza Archard. "Our Boys in Luzon: Eliza Archard Conner Praises the American Soldier." *Akron (Ohio) Tribune*, June 19, 1899.

———. "Women's World in Paragraphs." *Arizona Republican*, April 17, 1891.

Cowan, Ruth. "Adventure Seeker Finds It in Africa." *New York Times,* February 23, 1943.

———. "Feminine AEF Greeted by Air Raid in Africa." *Washington Post*, February 3, 1943.

———. "First WAACs to Join A.E.F. Sing Thru Sea Danger: Sleep in Blankets; How 'Eyes' Won Crew." *Chicago Tribune,* January 31, 1943.

———. "Folks Still Dress for Evening in Africa." *Washington Post,* February 9, 1943.

———. "Girl Reporter in North African Battle Area Rides a Tank to Check Upon Musicians." *Washington Post*, March 14, 1943.

———. "Great Opportunities Seen for Women in WAVES, WAACs." *Atlanta Constitution,* September 10, 1942.

———. "N.E. Ambulance Drivers Among Unsung Heroes of Fighting in Tunisia." *Daily Boston Globe*, March 5, 1943.

———. "WAACs Arrive in Africa Headed by a Boston Woman." *Daily Boston Globe*, January 31, 1943.

———. "WAACs Who Drive Jeeps Win Eisenhower's Praise." *Los Angeles Times*, February 7, 1943.

———. "War No Tea Party, WAACs Find in Africa." *Washington Post,* February 13, 1943.

———. "Women Reporters Hitchhike to Escape Advance of Nazis." *Ironwood (Michigan) Daily Globe,* February 26, 1943.

———. "Women's AEF Head Is Still Quite Feminine." *Washington Post,* January 31, 1943.

Coyne, Catherine. "Fearing Air Raid, Writer Puts on Steel Helmet, Then Falls Asleep." *Boston Herald*, August 1944.

Cramer, Robert B. "Little Stories of the War." *Atlanta Constitution*, September 3, 1898.

Daily Boston Globe. "Great Staff of Foreign Correspondents." July 23, 1942.

Dallam, Jr., Frank M. "The American Fighting Man." *Goodwin's Weekly*, September 18, 1918.

Dean, Teresa. "He Was a Daring Man." *Chicago Herald*, February 5, 1891.

Dew, Gwen. "Repatriates Tell Stories Of Jap Prisons: Talk to Internee of First Trade." *Chicago Daily Tribune*, December 3, 1943.

Dooly, Isma. "Corra Harris, in Her Georgia Valley, Back from Fighting Zone, Tells of Her Experiences in England, Belgium and France." *Atlanta,* February 7, 1915.

Dorr, Rheta Childe. "A Soldier's Mother in France." *Chicago Daily Tribune,* June 2, 1918.

Drachman, Rosemary. "Only Woman Correspondent on the Moroccan Front: Longworth's Sister as 'First Lady' of Fez." *Washington Post,* January 10, 1926.

Farwell, Mildred. "Tribune Writer in Thick of the Riot at Petrograd." *Chicago Daily Tribune*, July 20, 1917.

Fleeson, Doris. "Who Banned Maine Woman Correspondent from Return from Rio on Missouri?" *Daily Boston Globe,* August 29, 1947.

Frank Leslie's Popular Monthly. "Deaf-Mutes." May 1885.

From *London (Ontario) Mail.* "Mrs. Blake Watkins: And How She Proved Herself One of the Boys at Tampa." *New York Times*, July 3, 1898.

Galveston Daily News. "Glory of War Correspondents." September 18, 1898.

Hamm, Margherita Arlina. "Brown and Blue Boys: Soldier Life as Seen by a Woman Inspector. The Lighter Side of the War." *Washington Post*, July 31, 1898.

Holt, Carlyle. "Even More Attractive Than Photo, Says Holt." *Daily Boston Globe*, April 29, 1945.

Kansas City Journal. "A Woman War Correspondent." May 29, 1899.

———. "Miss Elsie Reasoner." August 8, 1898.

———. "Woman War Correspondent." March 29, 1899.

Kauffman, Reginald Wright. "The News Embargo." *North American Review,* 208, 757 (December 1918).

Kauffman, Ruth Wright. "Back In an Empty." *Outlook*, July 3, 1918.

Kirtland, Helen Johns. "A Woman on the Battle Front." *Leslie's Weekly Newspaper*, August 24, 1918.

Los Angeles Times. "A Blessing Disguise." July 31, 1898.

———. "WAACs Soon to Be Seen in Country's Major Centers: Graduates of Ft. Des Moines Scheduled for Assignment." August 9, 1942.

MacGowan, David. "Poisoned by Army Ration: Private Gibbons, Fifth Illinois, Eats Corned Beef and Dies." *Chicago Daily Tribune,* May 27, 1898.

McCardell, Lee. "Six Girls, No Chow, No Beds." *(Baltimore) Sun*, October 17, 1944.

McCutcheon, John T. "Mrs. [Mildred] Farwell Held Captive by Bulgars." *Chicago Daily Tribune,* December 21, 1915.

Miller, Lee. "France Free Again." *Vogue,* October 1944, 92–94, 129–134, 136, 143.

New York Daily Tribune. "Death of Miss [Anna] Benjamin: She Was the First Woman War Correspondent to Reach Santiago—Her Travels." January 22, 1902.

New York Times. "25 Drowned in Submarine Panic." November 29, 1915.

———. "Daniell Heads News Men: *Times* Correspondent Is Elected Head of London Association." May 7, 1942.

———. "Four Women Writers in Pacific." November 15, 1944.

———. "Honor to Writers Urged: Colleagues Would Allow Ribbons for War Correspondents." April 6, 1944.

———. "MacArthur Lauds Victims." May 1, 1942.

———. "Pen Names: The More Important of Those Which Authors Have Employed." November 17, 1900.

———. "Queries and Answers." September 8, 1900.

———. "Two News Women Honored for Work; Mrs. Roosevelt Presents $100 Prizes of Their Club at Front Page Ball; War Reporters Hailed." February 15, 1941.

———. "Women Publishers View War Changes." April 21, 1942.

———. "Women Will Jump at the Chance." April 6, 1910.

(New York) World. "The Ways of Woman Fair." March 12, 1891.

Newark (New Jersey) Daily Advocate. "Margherita Arlina Hamm." June 28, 1896.

———. "She's at the Front: Mrs. [Clara] Colby the Only Woman War Correspondent in Cuba." August 10, 1898.

New Journal and Guide. "And Now a Woman War Correspondent." November 4, 1944.

New York Amsterdam News. "New War Correspondent." October 28, 1944.

Newsweek. "The Rhine Maidens." March 14, 1945.

Outlook. "A War-Correspondent on Crutches." January 14, 1899.

———. "Does the Red Cross Prolong War?" March 7, 1914.

Philadelphia Tribune. "War Correspondent." October 28, 1944.

Phillips, Bettye. *(Baltimore) Afro-American.* "Phillips' Hospital Room Is Meeting Place for Yanks." January 13, 1945.

———. "Regains Use of Arm, Leg, but Doctors Still Check." *(Baltimore) Afro-American.* December 2, 1944.

Phillips, Lieutenant Colonel Joseph B. "Women Correspondents Called Good Soldiers in North Africa." *Editor & Publisher*, 1943.

Pittsburgh Courier. "Covers War." October 28, 1944

Pittsburgh Dispatch. "A Heroine in Petticoats: Remarkable Experiences of a Pittsburg Lady during the War—Adventures in Field and Prison Pen." May 4, 1889.

Plaindealer (Kansas City). "War Correspondent." October 27, 1944.

Portsmouth (Ohio) Times. "American Girl Reporter Gets Taste of War." August 8, 1944.

Pyle, Ernie. "London Filled with Reporters for Invasion." *Atlanta Constitution,* May 11, 1944.

———. "Vet War Correspondents Scared." *Atlanta Constitution*, June 11, 1944.

R. "Woman Has No Business Reporting War, He Says." What People Talk About. *Daily Boston Globe,* March 16, 1945.

———. "A Rebuttal from 'R.'" What People Talk About. *Daily Boston Globe*, April 3, 1945.

(Richmond) Times Dispatch. "Our War Correspondent Creates Consternation." May 5, 1905.

Robb, Inez. "600 WAACs Will Make Up America's First Female AEF: 600 WAACs to Get Duty in England." *Washington Post*, August 25, 1942.

———. "At U.S. Army Camp in Africa: INS Woman Scribe Now with WAACs." *San Antonio Light*, February 1, 1943.

———. "Blood and Toil of British Women Free Millions of Men for War Jobs." *New York Journal-American*, January 12, 1942.

———. "Inez Robb Finds Beauty Shop—But No Soap in Hotel." *Atlanta Constitution*, May 12, 1943.

———. "Mail Arrival Brings Joy to WAACs Abroad." *Lima (Ohio) News*, February 2, 1943.

———. "Gunner from Flatbush Riddles Own Plane Downing 2d Nazi." *Atlanta Constitution*, March 17, 1943.

———. "Hard Winter but English 'Can Take It': Public Never Grouches Over War's Hardships, Correspondent Finds." *Syracuse Herald Journal,* February 10, 1942.

———. "Inez Robb Finally Gets Answer to Transport's $64 Question." *Atlanta Constitution*, March 13, 1943.

———. "Inez Robb Learns to Like Food While Stationed on African Front." *Atlanta Constitution,* May 15, 1943.

———. "Sergeant Is Glamour Girl of Africa." *Washington Post,* February 13, 1943.

———. "Tooth Brush Is Pressing Need for Soldiers in War Hospital." *Atlanta Constitution*, March 1, 1943.

———. "War Fails to Spoil Midwinter Cruise on Mediterranean." *Atlanta Constitution*, March 10, 1943.

———. "Woman War Correspondent." *Washington Post,* a series of articles that ran daily from May 11 to May 15, 1943.

Salt Lake Herald. "Off for Cuba: First Salt Lake Girl to Go There." June 27, 1898.

San Antonio Express. "Skedaddled for Safety: *London Telegraph's* Woman War Correspondent Couldn't Stand Fire." November 20, 1899.

San Antonio Express. "Woman War Correspondent Tells of Fight to the Front." August 2, 1943.

Saturday Evening Post. "Femininities." April 30, 1881.

Simonton, Ann. "Four American Women Who Have Been to the War." *New-York Tribune*, August 1, 1915.

St. Paul (Minnesota) Globe. "The Romance of the Only Woman War Correspondent." June 19, 1904.

———. "Girl Who Went to the Front." September 4, 1898.

Stevens, Edmund. "War Correspondent: Thrills, Danger and Boredom." *Christian Science Monitor*, June 11, 1943.

Syracuse Herald-Journal. "Biggest War News to Come: Starting Tomorrow in *The Herald-Journal*: Famous War Correspondents of the Chicago Daily News Foreign Service." March 2, 1941.

Telford, Emma Paddock. "Warships in Suda Bay: The First Sight of Crete to an American Passenger on the Way to Athens." *New York Times*, May 9, 1897.

Time. "A Letter from the Publisher." August 3, 1942.

———. "Foreign News: Out of Boredom." April 5, 1943.

———. "Foreign News: Retreat from Greatness." March 29, 1943.

———. "The Press: Cartwheel Girl." June 12, 1939.

Ward, Fannie B. "Red Cross in Cuba." *Los Angeles Times*, March 21, 1898.

———. "The Chilean War: A Correspondent Who Sides with Balmaceda." *Los Angeles Times*, July 12, 1891.

———. "Horrors of War: Past and Present Sufferings in Santiago de Cuba." *Los Angeles Times*, September 2, 1898.

(Washington) Evening Times. "Women's Auxiliary Ex-Prisoners of War: A Female War Correspondent Who Was Incarcerated in Castle Thunder." October 7, 1902.

Washington Post. "American Woman and a French Officer Are Wounded." October 22, 1918.

———. "Mrs. F.B. Ward Dead: Prominent Newspaper Writer, Traveler, and Lecturer." October 6, 1913.

———. "Reporter, Writer for Movies." May 15, 1973.

Williamson, Alice. "My Attempt to Be a War Correspondent: Being the Confessions of a Coward." *McClure's,* 43, no. 5 (September 1914): 66–76.

Wisconsin State Journal. "Soldiers Greet Girl Reporter." March 18, 1943.

Woods, Lewis. "Full News of War Promised by Davis." *New York Times*, July 11, 1942.

Wyoming State Tribune. "Assignment to War Front Brings Fame to Miss Peggy Hull." April 2, 1920.

CONTEMPORANEOUS LITERATURE AND AUTOBIOGRAPHIES

Baillie, Hugh. *Two Battlefronts: Dispatches Written by the President of the United Press Covering the Air Offensive Over Germany and the Sicilian Campaign, during the Summer of 1943*. New York: United Press Associations, 1943.

Black, Helen C. *Notable Women Authors of the Day*. Glasgow: David Bryce & Son, 1893.

Booker, Edna Lee. *News Is My Job: A Correspondent in War-Torn China*. New York: MacMillan, 1940.

Boughner, Genevieve. *Women in Journalism: A Guide to the Opportunities and a Manual of the Technique of Women's Work for Newspapers and Magazines*. New York: D. Appleton, 1926.

Bourke-White, Margaret. *Portrait of Myself*. New York: Simon and Schuster, 1963.

Bullard, F. L. *Famous War Correspondents*. Boston: Little, Brown and Company, 1914.

Carpenter, Iris. *No Woman's World*. Boston: Houghton Mifflin Company, 1946.

Chandler, Arthur D., ed. *The Papers of Dwight D. Eisenhower: The War Years*. Baltimore: Johns Hopkins University Press, 1970.

Chapelle, Dickey. *What's a Woman Doing Here? A Reporter's Report on Herself*. New York: William Morrow & Co., 1962.

Considine, Robert. *It's All News to Me*. New York: Meredith Press, 1967.

Cowles, Virginia. *Looking for Trouble*. New York: Harper & Brothers, 1941.

Daniell, Raymond. *Civilians Must Fight*. New York: Doubleday Doran, 1941.

Davis, Elmer and Byron Price. *War Information and Censorship*. Washington, D.C.: American Council on Public Affairs, 1943.

Ebener, Charlotte. *No Facilities for Women*. New York: Alfred A. Knopf, 1955.

Gallagher, Wes. *Back Door to Berlin: The Full Story of the American Coup in North Africa*. New York: Doubleday, 1943.

Gramling, Oliver and Associated Press Correspondents Around the World. *Free Men Are Fighting: The Story of World War II*. New York: Farrar and Rinehart, Inc., 1942.

Hemingway, Mary Welsh. *How It Was*. New York: Knopf, 1976.

Hiett, Helen. *No Matter Where*. New York: Dutton, 1944.

Higgins, Marguerite. *News Is a Singular Thing*. New York: Doubleday, 1955.

Hollingworth, Clare. *Front Line*. London: Jonathan Cape, 1991.

Hudson, Frederic. *Journalism in the United States, 1690–1872*. New York: Harper & Brothers, 1873.

Hughes, Helen MacGill. *News and the Human Interest Story*. Chicago: University of Chicago Press, 1940.

"Journalism Week, 1914: From Speeches by Newspaper Makers and Advertising Men at the University, May 18–22, 1914." *The University of Missouri Bulletin*, 15, no. 20 (July 1914).

Kirkpatrick, Helen P. *Under the British Umbrella: What the English Are and How They Go to War*. New York: C. Scribner's Sons, 1939.

Knickerbocker, H. R., et al. *Danger Forward: The Story of the First Division in World War II*. Washington, D.C.: Society of the First Division, 1947.

Koop, Theodore F. *Weapon of Silence*. Chicago: University of Chicago Press, 1946.

Kuhn, Irene. *Assigned to Adventure*. New York: J.B. Lippincott Company, 1938.

Leonard, John William, ed. *Woman's Who's Who of America: A Biographical Dictionary of Contemporary Women of the United States and Canada, 1914–1915*. New York: American Commonwealth Company, 1976.

Liebling, A. J. *The Wayward Pressman*. Garden City, NY: Doubleday, 1948.

McNamara, John. *Extra! U. S. War Correspondents in the Fighting Fronts*. Boston: Houghton Mifflin Company, 1945.

Members of the Overseas Press Club of America. *Deadline Delayed*. New York: Dutton, 1947.

Monks, Noel. *Eyewitness*. London: Frederick Muller Ltd., 1955.

Mydans, Carl. *More Than Meets the Eye*. New York: Harper, 1959.

Oestreicher, J. C. *The World Is Their Beat*. New York: Duell, Sloan and Pearce, 1945.

Oldfield, Barney. *Never a Shot in Anger*. New York: Duell, Sloan and Pearce, 1956.

Reiss, Curt, ed. *They Were There: The Story of World War II and How It Came About, by America's Foremost Correspondents.* New York: Books for Libraries Press, 1944.

Ross, Ishbel. *Ladies of the Press: The Story of Women in Journalism by an Insider.* New York: Harper, 1936.

Sergeant, Elizabeth Shepley. *Shadow Shapes: The Journal of a Wounded Woman.* Boston: Houghton Mifflin Co., 1920.

Shuman, Edwin Llewellyn. *Steps into Journalism: Helps and Hints for Young Writers.* Evanston, Illinois: Evanston Press Co., 1894.

Tietjens, Eunice. *The World at My Shoulder.* New York: MacMillan Company, 1938.

Treadwell, Mattie E. *The Women's Army Corps.* Washington, D.C.: Office of the Chief of Military History, 1954.

United States War Department Office of the Chief of Staff, *Field Service Regulations United States Army 1914: Text Corrections through December 20, 1916: Changes No. 5* (New York: Army and Navy Journal, 1916), 165–69.

United States War Department. *Regulations for War Correspondents Accompanying United States Army Forces in the Field.* Field Manual 30–26. Washington, D.C.: War Department, 1942.

United States Senate, Seventy-Eighth Congress, First Session, March 1, 1943.

Welch, Margaret H. "Is Newspaper Work Healthful for Women?" *Journal of Social Science* 32 (1894).

Willard, Frances E., and Mary A. Livermore, eds. *A Woman of the Century: Fourteen Hundred Biographical Sketches Accompanied by Portraits of Leading American Women in All Walks of Life.* Buffalo, NY: Charles Wells Moulton, 1893.

SECONDARY SOURCES

Abramson, Phyllis. *Sob Sister Journalism.* New York: Greenwood Press, 1990.

Allan, Stuart, and Barbie Zelizer, eds. *Reporting War: Journalism in Wartime.* New York: Routledge, 2004.

Allen, Ann. "The News Media and the Women's Army Auxiliary Corps: Protagonists for a Cause." *Military Affairs* 50 (April 1986): 77–83.

Anderson, Karen. *Wartime Women: Sex Roles, Family Relations, and the Status of Women during World War II.* Westport, CT: Greenwood Press, 1981.

Beasley, Maurine. "Recent Directions for the Study of Women's History in American Journalism." *Journalism Studies* 2, no. 2 (2001): 207–20.

Beasley, Maurine, and Sheila Jean Gibbons. *Taking Their Place: A Documentary History of Women and Journalism.* State College, PA: Strata Publishing, 2003.

Bederman, Gail. *Manliness and Civilization: A Cultural History of Gender and Race in the United States, 1880–1917.* Chicago: University of Chicago Press, 1995.

Belford, Barbara. *Brilliant Bylines: A Biographical Anthology of Notable Newspaperwomen in America.* New York: Columbia University Press, 1988.

Bentley, Amy. *Eating for Victory: Food Rationing and the Politics of Domesticity.* Urbana: University of Illinois Press, 1998.

Blanchard, Margaret A. "Freedom of the Press in World War II: Historiographic Essay." *American Journalism* 12 (Summer 1995): 342–58.

Bradley, Patricia. *Women and the Press: The Struggle for Equality.* Evanston: Northwestern University Press, 2005.

Broussard, Jinx Coleman. *African American Foreign Correspondents [A History].* Baton Rouge: Louisiana State University Press, 2013.

Butler, Judith. *Gender Trouble: Feminism and the Subversion of Identity.* New York: Routledge, 1990.

Cairns, Kathleen A. *Front-Page Women Journalists, 1920–1950.* Lincoln: University of Nebraska Press, 2003.

Campbell, D'Ann. *Women at War with America: Private Lives in a Patriotic Era.* Cambridge: Harvard University Press, 1984.

————. "Women in Combat: The World War II Experience in the United States, Great Britain, Germany, and the Soviet Union." *The Journal of Military History* 57, no. 2 (April 1993): 301–23.

Canning, Kathleen. "Gender and the Politics of Class Formation: Rethinking German Labor History." *American Historical Review* 97, no. 3 (June 1992): 736–68.

Canning, Kathleen, and Sonya O. Rose. "Gender, Citizenship, and Subjectivity: Some Historical and Theoretical Considerations." *Gender and History* 13, no. 3 (November 2001): 427–43.

Carroll, Berenice A., ed. *Liberating Women's History: Theoretical and Critical Essays.* Urbana: University of Illinois Press, 1976.

Chafe, William H. *The Paradox of Change.* New York: Oxford University Press, 1991.

Collier, Richard. *The Warcos: The War Correspondents of World War Two.* London: Weidenfeld & Nicolson, 1989.

Cooke, Miriam, and Angela Woollacott, eds. *Gendering War Talk.* Princeton: Princeton University Press, 1993.

Copeland David A. *Greenwood Library of American War Reporting: The Indian Wars & the Spanish-American War* (Westport, CT: Greenwood Press, 2005).

Copeland, David, Frank E. Fee, Jr., Mark Feldstein, and Linda Lumsden. "Debate and Reflection: How to Write Journalism History." *Journalism Studies* 7, no. 3 (2006): 463–81.

Covert, Catherine L. "Journalism History and Women's Experience: A Problem in Conceptual Change." *Journalism History* 8, no. 1 (Spring 1981): 2–6.

Crozier, Emmet. *American Reporters on the Western Front, 1914–1918.* New York: Oxford University Press, 1959.

Dell'Orto, Giovanna. *American Journalism and International Relations: Foreign Correspondence from the Early Republic to the Digital Era.* New York: Cambridge University Press, 2013.

————. *AP Foreign Correspondents in Action: World War II to the Present.* New York: Cambridge University Press, 2015.

Desmond, Robert William. *The Information Process: World News Reporting to the Twentieth Century.* Iowa City: University of Iowa Press, 1978.

————. *The Press and World Affairs.* New York: D. Appleton-Century Company, Inc., 1937.

————. *Tides of War: World News Reporting, 1931–1945.* Iowa City: University of Iowa Press, 1984.

Donnelly, Karen J. *American Women Pilots of World War II.* American Women at War. New York: Rosen Pub. Group, 2003.

Edwards, Julia. *Women of the World: The Great Foreign Correspondents.* Boston: Houghton Mifflin, 1988.

Edy, Carolyn. "Juggernaut in Kid Gloves: Inez Callaway Robb, 1900–1979." *American Journalism* 27, no. 4 (Fall 2010).

Elshtain, Jean Bethke. *Women and War.* New York: Basic Books, 1987.

Farrell, Grace. *Lillie Devereux Blake: Retracing a Life Erased.* Amherst: University of Massachusetts Press, 2002.

Foucault, Michael. *History of Sexuality: An Introduction, Volume 1.* New York: Random House, 1978.

Friedl, Vicki L. *Women in the United States Military, 1901–1995: A Research Guide and Annotated Bibliography.* Westport, CT: Greenwood Press, 1996.

Fussell, Paul. *Wartime: Understanding and Behavior in the Second World War.* New York: Oxford, 1989.

Gangadharan, Seeta Pena. "Public Participation and Agency Discretion in Rulemaking at the Federal Communications Commission." *Journal of Communication Inquiry* 33 (2009): 337–53.

Gellhorn, Martha. *The Face of War.* New York: Atlantic Monthly Press, 1988.

————. *The View from the Ground.* Boston: Atlantic Monthly Press, 1994.

Golombisky, Kim, and Derina Holtzhausen. "'Pioneering Women' and 'Founding Mothers': Women's History and Projecting Feminism Onto the Past." *Women and Language* 28, no. 2 (Fall 2005): 12–22.

Goralski, Robert. *World War II Almanac 1931–1945*. New York: Bonanza Books, 1981.

Gruhzit-Hoyt, Olga. *They Also Served: American Women in World War II*. Secaucus, NJ: Carol Pub. Group, 1995.

Hamill, Pete, ed. *A. J. Liebling: World War II Writings*. New York: Penguin, 2008.

Hamilton, John Maxwell. *Journalism's Roving Eye: A History of American Foreign Reporting*. Baton Rouge: Louisiana State University Press, 2009.

Hampton, Ellen. *Women of Valor: The Rochambelles on the WWII Front*. New York: Palgrave Macmillan, 2006.

Hartmann, Susan M. *The Home Front and Beyond*. Boston: Twayne Publishers, 1982.

Hegarty, Marilyn E. *Victory Girls, Khaki-Wackies, and Patriotutes: The Regulation of Female Sexuality during World War II*. New York: New York University Press, 2008.

Higonnet, Margaret Randolph, Jane Jenson, Sonya Michel, and Margaret Collins Weitz, eds. *Behind the Lines: Gender and the Two World Wars*. New Haven: Yale University Press, 1987.

Hoffmann, Joyce. *On Their Own: Women Journalists and the American Experience in Vietnam*. New York: Da Capo Press, 2008.

Hohenberg, John. *Foreign Correspondence: The Great Reporters and Their Times*. Syracuse: Syracuse University Press, 1995.

Honey, Maureen, ed. *Bitter Fruit: African American Women in World War II*. Columbia: University of Missouri Press, 1999.

———. *Creating Rosie the Riveter: Class, Gender, and Propaganda during World War II*. Amherst: University of Massachusetts Press, 1984.

Horten, Gerd. *Radio Goes to War: The Cultural Politics of Propaganda during World War II*. Berkeley: University of California Press, 2002.

Hudson, Linda S. *Mistress of Manifest Destiny: A Biography of Jane McManus Storm Cazneau, 1807–1878*. Austin: Texas State Historical Association, 2001.

Kaszuba, Dave. "Ringside, Hearthside: Sports Scribe Jane Dixon Embodies Struggle of Jazz Age Women Caught Between Two Worlds." *Journalism History* 35, no. 3 (2009): 141–50.

Kennedy, David M. *Freedom from Fear: The American People in World War II*. New York: Oxford University Press, 1999.

Kennedy, Edward, and Julia Kennedy Cochran. *Ed Kennedy's War: V-E Day, Censorship, and the Associated Press*. Baton Rouge: Louisiana State University Press, 2012.

Kitch, Carolyn. "A Genuine, Vivid Personality." *Journalism History* 31, no. 3 (Fall 2005): 122–37.

———. "Changing Theoretical Perspectives on Women's Media Images: The Emergence of Patterns in a New Area of Historical Scholarship." *Journalism and Mass Communication Quarterly* 74, no. 3 (Autumn 1997): 477–89.

Knight, Oliver. *Following the Indian Wars: The Story of the Newspaper Correspondents Among the Indian Campaigners*. Norman: University of Oklahoma Press, 1960.

Knightley, Phillip. *The First Casualty: The War Correspondent as Hero, Propagandist and Myth-Maker from the Crimea to Iraq*. London: Andre Deutsch, 2003.

Korte, Barbara. *Represented Reporters: Images of War Correspondents in Memoirs and Fiction*. New Brunswick, N.J.: Transaction Publishers, 2009.

Lande, Nathaniel. *Dispatches from the Front: A History of American War Correspondents*. New York: Oxford University Press, 1995.

Langley, Wanda. *Flying Higher: The Women Airforce Service Pilots of World War II*. North Haven, CT: Linnet Books, 2002.

Lerner, Gerda. *The Majority Finds Its Past: Placing Women in History*. Chapel Hill: University of North Carolina Press, 1979.

Lewis, John E., ed. *The Mammoth Book of War Correspondents*. New York: Carroll and Graf, 2001.

Lumsden, Linda J. "The Essentialist Agenda of the 'Woman's Angle' in Cold War Washington: The Case of Associated Press Reporter Ruth Cowan." *Journalism History* 33, no. 1 (Spring 2007): 2–13.

———. "Women's Lib Has No Soul." *Journalism History* 35, no. 3 (Fall 2009): 118–30.

Lutes, Jean Marie. *Front Page Girls: Women Journalists in American Culture and Fiction, 1880–1930.* Ithaca, NY: Cornell University Press, 2006.

MacKinnon, Stephen R., and Oris Friesen. *China Reporting. An Oral History of American Journalism in the 1940s.* Berkeley: University of California Press, 1987.

Mander, Mary S. *Pen and Sword: American War Correspondents, 1898–1975.* Urbana: University of Illinois Press, 2010.

Marzolf, Marion. *Up from the Footnote: A History of Women Journalists.* New York: Hastings House, 1977.

———. "American Studies—Ideas for Media Historians?" *Journalism History* 5 (Spring 1978): 13–16.

Mathews, Joseph J. *Reporting the Wars.* Minneapolis: University of Minnesota Press, 1957.

Matloff, Judith. "Unspoken: Foreign Correspondents and Sexual Abuse." *Columbia Journalism Review* (May/June 2007): 22–23.

May, Elaine Tyler. "Redrawing the Map of History." *The Women's Review of Books* (February 2000): 26–27.

McGovern, Charles F. *Sold American: Consumption and Citizenship, 1890–1945.* Chapel Hill: University of North Carolina Press, 2006.

Meyer, Leisa. *Creating G.I. Jane: Sexuality and Power in the Women's Army Corps during World War II.* New York: Columbia University Press, 1996.

Meyerowitz, Joanne. "AHR Forum: A History of 'Gender.'" *American Historical Review* (December 2008): 1346–56.

Milkman, Ruth. *Gender at Work: The Dynamics of Job Segregation by Sex during World War II.* Urbana: University of Illinois Press, 1987.

Miller, Jane Eldridge, ed. *Who's Who in Contemporary Women's Writing.* New York: Routledge, 2001.

Mills, Kay. *A Place in the News: From the Women's Pages to the Front Page.* New York: Dodd Mead, 1988.

Milton, Joyce. *The Yellow Kids: Foreign Correspondents in the Heyday of Yellow Journalism.* New York: Harper & Row, 1989.

Moorehead, Caroline. *Selected Letters of Martha Gellhorn.* New York: Henry Holt & Co., 2006.

Morgan, Sue, ed. *Feminist History Reader.* New York: Routledge, 2006.

Mott, Frank Luther. *American Journalism: A History, 1690–1960.* New York: Macmillan, 1962.

Mulligan, Timothy. *World War II Guide to Records Relating to United States Military Participation.* Rebecca L. Collier, Judith Koucky, and Patrick R. Osborn, eds. Washington, D.C.: National Archives and Records Administration, 2008.

O'Neill, James E., and Robert W. Krauskopf. *World War II: An Account of Its Documents.* Washington, D.C.: Howard University Press, 1976.

Publicity and Psychological Warfare Section, 12th Army Group. *Report of Operations (Final after Action Report).* 14 (1945).

Reilly, Tom. "Jane McManus Storms: Letters from the Mexican War, 1846–1848." *Southwestern Historical Quarterly* 85 (July 1981): 21–44.

Riley, Denise. *"Am I That Name?": Feminism and the Category of "Women" in History.* New York: Macmillan, 1988.

Roeder, George H. *The Censored War: American Visual Experience during World War Two.* New Haven: Yale University Press, 1993.

Romeiser, John. *Combat Reporter: Don Whitehead's World War II Diary and Memoirs.* New York: Fordham University Press, 2006.

Rosenberg, Emily S. "Gender." *Journal of American History* 77, no. 1 (1990): 116–24.

Rosenberg, Rosalind. *Divided Lives: American Women in the Twentieth Century.* New York: Hill and Wang, 2008.

Roth, Mitchel P. *Historical Dictionary of War Journalism.* Westport, Conn.: Greenwood Press, 1997.

Rupp, Leila J. *Mobilizing Women for War: German and American Propaganda, 1939–1945.* Princeton: Princeton University Press, 1978.

Savage, Barbara. *Broadcasting Freedom: Radio, War and the Politics of Race, 1938–1948.* Chapel Hill: University of North Carolina Press, 1999.

Schilpp, Madelon Golden and Sharon M. Murphy. *Great Women of the Press.* Carbondale: Southern Illinois University Press, 1983.

Scott, Joan W. "Unanswered Questions." *American Historical Review* (December 2008): 1422–29.

———. "Women and War: A Focus for Rewriting History." *Women's Studies Quarterly* 12, no. 2 (Summer 1984): 2–6.

Scott, Joan Wallach. *Gender and the Politics of History.* New York: Columbia University Press, 1999.

Scott, Joan Wallach, ed. *Feminism and History.* New York: Oxford University Press, 1996.

Scott, Mark. *"Bravo Amerikanski!" And Other Stories from World War II by Ann Stringer as told to Mark Scott.* Bloomington, IN: 1st Books Library, 2000.

Sheldon, Sayre P. *Her War Story: Twentieth-Century Women Write About War.* Carbondale: Southern Illinois University Press, 1999.

Sherry, Michael S. *In the Shadow of War: The United States Since the 1930s.* New Haven: Yale University Press, 1995.

Smith, Jeffery Alan. *War & Press Freedom: The Problem of Prerogative Power.* New York: Oxford University Press, 1999.

Smith, Wilda M. and Eleanor A. Bogart. *The Wars of Peggy Hull: The Life and Times of a War Correspondent.* El Paso: Texas Western Press, 1991.

Sorel, Nancy Caldwell. *The Women Who Wrote the War.* New York: HarperCollins, 1999.

Startt, James D., and William David Sloan. *Historical Methods in Mass Communication.* Northport, AL: Vision Press, 2003.

Stein, M. L. *Under Fire: The Story of American War Correspondents.* New York: Julian Messner, 1968.

Stempel, Guido H., III, David H. Weaver, and G. Cleveland Wilhoit, eds. *Mass Communication Research and Theory.* Boston: Allyn and Bacon, 2003.

Stokesbury, James. *A Short History of World War II.* New York: Morrow, 1980.

Stoler, Ann Laura. *Carnal Knowledge and Imperial Power: Race and the Intimate in Colonial Rule.* Berkeley: University of California Press, 2002.

Storm, Hannah and Helena Williams, eds. *No Woman's Land: On the Frontlines with Female Reporters.* London: International News Safety Institute, 2012.

Sweeney, Michael S. *From the Front: The Story of War Featuring Correspondents' Chronicles.* Washington, D.C.: National Geographic, 2002.

———. *Secrets of Victory: The Office of Censorship and the American Press and Radio in World War II.* Chapel Hill: University of North Carolina Press, 2001.

———. *The Military and the Press: An Uneasy Truce.* Evanston: Northwestern University Press, 2006.

"Table No. 523. Armed Forces Personnel—Summary of Major Conflicts." *United States Census Bureau, Statistical Abstract of the United States: 2003.* National Defense and Veterans Affairs.

Tuchman, Barbara W. *Practicing History.* New York: Alfred A. Knopf, Inc., 1981.

United States Army in the World War 1917–1919: Reports of the Commander-in-Chief, Staff Sections and Services Volume 13. Washington, D.C.: Center of Military History United States Army, 1991.

Voss, Frederick. *Reporting the War: The Journalistic Coverage of World War II: Volumes 1 & 2.* Washington, D.C.: Smithsonian Institution Press for the National Portrait Gallery, 1994.

Wagner, Lilya. *Women War Correspondents of World War II.* New York: Greenwood Press, 1989.

Washburn, Patrick. "The Office of Censorship's Attempt to Control Press Coverage of the Atomic Bomb During World War II." *Journalism Monographs* (April 1990).

Weinberg, Gerhard. *A World at Arms: A Global History of World War II.* Cambridge: Cambridge University Press, 1995.

Wertheim, Stanley. "Stephen Crane Remembered." *Studies in American Fiction* 4, no. 1 (Spring 1976): 45–64.

Whitt, Jan. *Women in American Journalism: A New History*. Urbana: University of Illinois Press, 2008.

Winfield, Betty H. *FDR and the News Media*. New York: Columbia University Press, 1994.

———. *Two Commanders-in-Chief: Free Expression's Most Severe Test*. Cambridge, MA: Joan Shorenstein Barone Center, 1992.

Yesil, Bilge. "'Who Said This Is a Man's War?': Propaganda, Advertising Discourse, and the Representation of War Worker Women during the Second World War." *Media History* 10, no. 2 (2004): 103–18.

Young, Iris Marion. *Intersecting Voices: Dilemmas of Gender, Political Philosophy, and Policy*. Princeton: Princeton University Press, 1997.

Zelizer, Barbie. "News: First or Final Draft of History?" *Mosaic* 2 (1993): 2–3.

Index

access to sources, 28, 33, 40, 93, 118
accreditation of war correspondents, 1–3,
    10; before 1914, 16, 17, 24, 27; World
    War I, 33–35, 38; World War II, 47,
    49–50, 52, 55, 81, 89, 93–97, 105, 107,
    111, 118, 121, 124, 125, 128, 143; with
    WAAC, 66–69, 70, 76; in the Pacific,
    85–86. *See also* regulation of war
    correspondents
Adams, Harriet Chalmers, 136
Addington, Sarah, 39, 45n32
advertising: as revenue source, 17, 21, 38;
    as war-time messages, 126; as means of
    promoting war correspondents, 54
age of war correspondents, 18, 55–56
air attacks, 52–53, 58, 60–61, 71, 81,
    83–84, 89, 107. *See also* Pearl Harbor;
    weaponry
Air Force, U.S., 5, 52–53, 72–73, 87–88,
    96, 107–108. *See also* SHAEF; WASP
Albania, 58
Algeria. *See* Algiers
Algiers, 71, 72, 74, 89
Allied Invasion, 70
American Expeditionary Forces (AEF), 34,
    66
Andrews, Esther, 136
Angly, Ed, 57–58
anonymity. *See* bylines; pseudonyms
Antwerp, 83
appearance. *See* physical appearance

Armistice, 36, 41
Army and Navy Journal, 28, 33
Army, U.S., 5, 18, 21, 28, 34–37, 38,
    48–51, 60, 70, 71, 72, 73, 81, 82, 96,
    107–109, 110. *See also* names of
    individual military units; Supreme
    Headquarters, Allied Expeditionary
    Forces; Women's Army Corps;
    Women's Auxiliary Army Corps
Arnold, Gladys, 143
Asia, 18, 27–28, 39–40, 41, 85, 111, 125.
    See also Pacific
Associated Press, 57, 65, 68, 69, 71, 73,
    74, 76, 81, 83, 84, 87, 97, 105, 107
Atkinson, Oriana, 143
Atlanta Constitution, 27, 28, 79n50
atrocities, news depiction of, 39–40, 83.
    See also casualties
audience. *See* readership
autobiography. *See* diaries; memoirs
Avery, Marjorie, 83, 101n21, 102n30, 143
awards; reporting, 58; campaign theater
    ribbons, 95, 111, 124; Medal of
    Freedom, 112; Pulitzer Prize, 1
Axman, Gladys, 136

Bailey, Muriel, 136
Balfour, Honor, 143
Baltimore Sun, 41
Barden, Judy, 143
Beale, Bill, 69

165

About the Author

Carolyn Edy teaches journalism at Appalachian State University in Boone, North Carolina, where she was named Outstanding Professor of 2015–2016 in the College of Fine and Applied Arts. She earned her master's and doctorate at the University of North Carolina at Chapel Hill. Her research on women war correspondents has been recognized with several grants and awards, including those awarded by the American Journalism History Association, Harvard University's Schlesinger Library, the Association for Journalism and Mass Communication, and the School of Journalism and Mass Communication at the University of North Carolina–Chapel Hill. She has published research related to women and the media in *American Journalism* and *Women & Health*, and she contributed to *The Multimedia Encyclopedia of Women in Today's World* (2011). Before she began teaching, she worked as a journalist, writing for local and national publications, including *American Demographics*, *Concord Monitor*, *Newsweek*, *U.S. News & World Report*, and *Yoga Journal*.